Discovering Artificial Economics

Discovering Artificial Economics

How Agents Learn and
Economies Evolve

David F. Batten

Westview Press
A Member of the Perseus Books Group

Copyright © 2000 by Westview Press, A Member of the Perseus Books Group

Published in 2000 in the United States of America by Westview Press, 5500 Central Avenue, Boulder, Colorado 80301-2877, and in the United Kingdom by Westview Press, 12 Hid's Copse Road, Cumnor Hill, Oxford OX2 9JJ

Find us on the World Wide Web at www.westviewpress.com

Library of Congress Cataloging-in-Publication Data
  Batten, David F.
  Discovering artificial economics : how agents learn and economies evolve / David F. Batten
    p. cm.
  Includes bibliographical references and index.
  ISBN 0-8133-9770-7
  1. Evolutionary economics.   I. Title.

HB97.3 .B38 2000

                                                              00-039877

The paper used in this publication meets the requirements of the American National Standard for Permanence of Paper for Printed Library Materials Z39.48-1984.

10 9 8 7 6 5 4 3 2 1

Contents

1 Chance and Necessity   1

2 On the Road to Know-Ware   45

3 Sheep, Explorers, and Phase Transitions   81

8 Artificial Economics   *247*

Illustrations and Tables

Tables

Preface

We live in an astonishingly complex world. Yet what we do in our everyday lives seems simple enough. Most of us conform to society's rules, pursue familiar strategies, and achieve reasonably predictable outcomes. In our role as economic agents, we simply peddle our wares and earn our daily bread as best we can.

So where on earth does this astonishing complexity come from? Much of it is ubiquitous in nature, to be sure, but part of it lies within and between us. Part of it comes from those games of interaction that humans play—games against nature, games against each other, games of competition, games of cooperation. In bygone eras, people simply hunted and gathered to come up with dinner. Today you can find theoretical economists scratching mysterious equations on whiteboards (not even blackboards) and getting paid to do this. In the modern economy, most of us make our living in a niche created for us by what others do. Because we've become more dependent on each other, our economy as a whole has become more strongly interactive.

A strongly interactive economy can behave in weird and wonderful ways, even when we think we understand all its individual parts. The resulting path of economic development is packed with unexpected twists and turns, reflecting the diversity of decisions taken by different economic agents. But an understanding of economic outcomes requires an understanding of each agent's beliefs and expectations and the precise way in which the agents interact. In a strongly interactive economy, the cumulative pattern of interactions can produce unexpected phenomena, emergent behavior that can be lawful in its own right. Yet this is far from obvious if we study economics.

Most of twentieth-century economics has been reductionist in character. Reductionism tries to break down complex economies into simpler parts, like industries and households, and those parts, in turn, into even simpler ones, like jobs and persons. Although this approach has enjoyed some success, it has also left us with a major void. Reductionism can never tell us how our economy really works. To find this out, we must combine our knowledge of the smallest parts, the individual agents, with our knowledge of their interactions to build up a behavioral picture of the whole economy. To date, macroeconomics has not devised a convincing way of doing this.

Almost thirty years of research have convinced me that the conventional wisdom in economics fails to explain how economies behave collectively and develop over time. There are several reasons for this. First, the key elements of our economy, human agents, are not homogeneous. They're amazingly diverse. Second, human reasoning is not just deductive, it's often inductive, intuitive, adaptive. Third, geographical and economic patterns that we take for granted have not been forged by economic necessity alone. They're the outcome of a highly evolutionary interplay between two different architects: the expected and the unexpected. Yet it's the world of the expected, where necessity rules, that dominates our classical views about social and economic behavior. This classical economic world is a fully deterministic one, a world of stasis resting at a stable equilibrium.

A world at rest is a world that isn't going anywhere. Static determinism has been bought at the expense of structural change. Our world is not static, but incredibly dynamic. And it's this dynamic world, where chance reigns supreme, that has triggered most of our economy's significant developments. To learn how to live with the unexpected, we must look into this dynamic world more deeply. And that's precisely what this book does. What we find is a world that's often far from equilibrium, a world that's teeming with complex interactions between coevolving agents, a world that literally begs us to be more adaptive. These are the real games that agents play. In short, we live in a world of morphogenesis, working to shape our future just as it has carved out our past.

What follows is a search for the laws of complexity that govern how human agents interactively alter the state of economies. Economies don't merely evolve over time, they coevolve. What people believe affects what happens to the economy, and what happens to the economy affects what people believe. Such positive feedback loops are the signature of coevolutionary learning. Some investment gurus call this process "reflexivity." In a nutshell, success or failure for various agents depends on which other agents are present, because their own state depends on the states of these other agents. Agents learn and adapt in response to their unique experiences, such that the aggregate economy evolves in a manner determined by the pattern of their interactions. An increasing returns economy can catalyze unforeseen chain reactions of change, so much so that the collective outcome can surprise everyone. Economies can and do self-organize. Sometimes something unexpected emerges.

Some of this emergent behavior is discussed and illustrated in the pages of this book, which takes a look at a handful of unexpected socioeconomic changes during the past millennium. We find ourselves poised on the threshold of a new kind of social science: the science of surprise. Oddly enough, we seem to be performing in a prearranged way, as if under the spell of an invisible choreographer. The characteristic style of this choreographer suggests an implicit faith in two things: adaptive learning and self-organization. If this is true, then the social sciences are entering a new era, one in which more and more economists will conduct experiments inside their own computers. Instead of traditional, closed-form models, the new scientific tool for these lab experiments will be agent-based simulations. Welcome to the Age of Artificial Economics!

David F. Batten

Credits

*A*lthough most of the figures in this book were designed and drawn by Barrie Bilton and myself, I am grateful to the following for permission to reproduce the material used in creating the figures and tables listed below. Strenuous effort has been made to contact the copyright holders of this material. Any omissions or corrections brought to my attention will be included in future editions.

Figure 1.1, from N. R. Hanson, *Patterns of Discovery*, Figures 4 and 5, page 13. Copyright © 1965 by Cambridge University Press. Reprinted with the permission of Cambridge University Press.

Figure 1.7, from Per Bak, *How Nature Works: The Science of Self-Organized Criticality*, Figure 11, page 47. Copyright © 1996 by Springer-Verlag. Reprinted with their permission.

Figure 1.8, from Benoit Mandelbrot, "The Variation of Certain Speculative Prices," *Journal of Business*, volume 36, Figure 5, page 405. Copyright © 1963 by the University of Chicago Press. Reprinted with their permission.

Figure 2.4, from W. Brian Arthur, "Inductive Reasoning and Bounded Rationality," *American Economic Association, Papers and Proceedings*, volume 84, page 409. Copyright © 1994 by the American Economic Association. Reproduced with their permission.

Figure 3.5, adapted from Stuart A. Kauffman, *The Origins of Order: Self-Organization and Selection in Evolution*, Figure 7.4, page 308. Copyright © 1993 by Oxford University Press.

Figure 3.8, copyright © London Regional Transport. Reprinted with permission.

Table 4.1 adapted from Paul Bairoch, *Cities and Economic Development*, Table 8.1, page 128. Copyright © 1988 by the University of Chicago Press.

Figures 4.1 and 4.2, from Alistair I. Mees, "The Revival of Cities in Medieval Europe," *Regional Science and Urban Economics*, volume

5, Figure 1, page 407, and Figure 3, page 409. Copyright © 1975 by North-Holland. Reprinted with permission of Elsevier.

Figure 5.1, from *Scientific American,* January 1989, page 85. Courtesy of Gabor Kiss.

Figure 5.2, from Edward L. Ullman, *American Commodity Flow,* Map 1, page 3. Copyright © 1957 by the University of Washington Press. Reprinted by permission.

Figure 5.3, from C. W. Wright, *Economic History of the United States,* Figure 15, page 262. Copyright © 1949 by McGraw-Hill. Reprinted with their permission.

Table 5.1, adapted from Tables 1 and 4 in G. R. Taylor, "American Urban Growth Preceding the Railway Age," *Journal of Economic History,* volume 27, pages 311–315 and 322–323. Copyright © 1967 by the Economic History Association at the University of Pennsylvania.

Figure 5.8, courtesy of Denise Pumain.

Figure 6.5, from Ofer Biham, Alan Middleton, and Dov Levine, "Self-Organization and a Dynamical Transition in Traffic-Flow Models," *Physical Review A*, volume 46, Figure 3, page R6125. Copyright © 1992 by the American Physical Society.

Figure 6.6, from Kai Nagel and Steen Rasmussen, "Traffic at the Edge of Chaos," in *Artificial Life IV*, ed. R. A. Brooks and P. Maes, Figure 4, page 226. Copyright © 1995 by the MIT Press. Reprinted with their permission.

Figures 7.2 and 7.7, adapted from A. J. Frost and Robert R. Prechter, *Elliott Wave Principle,* Figure 1, page 19; Figures 73 and 74, page 104. Copyright © 1978 by McGraw-Hill.

Figures 7.4 and 7.9, from *Commodity Research Bureau's Chart Futures Service.* Copyright © 1993 by Knight-Ridder Financial Publishing. Reprinted with their permission.

Figure 7.6, adapted from H-O Peitgen and D. Saupe, *The Science of Fractal Images.*

Acknowledgments

Shortly after I moved to Sweden in 1986, Åke E. Andersson suggested that a book be written on knowledge, networks, and economic development. He envisaged that the two of us would join forces with our creative colleague in Kyoto, Kiyoshi Kobayashi. That book remains unwritten. In the meantime, Åke has written at least five books on this subject in Swedish, and Kiyoshi has probably written the equivalent of five in Japanese. Despite my natural command of the English language, this is my first. Some of us are living proof of the pervasiveness of slow processes!

Immense thanks are due to Åke for his inspiring insights into slow and fast processes, the C-society, and the catalytic role of networks. While Director of the Institute for Futures Studies (IFS) in Stockholm, he provided generous grants supporting the transformation of my thoughts into written words. Given the institute's stimulating atmosphere, perhaps it's not surprising that I hastened slowly! Timely reminders and pragmatic suggestions came from a scientific ringmaster at the IFS, Folke Snickars. Gradually, a draft manuscript began to take shape, aided by creative IFS residents and visitors. Helpful in many ways at this early stage were Martin Beckmann, John Casti, Börje Johansson, T. R. Lakshmanan, Don Saari, Peter Sylvan, and Wei-Bin Zhang.

After my return to Australia, an unexpected phase transition occurred: I lost my enthusiasm for the manuscript. A critical review by Kevin O'Connor identified the need for a major rewrite. Fortunately, stays at Monash and Curtin Universities revived my flagging morale. The rewrite was duly completed. Special thanks go to Kevin and a close friend, Barry Graham, for organizing these opportunities. Further suggestions by Bertil Marksjö and two anonymous reviewers have generated valuable refinements to the final manuscript.

Though it may appear to be the work of one author, this book is precisely the opposite. It's packed with the creative ideas of many gifted scholars. Two scientists who inspired me in the early days were the joint pioneers of self-organization: Hermann Haken and Ilya Prigogine. More recently, the work of the Santa Fe Institute, notably that of Brian Arthur and Stuart Kauffman, has left an indelible impression. In addition to the IFS scholars mentioned above, many others have helped to shape various parts of the manuscript. Among these, I want to thank Chris Barrett, Sergio Bertuglia, Dimitrios Dendrinos, Manfred Fischer, Britton Harris, Jeff Johnson, Dino Martellato, and Michael Sonis. Organizational support from CERUM in Umeå (where it all started), the Regional Planning Group at the Royal Institute of Technology in Stockholm (who provided a second office), and the Swedish Council for Building Research (who funded my research chair in Sweden) is also gratefully acknowledged.

Throughout writing periods in Australia and Europe, my wife, Jenny, has been a marvelous helper in many different ways. In addition to amusing our daughter, Sofie, and thereby freeing up time for me to write, she has played an invaluable role by assisting with the research for the book and adapting to my frequent outbursts of joy and frustration.

D. F. B.

The social process is really one indivisible whole. Out of its great stream the classifying hand of the investigator artificially extracts economic facts.

—Joseph A. Schumpeter

one

Chance and Necessity

Everything existing in the universe is the fruit of chance and of necessity.

—**Democritus**

"Wetting" the Appetite

According to the MIT economist Paul Krugman, we're caught up in the "Age of Diminished Expectations."[1] Despite the recent resurgence in U.S. growth, many other parts of the global economy are not doing well, compared with previous expectations. This unhealthy mixture of bliss and disaster has triggered a great deal of critical debate about economics. In many parts of the Western world, it's been the age of the *policy entrepreneur*: that economist who tells politicians precisely what they want to hear. Thankfully, the nonsense preached by some of these opportunists has been condemned by most serious economists.[2] But the fallout still lingers. In the eyes of an unforgiving public, misguided policy entrepreneurship has undermined the credibility of economics as a trustworthy discipline.

Oddly enough, the problem with economics is much more challenging than most policy entrepreneurs and many academic economists would have us believe. The truth is that we know very little about how people, societies, and economies are likely to change as time goes on. But admission of ignorance is hardly a suitable trait for a policy entrepreneur or an academic, so it's difficult to get this message of uncertainty across to the public.

Krugman tells an amusing story of an Indian-born economist, who tried to explain his personal theory of reincarnation to his

1

graduate economics class: "If you are a good economist, a virtuous economist," he said, "you are reborn as a physicist. But if you are an evil, wicked economist, you are reborn as a sociologist."[3] If you happen to be a sociologist, you'd have every right to be upset by this. How could a subject that's fundamentally about human beings, with all their idiosyncrasies, possibly hope to solve its problems with the mathematical certainty of the hard sciences? You're probably thinking that there's too much mathematics in the economics journals. Economics is not just mathematics. Fondly enough, the Indian-born economist was making a different point. His real message was that the more we learn about the economy, the more complicated it seems to get. Economics is a *hard* subject. Economists like Krugman believe that it's harder than physics.[4]

Is economics harder than physics? Before we try to answer this question, let's hear what another well-known economist has to say. Paul Samuelson feels that we can't be sure whether the traditional methods of the physical sciences—observation, quantitative measurements, and mathematical model building—will ever succeed in the study of human affairs.[5] Part of his reasoning is that physics relies on controlled experiments, whereas in the socioeconomic fields it's generally impossible to perform such experiments. Nevertheless, experiments in the form of computer simulation have begun in earnest in the social sciences. In the short space of twenty years, a small group of evolutionary economists have embarked on a fascinating journey toward wider use of experimental methods. As we'll see shortly, agent-based simulation is at the forefront of this new world of economic theorizing.

Samuelson also claims that physics is not necessarily as lawful as it appears, because the so-called laws of physics depend subjectively on one's point of view. How we perceive or interpret the observed facts depends on the theoretical spectacles we wear. Part of his argument is based on an ambiguity drawn from the visual perception of art. Take a close look at Figure 1.1. Do you see birds gazing to the left or antelopes staring to the right? Perhaps you see rabbits instead of antelopes? All answers are admissible, but someone who has no knowledge of living creatures might say that each shape is simply a continuous line between two points plus a closed curve that, unlike a bird or an antelope or a rabbit, is topologically

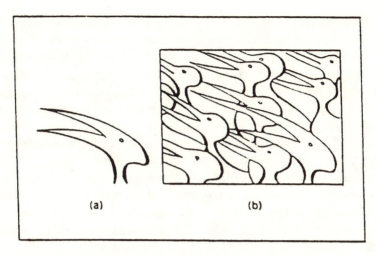

(a)   (b)

FIGURE 1.1   Reality can differ depending on the kind of glasses a person is wearing.

equivalent to a straight line plus a circle. There's no universal truth in a picture like this. Multiple impressions prevail.

Samuelson's point about the subjectivity of science is an important one. Various leading schools of scientific thought argue that physical reality is observer-created.[6]. If there are doubts about the existence of a unique, observer-independent reality in the physical world, what are our chances of coming up with universal laws that are mathematical in the fuzzy world of human decisionmaking? Rather slim, one would think. But before we launch into a deeper discussion of how law-abiding our socioeconomic behavior might be, let's take a closer look at the conventional view of what physics and economics are construed to be.

Physics is the science of matter and energy and their interactions. As such, it does very well at explaining simple, contained systems—such as planets orbiting the sun. In classical physics (and in chemistry, for that matter), the conceptual palette used to paint the big picture is thermodynamics. Of great significance in this field is the equilibrium state, that full stop at the end of all action.

To gain a mental picture of a state of equilibrium, consider what would happen if you released a marble near the top of a mixing bowl, pushing it sideways. There are no prizes for guessing where it will end up. After rolling around briefly, it falls to the bottom of the bowl under the influence of gravity. Eventually it settles in the center where its motion ceases. The convex shape of the bowl "attracts" the marble to its base. In mathematical jargon, this point of stability is even called an *attractor*. Once it reaches that safe haven, it's pretty much like the equilibrium state of a chemical reaction. It's trapped in a minimum energy state. To simplify matters, we'll just say that it's trapped in the world of *stasis*.7

A system at a stable equilibrium *is* trapped. It's like a crystal, not doing anything or going anywhere. It becomes immortal, forever frozen into an ordered state. With the advent of Newtonian mechanics, much of physics found itself locked inside this world of stasis. And for very good reasons. Newton's laws of motion strengthened our faith in this immortal world, because his laws are a classical example of determinism. At the dawn of the twentieth century, most physicists agreed that the fundamental laws of the universe were deterministic and reversible. The future could be uniquely determined from the past. All that occurred had a definite cause and gave rise to a definite effect. Since predictability was the ruling paradigm, a mathematical approach worked perfectly.

But this kind of physics breaks down badly if called upon to explain nature and all its magic. Imagine trying to forecast weather patterns using the properties of a stable equilibrium. Faced with these stark realities, physics was forced to move on. And move on it has. The advent of quantum physics made sure of that. As we enter the new millennium, a large number of physicists will have agreed that many fundamental processes shaping our natural world are stochastic and irreversible. Physics is becoming more historical and generative. Of course, headaches like weather forecasting will remain. Despite massive expenditure on supercomputers and satellites, predicting the weather remains an inexact science. Why? Because it rarely settles down to a quasi-equilibrium for very long. On all time and distance scales, it goes through never-repeating changes. Our climatic system is a complex dynamic system.

Unlike physics, economics has hardly changed at all. Despite the rumblings of a handful of evolutionary economists, its central dogma still revolves around stable equilibrium principles. Goods and services are assumed to flow back and forward between agents in quantifiable amounts until a state is reached where no further exchange can benefit any trading partner. Any student of economics is taught to believe that prices will converge to a level where supply equates to demand.

Boiled down to its bare essentials, equilibrium economics is no more sophisticated than water flowing between two containers.[8] Suppose a farmer owns two water tanks, which we'll call "A" and "B." A contains eighty liters of rainwater, while B has twenty liters. One day the farmer decides to combine his water resources by linking the tanks. He lays a pipe from A to B, allowing water to flow between them until the levels in each are identical (see Figure 1.2).[9] For all intents and purposes, this balanced equilibrium outcome is imperturbable. Obviously, the water level in each tank will always match perfectly unless the pipe is blocked.

Now substitute fruit for water. Suppose that farmer A has a case of eighty apples and farmer B a bag of twenty oranges. Because farmer A is fond of oranges and farmer B loves apples, they agree that an exchange would serve their joint interests. Apples being far more plentiful than oranges, farmer B sets the price: four apples for every orange. They agree to trade. Farmer A parts with forty apples in return for ten oranges. Both end up with fifty pieces of fruit. Being equally satisfied with the outcome, there's no point in trading further. Displaying perfect rationality, each farmer deduces the optimal strategy. The equilibrium outcome turns out to be predictable and perfectly stable. Just like the two tanks of water.

A stable equilibrium *is* the best possible state in a static world. There's simply nowhere better to go. Everything adds up nicely and linearly. The effect on the water level of adding additional liters of water is proportional to the number of liters added. Generalizing to many agents simply corresponds to connecting more tanks together. In physics, this kind of treatment is referred to as a "mean field approximation." A single macrovariable, such as the water level, is considered. Many traditional economic theories are mean field theories, to the extent that they focus on the macrovariables that are associated with an equilibrium state. Examples are GNP (gross national product), the interest rate, and the unemployment rate.

Mean field theories work quite well for systems that are static and ordered. They also work well for systems that are full of disorder.

6

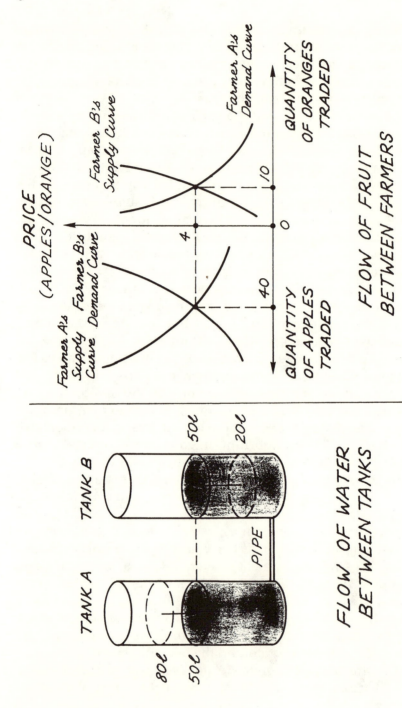

FIGURE 1.2   The behavioral paradigm underpinning equilibrium economics is the same as the one governing liquids at rest.

However, they don't work well for systems that are subject to diversity and change. For example, they don't work well when differences in economic agents' behavior become so significant that they can't be overlooked. Furthermore, they don't work well if our economy happens to be at or near a bifurcation point, such as a critical stage of decisionmaking. In short, they don't work well if we wish to understand all those weird and wonderful ways in which the economy really works.

The point of departure for this book, in fact, is that our economic world is *heterogeneous and dynamic*, not homogeneous and static. It's full of pattern and process. Development unfolds along a trajectory that passes through a much richer phase space, one in which multiple possibilities abound. Although this creates spectacular diversity, it also poses a major problem. How do we predict likely outcomes, least of all the whole development process, if we don't know what the system's trajectory looks like along the way? It's mostly impossible to predict details of this trajectory unless we know exactly what the system's initial state was. And many other questions arise. Does the system reach any equilibrium state at all? If it does and such equilibria are temporary, when will it move on? What happens when it's far from equilibrium?

In a dynamic economy, traditional equilibrium models only provide a reasonable description of the state of an economic system under very limited circumstances: namely if the system just happens to evolve towards a fixed-point attractor. We can think of a fixed-point attractor as a point along the way, with a signpost saying: "Endpoint: all motion stops here!" Under different conditions, however, an economic system may never reach such a point. There's growing evidence that certain economic processes may never come to such a dead end.[10] Instead, some may converge towards a periodic attractor set, or to a chaotic attractor.[11] Because periodic attractor sets are unstable, one imagines that their signposts might say: "Resting place: stop here briefly!" A suitable sign for a chaotic attractor will be left to the avid reader's imagination.

What, then, is the best possible state in a dynamic world? This is a very thorny question to answer. Consider the following statement in a recent book exploring facets of the new science of complexity: "In the place of a construction in which the present implies the future, we have a world in which the future is open, in which time is a construction in which we may all participate."[12] These are the words of the Belgian chemist, Ilya Prigogine, 1977 Nobel laureate in chemistry for his novel contributions to nonequilibrium thermodynamics and the process of self-organization. They remind us that in an open, dynamic world, we find evolution, heterogeneity, and instabilities; we find stochastic as well as deterministic phenomena; we find unexpected regularities as well as equally unexpected large-scale fluctuations. Furthermore, we find that a very special kind of transformation can occur. Many systems *self-organize* if they're far from equilibrium. Obviously, we must postpone our discussion of what constitutes the best possible state in such a world until we know much more about it. We'll look at the nitty-gritty of self-organization in the next section.

One thing is certain: We live in a pluralistic economy. Pluralism stems from the fact that trajectories of economic development depend on the deterministic and the stochastic. Moreover, some processes are reversible, whereas others are irreversible. Since there's a privileged direction in time, what we're beginning to realize is that many economic phenomena appear to be stochastic and irreversible. For example, an economy that started as a primitive, agrarian one may eventually develop a more sophisticated, multisectoral structure. By evolving toward a more complex state, an economy gives the impression that it can never return to its original, primitive state. But the more sophisticated it becomes, the more difficult it is to predict what it will do next.[13] To understand the multitude of ways in which economies can change, we must acknowledge the existence of stochastic processes—those whose dynamics are nondeterministic, probabilistic, possibly even random and unpredictable. A high degree of unpredictability of the future may well be the hallmark of human endeavor, be it at the individual level of learning or at the collective level of history making.

Another Nobel laureate in the natural sciences, the biologist Jacques Monod, puts the argument for pluralism concisely: "Drawn out of the realm of pure chance, the accident enters into that of necessity, of the most implacable certainties."[14] Our world is pluralistic because two "strange bedfellows" are at work together: chance and necessity. Chance events, or accidents of history, play a vital role whenever an economy's trajectory of development is confronted with alternative choice possibilities. We can

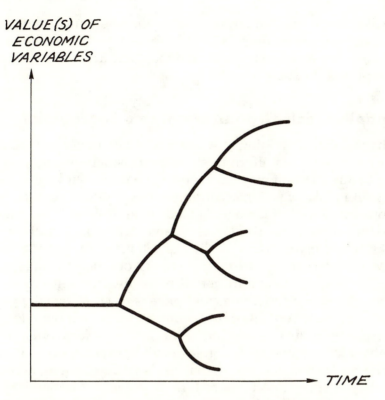

FIGURE 1.3   Chance and determinism are coevolutionary partners in the evolution of a complex economy.

think of them as key moments of decision. Technically, they're points of instability or bifurcation. Alternative pathways into the future introduce an element of uncertainty, which, in turn, invalidates simple extrapolations (see Figure 1.3). Under these conditions, prediction of future economic outcomes becomes impossible.

This book will argue that we live under just such conditions. More exactly, we're both spectators and participants in a dynamic, pluralistic economy. Patterns of economic evolution change by way of fluctuations in time and space. The interesting thing is that seemingly simple interactions between individual agents can accumulate to a critical level, precipitating unexpected change. What's even more surprising is that some of this change can produce patterns displaying impressive order. Order through fluctuations, if you like. We're left wondering whether the sole source of this order is "chance caught on the wing," as Monod suggests. On the surface at least, there seems to be more to it than that. The rest of this book attempts to find out.

Sandpiles, Self-Organization, and Segregation

Perhaps you're beginning to wonder whether a dynamic economy ever reaches any equilibrium state? Surprisingly enough, the answer to this question may have more in common with piles of sand than with tanks of water, according to the physicist Per Bak.[15] Decisions made by human agents tend to be discrete, like grains of sand, not continuous, like levels of tank water. Many decisions are sticky. So are many prices. We buy or sell many capital goods only when the need arises or the opportunity of a bargain presents itself, remaining passive in between. We buy or sell stocks and shares only when some threshold price is reached, remaining passive in between. Very few of us *continually* adjust our own holdings in response to fluctuations in the market. In other words, there's plenty of friction in real economies, just like in sandpiles.[16] It might just be the friction of distance that binds villages, towns, and cities together in special patterns to form a stable, yet dynamic, economy. Oddly enough, it's also friction that prevents a sandpile from collapsing completely to a flat state. It may even be responsible for a special kind of dynamic equilibrium.

No doubt you're thinking to yourself: "Economic agents can think but grains of sand can't think! Surely economics must be more sophisticated than sandpiles!" Perhaps you're right. But before we start to delve more deeply into the quirks and foibles of economic agents, let's explore a few of the surprising features of "unthinking" sandpiles. Try the following experiment in your backyard sandpit. Starting from scratch on a flat base, build up a pile by randomly adding sand at the center; slowly and carefully, a few grains at a time. Notice how the grains tend to stick together. The peaked landscape formed by the sand doesn't revert automatically to the flat state when you stop adding sand. Static friction keeps the pile together. Gradually it becomes steeper. Then a few small sand slides start to occur. One grain lands on top of others and topples to a lower level, causing a few other grains to topple after it. In other words, that single grain of sand can cause a local disturbance, but nothing dramatic happens to the pile as a whole.

At this formative stage, events in one part of the pile have no effect on other grains in more distant parts of the pile. We might say that the pile is only weakly interactive, featuring local disturbances between individual grains of sand. As you add more grains and the slope increases, however, a single grain is more likely to cause a larger number of others to topple. If you've created it properly, eventually the slope of your pile will reach a stationary state—where the amount of sand you add is balanced on average by the amount falling off.

There's something very special about this stationary state. Remember that you're adding sand to the pile in the center, but the sand that's falling off is at the edges. For this to happen, there must be communication between grains at the center and grains at the edge. How on earth could grains of sand communicate with each other? What transforms this collection of grains from a weakly interactive to a strongly interactive pile? Perhaps there's communication throughout the entire pile. In the words of its discoverer, Per Bak, the sandpile has *self-organized*. It has attained a self-organized critical state.

The marvelous thing about self-organization is that it can transform a seemingly incoherent system into an ordered, coherent whole. Weakly related grains of sand suddenly become a strongly interactive sandpile. Adding a few grains of sand at a crucial stage transforms the system from a state in which the individual grains follow their own local dynamics to a critical state where the emergent dynamics are global. This is a transition of an unusual kind: a *nonequilibrium phase transition*. Space scales are no longer microscopic; suddenly they're macroscopic. A new organizing mechanism, not restricted to local interactions, has taken over. Occasional sandslides or *avalanches* will span the whole pile, because the sandpile has become a complex system with its own emergent dynamics. What's most important is that the emergence of the self-organized critical state in the sandpile, with its full range of avalanche sizes, could not have been anticipated from the properties of the individual grains.

Now go back to your own sandpit again. Once you've reached this critical state, try adding more sand. See how it slides off. Try adding wet sand instead. Wet sand has greater friction, so the avalanches will be smaller and local for a while. Your pile becomes steeper. But eventually it will return to the critical state with systemwide avalanches again. Admittedly it's not an easy experiment to conduct successfully. So you may need to try the whole thing again if you're not convinced. The pile always bounces back whenever you try to force it away from this critical state. Formally speaking, it exhibits homeostasis. In other words, it's resistant to small perturbations.

Another fascinating thing is that the whole sandpile evolves to this critical state independently of any intentions on your part. You can't force it to do something else. In fact, you can't control it at all. All you can do is add sand, a few grains at a time. Nobody knows the sandpile's initial conditions. Whatever they happen to be is of no significance anyway. Repeated experiments produce the same result. In the words of Stuart Kauffman, Santa Fe Institute scientist and devout advocate of self-organization, this kind of emergent order seems to be the work of an "invisible choreographer."[17] An ordered pattern has sprung up from nowhere. Order through fluctuations, if you like. Technically speaking, this critical state is an attractor for the dynamics. It's a dynamic equilibrium.

We can now return to that challenging question posed earlier. What's the best possible state in a dynamic world? With all its fluctuations, perhaps the self-organized critical state doesn't strike you as being the very best possible state. But it might just be the best of all those states that are dynamically feasible and more or less efficient from a collective viewpoint.

So what, you might say! This still has nothing to do with economics. Yes, I remember. People can think, but grains of sand can't think. So it's time to take a look at some of those quirks and foibles of human nature. To introduce the human element, we turn to work done a generation ago by Harvard's Thomas Schelling.[18] His ideas on complexity and self-organization were summed up in a deceptively simple account of how people in a city could become segregated. In this section, we'll simply describe the model and its results. In later chapters, we'll elaborate on the implicit features of Schelling's important work. In particular, we'll look at other collective outcomes that were neither expected nor intended by the agents who engineered them. Such outcomes turn out to be instances of self-organization, that is, emergent order through fluctuations.

In Schelling's model, there are two classes of agents. He thought of them as blacks and whites, but they could be any two classes of individuals that have some cultural difficulty in getting along together—for example, boys and girls, smokers and nonsmokers, butchers and vegetarian restaurants. Instead of a sandpit, a chessboard can play the role of our "simplified city." Think of the sixty-four squares as a symmetrical grid of house locations, although the principles hold just as convincingly over much larger (and irregularly shaped) domains.

The key thing is that each agent cares about the class of his immediate neighbors, defined as the occupants of the abutting squares of the chessboard. Preferences are honed more by a fear of being isolated rather than from a liking for neighbors of the same class. It's pretty obvious that such preferences will lead to a segregated city if each agent demands that a majority of his neighbors be the same class as himself. But the novelty of Schelling's work was that he showed that much milder preferences, preferences that seem to be compatible with an integrated structure, typically lead to a high degree of segregation, once the interdependent ramifications of any changes are considered.

Consider the following simple rule: An individual who has one neighbor will try to move only if that neighbor is a different class; one with two neighbors wants at least one of them to be of the same class; one with three to five neighbors wants at least two to be his or her class; and one with six to eight neighbors wants at least three of them to be like him or her.[19] At the level of each individual, this rule of neighborhood formation is only mildly class-conscious. For example, with these preferences it's possible to form an integrated residential pattern that satisfies everybody. The familiar checkerboard layout, where most individuals have four neighbors of each class, does the trick as long as we leave the corners vacant.

Nobody can move in such a layout, except to a corner. There are no other vacant cells. But nobody wants to move anyway. Because it's an integrated equilibrium structure, there's no incentive to change it. But what if a few people are forced to move? What if three neighbors, who happen to work together, are transferred by

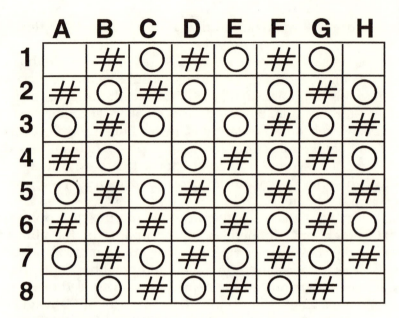

FIGURE 1.4a   The residential pattern before the chain reaction of moves.

their company? They must sell their homes and move to another city. Will the integrated equilibrium remain? Let's try to find out.

After they move out, the neighborhood layout looks like the chessboard shown in Figure 1.4a. The departing workmates vacate the squares located at coordinates C4, D3, and E2. Once they move out, other nearby neighbors of the same type suddenly feel too isolated. For example, residents at D1 and F1 discover that only one of their four neighbors is the same type as they are. Thus they decide to move to locations where the neighborhood rule is satisfied again, say A1 and H8.

A self-reinforcing pattern of interdependency quickly becomes evident. Another resident can become unhappy because the departing resident tips the balance in his neighborhood too far against his own class or because his arrival in a new location tips the balance there too far against agents of the other class. Surprisingly, our integrated equilibrium begins to unravel. An unsatisfied individual at C2 moves to C4, leaving another at G2 with nowhere

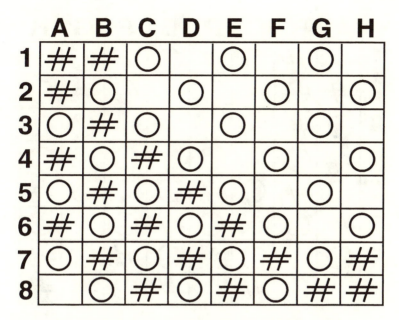

FIGURE 1.4b The residential pattern after the chain reaction of moves.

to go. G2 has no alternative but to move out of the city completely, precipitating a chain reaction of moves in response to his decision. Residents at F3, H3, G4, H5, E4, F5, and G6 all follow suit. Despite the fact that agents have only mild preferences against being too much in the minority, some of them are forced to move out, and pockets of segregation begin to appear on our chessboard city (see Figure 1.4b).

There are now forty-nine agents residing in the city. Let's trigger some more change by removing another nine of them using a random number generator, then picking five empty squares at random and filling them with a new class of agent on a 50/50 basis. In a similar manner, Schelling showed that an equilibrium like that in Figure 1.4a was unstable with respect to some random shuffling and that it tends to unravel even further. Figure 1.5a shows the result after my random number generator has done the job.

It's clear that some other residents will now be unhappy with their locations and will move (or move again). Seemingly simple

	A	B	C	D	E	F	G	H
1		#	O		O		O	
2	#	O				O	#	O
3	O	#	O				O	
4	#	O		O		O	O	O
5		#	O	#	O		O	#
6	#	O	#	O	#	O		O
7	O		O	#	O	#	O	#
8		O	#		#	O	#	#

FIGURE 1.5a   Scrambling the pattern a little more leads to . . .

moves provoke responses. Thus a new chain reaction of moves and countermoves is set in motion. To simulate this chain reaction on a computer, the order in which people move and the way they choose their new location would need to be specified. As we're doing this by hand on a chessboard, we can watch the structure evolve. When it finally settles down, my series of moves leads to the layout shown in Figure 1.5b.[20]

What a surprise! Even though the individuals in our city are tolerant enough to accept an integrated pattern, they end up highly segregated. Even though their concerns are local—they only care about the class of their immediate neighbors—the whole chessboard city gets reorganized into homogeneous residential zones. How remarkable that short-range interactions can produce large-scale structure. Like the sandpile we discussed earlier, our chessboard city has been engaged in a process of self-organization. Large-scale order has emerged from a disordered initial state. Seg-

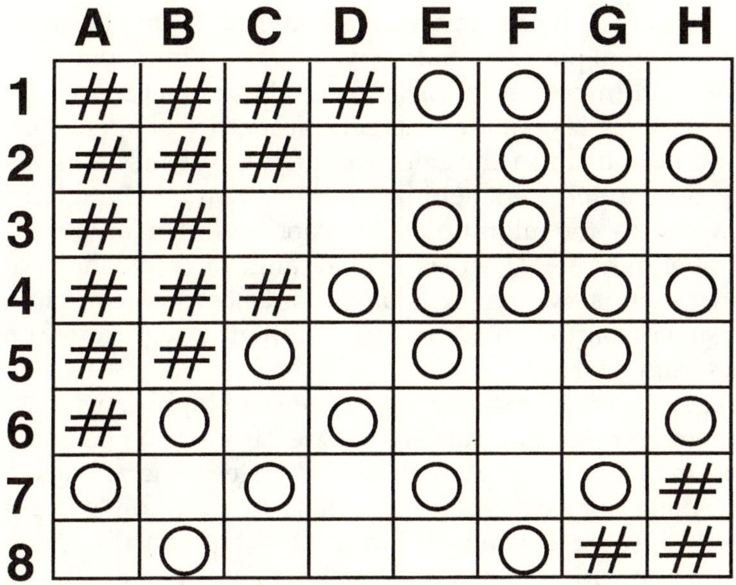

	A	B	C	D	E	F	G	H
1	#	#	#	#	O	O	O	
2	#	#	#			O	O	O
3	#	#			O	O	O	
4	#	#	#	O	O	O	O	O
5	#	#	O		O		O	
6	#	O		O				O
7	O		O		O		O	#
8		O				O	#	#

FIGURE 1.5b   A highly segregated city.

regation may not be our favorite form of order, but it's order nevertheless. All of our city-dwellers in Figure 1.5b are now content.

This large-scale order emerges because the original state—the integrated pattern shown in Figure 1.4a—is *unstable*. Scramble it a little and you trigger a chain reaction of moves that eventually produces a strongly segregated city. We could say that you get *order from instability*. This is another hallmark of self-organization.

The interesting thing is that such a chain reaction of moves never would have happened if class consciousness had been slightly weaker. Schelling fine-tuned his rules very carefully. He specified that each resident would be satisfied only if at least 37.5 percent of his or her neighbors were of the same class. If that figure had been slightly lower, say 33.3 percent, then only two residents in Figure 1.4a—those located at positions D1 and F1—would have wanted to move. Once they had moved—say to A1 and H1—then everyone else in the city would have been satisfied. In other words, the original integrated equilibrium would have remained stable.

Conversely, if the figure had been 50 percent, then a highly segregated residential pattern would have appeared immediately.

There is an important message here about emergence. As John Holland has suggested, the emergent properties of agents' interactions are bound up in the selection of rules or mechanisms that specify the model. In Schelling's model, a small change in class consciousness—the migration rule—can result in a large change in the number of moves. There is a small range over which the degree of segregation is by no means obvious. Once class consciousness exceeds a critical threshold, however, a highly segregated pattern appears immediately.

The sudden and unexpected appearance of highly segregated areas, when the migration rule is increased from 33.3 percent to 37.5 percent, is indicative of a qualitative change in the aggregate pattern of behavior. We might say that the location pattern has "flipped" into an entirely different state. In fact this nonlinear change is indicative of something like a *phase transition*. Alternatively, it's the kind of nonlinear jump portrayed in percolation theory. Both of these abrupt transitions are shown in Figure 1.6. At first the integrated equilibrium remains rather stable to slight increases in class consciousness. Then, rather suddenly, the number of moves skyrockets dramatically. Although we cannot be sure that the whole city ever reaches a state of self-organized criticality, various avalanches of change (in the form of clusters of migration of different sizes) will occur, just like those sandslides we referred to a little earlier. Global order emerges from the expanding reach of local interactions.

The idea that local interactions can produce global structure—through nonequilibrium phase transitions—came from the pioneering work of some physicists and chemists studying self-organization in physical systems.[21] Yet Schelling's model permits us to see exactly how the process works in a socioeconomic context. To some extent, of course, the model oversimplifies urban realities. The tendency is to divide the whole city into vast # and O areas. What typically happens in a real city is that the chain reaction of moving households dies out at some point, leaving the city locked into various # and O domains of different sizes. And the resulting classes of individuals are not simply two-dimensional. They're n-dimensional, so much so that it's sometimes difficult to

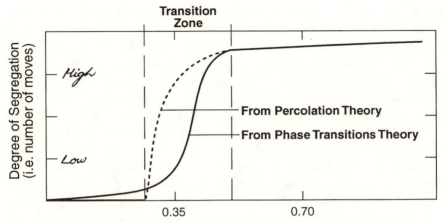

FIGURE 1.6 **A highly segregated city can be triggered by a very small change in class consciousness.**

discern the true class or "colors" of all your neighbors. Despite these drawbacks, Schelling's insights were well ahead of their time, and the rich dynamics contained therein are extraordinary.

Power Laws and Punctuated Equilibria

Odd as it may seem, Bak's sandpile experiment and Schelling's segregation model have plenty in common. First and foremost, both are examples of self-organizing systems. They develop macroscopic order without interference from any outside agent. Nothing more than the local, dynamic interactions among the individual elements are needed to produce this global order. Each system gets transformed from a state where individual elements follow their own local rules to one displaying an emergent, global pattern. Space scales that were once microscopic suddenly become macroscopic. Even more mysteriously, an unexpected and unpredictable chain reaction of events produces this coherent, stationary state.

What an incredible discovery! A mysterious process called self-organization can transform disordered, incoherent systems into ordered, coherent wholes. What's even more amazing is that each emergent whole could not have been anticipated from the properties of the individual elements. Order from incoherence. Who would have thought that a coherent sandpile could result from so many weakly interactive grains of sand? Who would have thought that a strongly segregated city could result from such weakly sensitive rules about local neighborhood structure?

But that's not all. Once these systems reach a state of spontaneous order, their holistic behavior seems to follow a dynamic pattern that is lawful in its own right. Take sandpiles first. Minor disturbances to a self-organized sandpile can trigger avalanches of all different sizes. Most of these avalanches are small, toppling only a few grains at a time. Some are much larger. Now and then, an avalanche collapses the entire pile. If we were clever and patient enough, we could measure how many avalanches there are of each size, just like earthquake scientists measure how many earthquakes there are of each magnitude. Let's skip this step and assume that we already have the data. An interesting thing might happen if we could plot the size distribution of avalanches on double logarithmic paper. The likely outcome is shown in Figure 1.7.

Surprisingly, the result is a straight line. The x-axis shows the size class, c, to which each avalanche belongs, whereas the y-axis shows how many avalanches, $N(c)$, occurred in that size class. Linearity on a log-log plot confirms that the number of avalanches is given by the simple power law:

$$N(c) = c^{-s}$$

Taking logarithms of both sides of this equation, we find that

$$log\ N(c) = -s\ log\ c$$

Thus the exponent s is nothing more than the slope of the straight line formed when log $N(c)$ is plotted against log c.

Now reconsider Schelling's segregated city. Chain reactions of relocation—like the sequences of household moves that were triggered by small disturbances to the original, integrated equilibrium—bear a striking resemblance to the avalanches of change depicted in Figure 1.7. For starters, the majority of such chain reac-

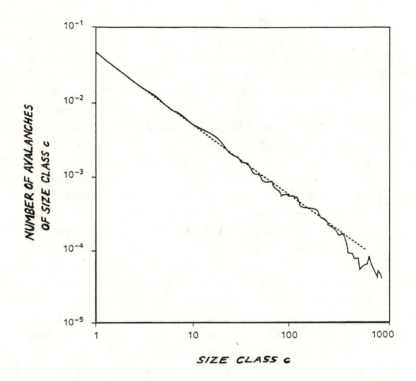

FIGURE 1.7 The size distribution of avalanches in Bak's sandpile model obeys a power law.

tions in a city tend to be small in terms of spatial scale. Most of them die out locally. But the few larger ones affect a bigger catchment area of residents. Very occasionally, a modest disturbance in a city can trigger a huge chain reaction of responses across the city. Such a skewed size distribution of chain reactions has much in common with the distribution of avalanches underpinning the sandpile model. If we were to collect the data or compute the possibilities exhaustively, the size distribution of chain reactions in our chessboard city would surely obey a power law distribution. Once again, the aggregate pattern of potential moves may be lawful in its own right.

There's another reason for suspecting that the size distribution of chain reactions leading to segregation may conform to a power law. Schelling's chessboard city, together with his rules determining moves to other locations, corresponds to a two-dimensional cellular automaton. Cellular automata were originally put into practice by John von Neumann to mimic the behavior of complex, spatially extended structures.[22] Because they're really cellular computers, today they're being put to use as simulators, designed to help with time-consuming calculations by taking advantage of fast parallel processing.[23] Since cellular automata employ repetitive application of fixed rules, we should expect them to generate self-similar patterns. Indeed, many do produce such patterns. If Schelling had used computer simulation to explore a much larger chessboard city, self-similar patterns of segregation may have even been visible in his results. Being akin to periodicity on a logarithmic scale, such self-similar patterns would conform to power laws.

Although it's too early to say for sure, it's likely that many dynamic phenomena discussed in this book obey power laws.[24] Power laws mean scale invariance, and scale invariance means that no kinks appear anywhere. Economic change may be rife with scale invariance. Over one hundred years ago, the Italian economist Vilfredo Pareto found that the number of people whose personal incomes exceed a large value follows a simple power law.[25] In some socioeconomic contexts, of course, linearity may break down at the smaller and larger scales. The fact that scaling usually has limits does no harm to the usefulness of thinking "self-similar." In the next section, we'll look more closely at scale invariance in economics. We'll take a further look at power laws when we discuss urban evolution in Chapter 5.

Yet another observation links sandpiles to economies. A great many unexpected socioeconomic changes may be nothing more than large avalanches that "punctuate" the quiescent state of affairs. Once it reaches a self-organized critical state, for example, a sandpile exhibits *punctuated equilibrium* behavior. In 1972, paleontologists Nils Eldredge and Stephen Jay Gould argued that evolutionary change is not gradual but proceeds in "fits and starts."[26] Long periods of stasis are interrupted, or punctuated, by bursts of dramatic change. Perhaps the most spectacular examples of such punctuations are the Cambrian explosion (500 million years ago) and the extinction of dinosaurs (about 60 million years ago). Out of the Cambrian explosion came a sustainable network of species, believed to be the collective result of a self-organized, learning process. The evolution of single species are thought to follow a similar pattern.

The theory of punctuated equilibria melds together stasis and adaptive change associated with speciation. Stasis recognizes that most species hardly change at all once they show up in the fossil record. But these quiet periods are interrupted occasionally by shorter periods, or punctuations, during which their attributes change dramatically. Speciation recognizes that major evolutionary change comes from new species, mutants that tend to show up unexpectedly. Again we find two worlds at work—speciation and stasis, punctuation and equilibria, chance and necessity.

Oddly enough, punctuated equilibria have turned up in many other places. For example, Kauffman and his colleagues at the Santa Fe Institute have produced computer algorithms that exhibit this kind of behavior: relatively long periods of stasis interrupted by brief periods of rapid change. The dramatic changes are not coded into the programs in advance. They appear spontaneously and unexpectedly from within the programs themselves. Tom Ray, a naturalist from the University of Delaware, created an experimental world inside his computer. The digital life he created is capable of replication and open-ended evolution.[27] Part of the open-ended repertoire displayed by Ray's digital world includes "periods of stasis punctuated by periods of evolutionary change, which appears to parallel the pattern of punctuated equilibrium described by Eldredge and Gould."

Another scene of punctuated calm is the scientific world. Remember the book *The Structure of Scientific Revolutions,* a best-seller in the sixties written by Thomas Kuhn?[28] Kuhn's central observation was that science proceeds for long periods as status quo paradigms, interrupted occasionally by creative spurts that finally force out the old paradigm in favor of a new one. The new arrival handles the anomalies swept under the table by its predecessor. Kuhn also argued that the historian constantly encounters many smaller, but structurally similar, revolutionary episodes that are central to scientific advance. Because the old must be revalued and reordered when assimilating the new, discovery and invention in the sciences are intrinsically revolutionary.

Economies also evolve in fits and starts. The Austrian economist Joseph Schumpeter coined the term *industrial mutation* for the process of creative destruction that incessantly revolutionizes the economic structure from within, destroying the old one and creating a new one. He further states: "Those revolutions are not strictly incessant; they occur in discrete rushes which are separated from each other by spans of comparative quiet. The process as a whole works incessantly however, in the sense that there always is either revolution or absorption of the results of revolution, both together forming what are known as business cycles."[29]

In one form or another, the idea of punctuated equilibria looks to be at the heart of the dynamics of complex systems. In fact, the footprints of power laws and punctuated equilibria can be found everywhere. They turn up in the frequency distribution of many catastrophic events—like floods, forest fires, and earthquakes. They're also thought to be responsible for the music most listeners like best—a succession of notes that's neither too predictable nor too surprising. In each case, the activity going on is relatively predictable for quite long periods. Suddenly this quiescent state is interrupted by brief and tumultuous periods of major activity, roaming and changing everything along the way. Such punctuations are another hallmark of self-organized criticality.

Large, intermittent bursts of activity lie beyond the world of stasis. They can change the very nature of the system itself. Their effects can be self-reinforcing. Self-organization affects form and structure in a fundamental way. A world ripe with punctuations is a world of *morphogenesis*. The process of morphogenesis is ubiquitous in history, biology, and economics. We can think of morphogenesis as a topological conflict, a struggle between two or more attractors. In the next section, we'll look for further footprints, direct evidence of self-organizing tendencies in the economic marketplace.

Bulls, Bears, and Fractals

One of the most baffling puzzles in financial markets is the fact that academic theorists, by and large, see markets quite differently from the way that actual traders see them. Academics see investors as being perfectly rational, thus ensuring that markets are efficient in the sense that all available information is discounted into current prices. The sole driving force behind price changes for any stock or commodity is assumed to be new information coming into the market from the outside world. Traders process this information so efficiently that prices adjust instantaneously to the news. Because the news itself is assumed to appear randomly, so the argument goes, prices must move in a random fashion as well.

Known as the efficient markets hypothesis, this notion was first put forward by the little-known French mathematician Louis Bachelier.[30] It's a long-standing equilibrium theory that suggests that prices are unpredictable, and therefore technical trading using price charts is a waste of time and money. Why is it, then, that newspapers and financial tabloids still feature graphs and advertisements by self-styled "chartists" claiming to be able to predict future price movements? Technical traders feel the geometry of price histories is important. As a result, they view markets quite differently from academics. Not only do they believe that technical trading can be profitable, but some of them have demonstrated that it *can* be consistently profitable. They also believe that factors such as market "psychology" and "herd" effects influence price changes.

Which group should we believe? It's a difficult question to settle empirically. Markets do seem to be reasonably efficient. Despite this, statistical tests and real results have shown that technical trading can produce modest profits over time.[31] Other tests have shown that trading volume and price volatility are more volatile in real markets than the standard theory predicts.[32] Temporary bubbles and slumps, like the major crash in 1987, seem well beyond the scope of rational adjustments to market news. Although a spate of economists have looked for signs that prices are being generated by chaotic mechanisms, we shall not dwell on these tests here. It suffices to say that the evidence implicating chaos as a factor influencing price fluctuations in financial markets is mixed.[33] But there's growing evidence that markets do undergo phase transitions between two different regimes of behavior: the simple and the complex. Could it be that chance and necessity are at play again?

What interests us most is that price histories do exhibit geometrical regularities. Charles Dow, one of America's earliest students of stock market movements, noted a certain repetition in various price gyrations. Dow observed that the market in its primary uptrend was characterized by three upward swings. But at some point in every upswing, there was a reverse movement canceling three-eighths or more of that swing. Dow's principles motivated Ralph Elliott to develop his wave principle, which asserts that market behavior trends and reverses in recognizable patterns. The ever-changing path of prices reflects a basic harmony found in nature. Elliott isolated thirteen patterns, or "waves," that recur in markets and are repetitive in form, but not necessarily in time or amplitude.[34] He also described how these patterns link together to form larger versions of the same patterns. Without realizing it, he had discovered patterns of self-similarity on different timescales.

Remarkably, Elliott reached his conclusions fifty years before the advent of the science of fractals. Yet his findings showed that historical price patterns bear a striking resemblance to the fractal character of the natural world. Benoit Mandelbrot's studies of fractals and multifractals have confirmed that nature and markets abound with a special symmetry. He analyzed daily and monthly data for the variation of cotton prices over different periods, drawing on statistics spanning more than a century. Then he counted how often the monthly variation was between 10 and 20 percent, how often it lay between 5 and 10 percent, and so on. After plotting the results on a double logarithmic plot, he found that the resulting distributions of price changes in different periods were horizontal translates of each other (see Figure 1.8). Furthermore, their shape conformed to a familiar pattern: the ubiquitous power law.[35]

Mandelbrot was the first to interpret such power laws in terms of scaling. The unifying concept underlying fractals and power laws is self-similarity: invariance against changes in scale or size. Finding the power law distribution in financial data was a major discovery. It showed that small-scale patterns combine to form similar patterns at larger scales.[36] Mandelbrot looked at price variations for other commodities, finding similar patterns that matched across different timescales. His scaling principles echo Elliott's observation that the market traces out characteristic patterns at all levels or trend sizes.

However, price charts themselves are not self-similar. A more exact term for the resemblance between the parts and the whole in financial markets is *self-affinity*. Mandelbrot concluded that much in economics is self-affine. Two renormalized price charts will never be identical, of course, but their resemblance over different timescales

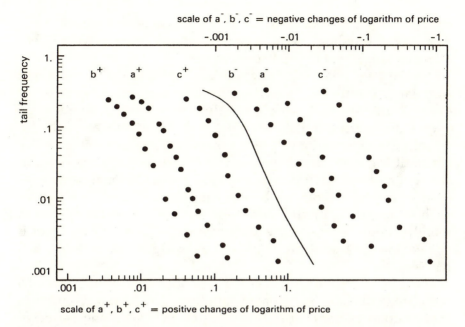

FIGURE 1.8 **The original evidence for scaling in economics: Mandelbrot's observation that variations in the spot price of cotton obey a power law.**

can be striking and worthy of our attention. Such price variations are "scale-free" with no typical size of variations, just like the sand-pile avalanches that we discussed in the previous section. As remarkable as it may seem, markets and sandpiles have something in common after all. In Chapter 7, we'll return to the issue of price fluctuations, fractals, and self-affinity in financial data.

Until very recently, most economists (and all policy entrepreneurs) ignored Mandelbrot's important work, presumably because it didn't fit into the traditional picture. Classical economists have a tendency to discard large events, attributing them to specific abnormal circumstances—such as program trading in the case of the crash in October 1987. If you happen to believe in the world of stasis, it would be difficult to believe in a general theory of events that occur just once! Yet history is riddled with such events. The paleontologist Stephen Jay Gould, co-inventor of the theory of punctuated equilibria, argues that in many sciences, we're compelled to engage in "storytelling" because particular outcomes are contingent on many single and unpredictable events.

Despite their potentially devastating consequences, the fact that rare, large events might follow the same law as a host of small events suggests that there's nothing very special about large events. Furthermore, they may not even be so rare after all. Although the magnitude of price movements may remain roughly constant for more than a year, suddenly the variability may increase for an extended period. Big price jumps become more common as the turbulence of the market grows. Then one observes such spikes on a regular basis—sometimes as often as once a month. Should such occurrences be regarded as abnormal? Not if one believes in fractal geometry and the scaling properties of such markets.

The important thing to learn from phenomena such as self-organized criticality, punctuated equilibria, and fractal geometry is that complex patterns of behavior are created by a long period of evolution. A universal law of economics, for example, cannot be understood by studying economic change within a time frame that is short compared with the economy's overall evolution. Mandelbrot's work spanned five human generations. Suddenly that familiar phrase "you cannot understand the present without understanding the past" takes on a deeper and more exact meaning.

I hope that you're beginning to sense how and why disciplines like geophysics, biology, and economics differ from physics. Modern physicists are accustomed to dealing with probabilistic theories in which the specific outcome of an experiment cannot be predicted. Only certain statistical features can be determined with any accuracy. Statistical mechanics, quantum mechanics, and chaos theory are important theories in physics that are of a statistical nature. What makes geophysics, biology, and economics different is that their outcomes impinge on our everyday lives as human beings. The fact that we may understand the statistical properties of earthquakes is of little consolation to those who have suffered from one large, devastating earthquake. A similar statement can be made about biological and economic catastrophes. Many affect us personally.

It's quite correct to attribute the variability of things, and thus their complexity, to contingency. History depends on freak accidents, so if the tape of history is replayed many times with slightly different initial conditions, the outcome will be different each time. The creation of each new nation, for example, usually involved a long series of events, each of crucial importance for the eventual outcome. Because of this, even the pioneers involved in such efforts had little idea of what the likely outcome would be. Wherever contingency is pervasive, detailed long-term prediction becomes impossible. For example, many kinds of economic changes are unpredictable. But that very fact doesn't mean that they're also unexplainable. The main problem with understanding our economic world is that we have no reliable benchmarks with which to compare it.

Fortunately, a few economists have recognized the important role of history and chance events in economic development. We'll sample some of their ideas in the next section, before moving on to a more detailed discussion of some of them in the chapters that follow.

Stasis and Morphogenesis

In case you're still wondering if equilibrium economics is really like tank water, here's another way of testing the analogy. It comes from the youthful field of cybernetics, which deals mostly with self-regulating and equilibrating systems. Thermostats, physiological regulation of body temperature, and automatic steering devices are examples of self-regulating systems. So are equilibrium economies and our tank water example. They're all systems in which negative feedback processes tend to counteract, or cancel out, deviations from the equilibrium state. In other words, they all possess *negative feedback loops*. Such loops promote stability in a system, because they tend to negate change.

Negative feedback is *assumed* to occur in economics. The belief is that economic actions will force the economy back to a stable equilibrium point because of the respective shapes of the supply and demand curves. You can see the logic behind this self-regulating process in Figure 1.9. Suppose the apple farmer (whom we met earlier) sets his price initially at p_A. Before long, he realizes that he's not selling as many apples as he would like. Supply exceeds demand. He's building up an unwanted surplus, some of which

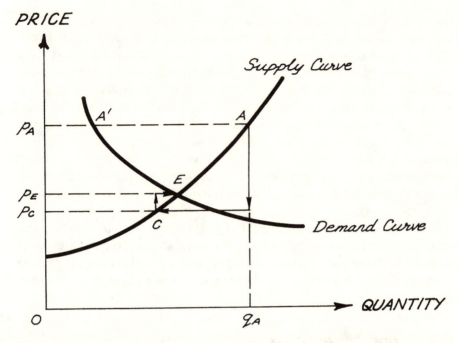

FIGURE 1.9   Negative feedback loops ensure stability and equilibrium in the economic marketplace.

will soon turn bad. So he drops his price to p_C. A little later, he sells out of apples. Demand has outstripped supply. Thinking that he must have set his price too low, he increases it again. As if guided by an "invisible hand," he finally converges on the equilibrium price, p_E.

Negative feedback loops like this are fine in principle. They seem to provide a stabilizing influence in an otherwise volatile marketplace. But does our economy really work this way in practice? Many believe that it has done so in the past and still does to some extent. It's certainly true that the price of a specific brand-name product, like a McDonald's cheeseburger or a Diet Coke, may not vary greatly from place to place. Although primary products do vary in price from season to season, Tasmanian apples and California oranges may not vary greatly when their prices are measured from place to place at the same point in time. Any difference might simply be due to differences in transportation costs to the market-place. The prices of various manufactured goods, like clothing or sports equipment, never seem to vary greatly when we shop around at different stores.

But how can we be sure that all the producers of the same product will behave in this way? The truthful answer is that we can't. In addition to all the sales, discounts, consumer loyalty privileges, and never-ending suite of devious tactics that firms introduce to attract buyers away from their competitors, there's another reason why it's hard to believe in the broad existence of equilibrium prices. Take a look at Figure 1.10. It shows a typical average cost curve faced by an "efficient" manufacturing firm over the long run. Cost per unit of output is plotted against output. The firm is efficient in the sense that it adopts a least-cost method of production for the level of output involved. Efficient production possibilities lie on the thick black line. For example, producing output OB at a cost of Ob can be done using the least-cost technique. Cost levels above Ob are inefficient, whereas cost levels below Ob are impossible at that level of output.

Strangely enough, two different kinds of economic worlds are implicit in this one curve. The one that we've been discussing, the negative feedback world, lies to the right of the point C. At smaller output levels than OC, a very different regime prevails. In this region, positive feedback mechanisms prevail. An expansion in production results in a decrease in costs per unit of output. On average, each unit of output becomes cheaper to produce. Under these conditions, a firm has every incentive to expand production as much and as quickly as possible, because the firm can then enjoy scale economies, that is, *increasing returns to scale*. Beyond OC, however, the curve begins to rise, signifying that unit costs have changed direction. Now they're increasing rather than decreasing. At these higher output levels, negative feedback loops prevail and the firm faces *diminishing returns to scale*.

Conventional economic theory tends to frown upon the left-hand part of this curve. Yet this is a realistic and most profitable cost structure for a firm. Why would any serious analyst want to overlook part of it? One answer is that Zone 2 is much simpler to model and understand than Zone 1. Negative feedback loops serve to stabilize the economy; any major changes will be offset by the

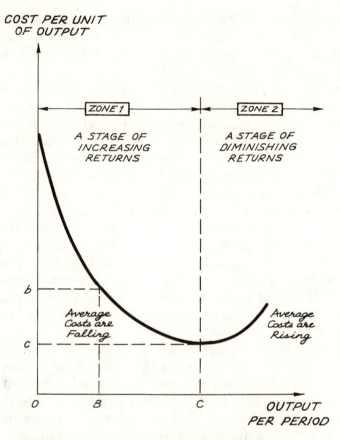

FIGURE 1.10   The typical average cost curve faced by an efficient firm embodies two starkly different economic worlds.

reactions they generate. A stable, closed economy is a predictable economy—easily identified and interpreted.[37] This classical world of diminishing returns is epitomized by the agricultural sector. Suppose a wheat farmer wants to expand production. Because of the scarcity of arable land, eventually he'll have to pay more for suitable land or put up with land that's less suitable for wheat. This pushes unit costs up, reducing unit profits. Hence the label "diminishing returns."

Primary producers are plagued by an additional problem. If there are too many wheat producers competing for scarce parcels of land, for example, wheat prices may come under downward pressure. As prices fall toward average production costs, some farmers will struggle to earn any profits. In this so-called world of perfect competition, profits are marginal at best. As we've said earlier, perfect competition belongs to the world of stasis, a world at equilibrium—stable, predictable, and resistant to change. What's rarely said, however, is that firms in such a world are flirting with extinction. Once we picture it as part of a dynamic economy, the true identity of a competitive equilibrium reveals itself. Basically, it's a dead end. Instead of engendering a perfect marketplace, negative feedback breeds extinction!

Feedback processes can also be positive. In many sectors of our economy, the stabilizing forces needed to maintain an equilibrium state are absent. Instead, radically different forces prevail. Positive feedback loops amplify the effects of small initial changes.[38] High-tech monopolies and oligopolies are a good example. They belong to a vastly different world, a world of increasing returns. Whereas diminishing returns imply a single equilibrium point for the economy, increasing returns imply many possible states. Such open-ended pluralism presents two problems. First, there is no certainty that the particular outcome selected from among the many alternatives will be optimal. Nor can it be predicted in advance. Chance dominates over necessity. Second, once a particular economic outcome is selected, that choice may become securely "locked in," thereafter tending to prevail regardless of its advantages or disadvantages.

Classical theories of industrial location have tended to resist the idea that historical chance plays a role. For example, the Santa Fe Institute economist Brian Arthur has noted two different views in the German literature on spatial economics.[39] The first, associated with the writings of von Thünen, the early Weber, Predöhl, Christaller, and Lösch saw the spatial evolution of industry as *predetermined*—by geographical endowments, transport possibilities, and economic needs. In this view, locational history does not matter. The key factors are geographical differences, shipment costs, market interactions, and the spatial distribution of prices and rents. The outcome is easily predictable: a unique equilibrium pattern. Because this is a static and unique view of the locational world, Arthur calls it *stasis*.

The second view regarded industry location as *path-dependent*— more like an organic process with new industry influenced by, and thus reinforcing, the locational landscape already in place. Included among this group were the later Weber, Engländer, Ritschl, and Palander. Although there's still a role for geographical endowments and economic factors (such as transportation costs) in this view, the dominant driving forces are agglomeration economies. Engländer and Palander were severe critics of Weber's theory on this point, claiming that he grossly underemphasized the actual development process and the historical advantages of existing production points as self-reinforcing centers of agglomeration. In a path-dependent world, chance events in history play a crucial role. We'll refer to this view as *morphogenesis.*

Here's a modern example of path dependence. Japan Railways East, believed to be the largest carrier in the world, ran into some water problems when it was building a train line through the mountains of Tokyo. As engineers made plans to drain the water out of the tunnel, the company learned that the workers were drinking it because it tasted good. So JR East decided to bottle and sell it as a premium mineral water. It became so popular that vending machines were installed on JR East's platforms and a home-delivery service was launched. A new $75 million-a-year beverage industry had been triggered by nothing more than an accidental discovery. Once again, such an outcome could not be foreseen in advance. Chance ruled out determinism. Morphogenesis reigned supreme.

Whether small events in history matter in determining the pattern of settlement, growth and change in an economy reduces, strangely enough, to a question of topology. In the matter of industrial location, it hinges on whether the underlying structure of locational forces guiding the location pattern is convex or nonconvex.[40] History does matter when the these forces are nonconvex, and nonconvexity stems from some form of agglomeration or increasing returns in space. Path dependence can be illustrated by a firm's decision to locate its headquarters in one of several alternative cities (or regions). I'll discuss agglomerative forces more fully in Chapter 5, where Chicago's development is portrayed as a path-dependent, coevolutionary process.

Agglomeration is a powerful force. Firms that are not heavily reliant on raw material locations, but are more sensitive to their industry's learning curve, are often attracted by the presence of other like-minded firms in a region. Some densely settled regions can offer better infrastructure, more diverse labor markets, more specialized services, and more opportunity to do business face to face. They may also provide an active forum for the continuous exchange of ideas. This is a vital part of Arrow's "learning by doing."[41] Under these conditions, the world of morphogenesis dominates.

Brian Arthur has suggested the following example.[42] Stasis would see today's electronics industry in the United States distributed across the country, but with a substantial part of it in California (e.g., Silicon Valley)—because that location is close to Pacific sources of supplies and because it has better access to skilled labor and to advances in academic engineering research. By way of contrast, morphogenesis would see concentrations of high-tech industry, like Silicon Valley, as largely the outcome of chance events—such as the vision of the vice president of Stanford University, Frederick Terman, who just happened to support a few key entrepreneurs—the Hewletts, the Varians, the Shockleys—who then decided to set up shop near Stanford in the 1940s and 1950s. The attractive work environment that they helped to create made subsequent location there very attractive for the thousand or so firms that followed them. If Terman or those key entrepreneurs had thought or acted differently, Silicon Valley might have happened somewhere else.

Stasis or morphogenesis? Which explanation is correct? It's likely that most of the locational patterns we observe today have been forged by a mixture of chance and necessity, rather than by either element alone.[43] Whenever industry and people are attracted to places where resources of interest are already gathered, those small concentrations established initially by chance will have sown the seeds of the resulting urban configurations. To the extent that the locational choices of the pioneering agents were preordained by geographical or economic needs, however, the resulting configurations will reflect pure necessity.

The important point to note is that positive feedback loops never let the economy return to its original state. Even an accidental (or seemingly insignificant) kick-start will cause divergence from the initial condition. This has troubled conventional economic theorists for decades. Most have refused to tackle the complexities of increasing returns economics, preferring to deny their importance. Given the lack of attention devoted to them, it's surprising to find that positive feedback processes are so ubiquitous in societies: the evolution of living organisms, the accumulation of knowledge and physical capital, the rise of specific cultures, for example. Because the term morphogenesis is used in cybernetics to cover this category of feedback processes, for ease of exposition we'll regard all economic systems that are governed by positive feedback loops as belonging to the world of morphogenesis.

Once we start to think of development as a life-cycle process of evolution, the respective roles of positive and negative feedback loops—or increasing and diminishing returns—fall into place. Consider the forces behind the typical S-shaped growth curve in population dynamics. The binding constraint is carrying capacity. When the population is well below this upper limit, it's being driven by a positive feedback loop. Additions to population increase in proportion to population itself. Thus it expands exponentially. This self-reinforcing process produces the initial upward sweeping part of the curve. As population nears carrying capacity, however, a dormant negative feedback loop becomes active, interacting nonlinearly with the positive feedback loop, neutralizing its influence and converting the system to a search for an equilibrium at the population limit. As Jay Forrester suggests, S-shaped growth curves depict shifting loop dominance at different times.[44]

Such S-shaped curves also form part of the trajectory traced out by the product life cycle. Like humans, products pass through a familiar sequence of recognizable stages. Self-reinforcing stages of the human life cycle include incubation, infancy, adolescence, and young adulthood. Here, positive feedback loops underpin the growth process. By the time we reach middle age, however, negative feedback loops have taken over. Their growing influence eventually leads to senility. Death—that ultimate equilibrium state of human existence—follows thereafter.

Stages of the product life cycle follow a similar pattern. Invention, innovation or imitation, and rapid growth correspond to self-reinforcing stages of market growth. They're the hallmarks of an increasing returns economy. Once competitive turbulence sets in, however, market share stabilizes and begins to decline. A mature,

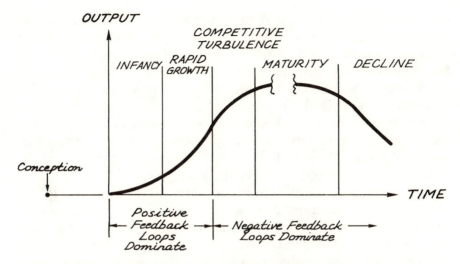

FIGURE 1.11   The life cycle of a product features positive and negative feedback loops in shifting proportions.

stable, saturated market confirms that diminishing returns have taken over. Even products cannot avoid senility, with rapidly declining market share signaling the ultimate death knoll.

Unless a firm is unusually innovative, it can expect to enjoy increasing returns only in the early stages of the cycle. Before final choices are locked in, the development process is characterized by a high degree of risk and uncertainty. Learning processes are rapid but haphazard. Many different solutions are possible, and frequent major changes are necessary. Chance invariably takes a hand. A host of ideas and products are triggered by accidental discovery or even by mistake. Any accidental kick-start in the invention process triggers the divergence mentioned earlier. But the high initial costs of research and testing usually become a distant memory once production expands and the cost per unit of output begins to fall. The stage of increasing returns takes over, bestowing on the firm a temporary period of competitive advantage over its rivals. Chance can breed windfall profits.

Economists can now explore the challenging terrain of increasing returns with much better equipment than they could a few decades ago. The early chapters of Adam Smith's *Wealth of Nations* placed considerable emphasis on increasing returns to explain both specialization and economic growth. Since then, many others have taken up the challenge. What they're discovering is a world of growing complexity. Among the early pioneers were A. A. Cournot, Alfred Marshall, Allyn Young, Edward Chamberlin, Joan Robinson, Gunnar Myrdal, and Nicholas Kaldor. Today's champions of increasing returns are led by Brian Arthur, Paul Krugman, and Paul Romer. Some of their work will be discussed in more detail as our story unfolds in the ensuing chapters.

In the words of Brian Arthur, an increasing returns world is a world of evolution rather than equilibrium, a world full of instability and chance events.[45] It's also a world of process and pattern change, placing it in the world of morphogenesis. If one firm gets ahead by historical accident or innovation, increasing returns serve to magnify this advantage. Regardless of its ultimate efficiency, a product can "lock in" considerable advantages by being first. Chance events in the past may have set the wheels in motion. But once they're turning, increasing returns turn them even more quickly—breeding uncertainty and instability. In brief, the state of increasing returns is the tendency for that which gets ahead to get further ahead.

In stark contrast, the state of diminishing returns is the tendency for that which falls behind to fall further behind. Such conditions tend to dominate during the later stages of the product life cycle. Once a product has become standardized, further innovation becomes marginal at best. Improvements are only incremental. Low-cost imitation takes over. The emphasis switches to productivity, marginal improvements, and cost control. Saturated markets breed numerous competitors, and unit profits are thin. The classical zero-profit equilibrium of economic theory is a reasonable approximation of the ultimate dead-end state of this frozen world. For the firms involved, death is imminent. Without fresh innovation, diminishing returns signal that the market and its customer base have matured and that the risk of extinction is growing.

Our analysis reveals two economic worlds: the seemingly static one (stasis) is heavier on resources, lighter on know-how, and subject to diminishing returns; the dynamic one (morphogenesis) is lighter on resources, heavier on know-how, and subject to increasing returns. These two worlds are readily visible in the economies of the past and the present. Our traditional mainstays of economic life—agriculture and manufacturing—have been surrendering market share on a global basis to dynamic newcomers built around newer technology. Instead of processing resources, these pioneers of high-tech products process knowledge and information. Instead of applying raw energy, they apply new ideas. The relentless pace of change in this high-tech world is nothing short of remarkable. Chance is setting such a cracking pace that necessity has trouble simply staying in touch.

On Learning Curves

To reiterate, two contrasting views of our economic world proliferate today: chance and necessity, punctuation and equilibria, morphogenesis and stasis (see Table 1.1). Our primary focus in the rest of book will be on morphogenesis—those chance events that

TABLE 1.1 Two Economic Worlds

NECESSITY	CHANCE
Stasis	Morphogenesis
Resource-Based	Knowledge-Based
Unique Outcome	Multiple Outcomes
Equilibrium	Path-Dependent
Mechanistic	Organic
Predictable	Unpredictable
Diminishing Returns	Increasing Returns
Convex	Nonconvex
Easy to Model	Difficult to Model
A SIMPLE WORLD	**A COMPLEX WORLD**

punctuate the calm, deterministic landscape of an economic system, propelling it into an uncertain future. Real economies evolve in fits and starts. Calm is nothing more than the precursor of storm. Morphogenesis and disequilibrium are more influential states in an evolving economy than stasis and equilibrium.

Recent simulation work in economics has also shown that rational expectations equilibria cannot be seen as stationary states of adaptive processes.[46] Instead of equilibrating, evolving economies adapt and select continuously. The work of nonequilibrium scientists like Ilya Prigogine and Peter Allen has revealed that self-organizing human systems possess an evolutionary drive that selects for populations with an ability to learn, rather than for populations exhibiting optimal behavior. Schumpeter was an early champion of the innovative entrepreneur. Creatively destructive entrepreneurs have been stoking the engine of economic change for centuries. The rest of this book attempts to unravel facets of their adaptive behavior.

Learning takes place individually and collectively. The collective learning process can be illustrated in the following way. Fundamental inventions spawn an early explosion of diverse forms as many tinkerers try out new variants on the basic invention. Tinkering occurs with very little real understanding of the likely consequences. After the early frenzy dies away, we settle down to finer, more incremental tinkering among a mere handful of designs that dominate. Once these better designs have been found, it becomes progressively more difficult to do much better. Variations become more modest. Such qualitative features are reminiscent of the Cambrian explosion: Branching radiation to create diverse forms is bushy at the base; then the rate of branching dwindles, extinction sets in, and a few final, major alternative forms persist.[47]

The more copies of an item produced by a firm, the more efficient production tends to become. Learning curves are a means of tracking such efficiency improvements by relating the unit costs of the firm to its accumulated output. According to empirical economists, the cost per unit for high-tech products entering the marketplace can fall by as much as half at each doubling of the number of units produced. Being heavy on know-how and light on resources, high-tech products typically have high R&D costs when compared with their unit production costs. As the technology matures, however, this rate of improvement slows considerably to a few percentage points. It may even start to rise if marketing costs become excessive. Being closely related to the product life cycle (Figure 1.11), the learning curve reveals a rapid improvement in performance at first, followed by an eventual slowdown and deterioration.

Formally speaking, then, learning curves relate unit costs to accumulated output. Let's plot such a curve for Microsoft's Windows software. Being a high-tech product in the early phase of its life cycle, it enjoys increasing returns to scale. In fact, the learning curve can be thought of as the result of economies of scale that just happen to be defined temporally.[48] The first disk of Windows entering the market cost Microsoft $50 million; the second and subsequent disks cost $3. For such high-tech products, the Nth unit typically costs about 1/Nth of the cost of the first unit produced. Once again, the special character of this property shows up when the logarithm of the cost per unit is plotted against the logarithm of the total number of units produced. The resulting straight line confirms an already familiar shape for this pattern of learning. Yes, it approximates another power law (see Figure 1.12).

How fascinating! Mathematically speaking, a learning curve appears to follow a power law. We're back to sandpiles again! Note how closely the linear plot resembles the one shown in Figure 1.7. In the early stages of a new product's life cycle, the power-law exponent may be near –1. This exponent approaches zero as the cycle runs its course. But the actual number, $N(c)$, could just as well be the number of sandpile avalanches of size c, or the number of fjords of length c, or the number of earthquakes with energy c. As Mandelbrot has shown, it could also be the number of months during which stock price variations exceeded a given fraction c. The message we're getting is that power laws may be rather ubiquitous in nature and in human endeavor.

Like sandpiles, fractals, and earthquakes, learning is a coupled dissipative process. Thus it can't be fully understood by limiting our study to a single human lifetime. Even an evolutionary approach is insufficient. Because it takes place individually *and* collectively, learning isn't just evolutionary; it's coevolutionary. Agents react to the moves of other agents. Each agent's decision affects the collective outcome, and in turn, this collective outcome influences the agents' future beliefs and decisions. Such outcomes

42

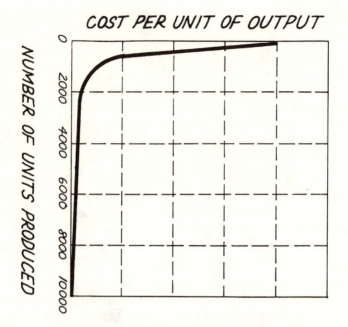

COST PER UNIT OF OUTPUT

NUMBER OF UNITS PRODUCED

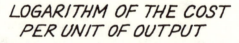

LOGARITHM OF THE COST
PER UNIT OF OUTPUT

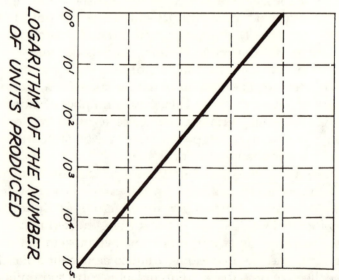

LOGARITHM OF THE NUMBER
OF UNITS PRODUCED

**FIGURE 1.12   The initial learning curve for Microsoft
Windows obeys a power law.**

may be quite different from what each agent expected or intended. Unexpected outcomes can trigger avalanches of anxiety and uncertainty, causing each agent to react and modify his view of the world. Because such avalanches of economic change vary greatly in magnitude, perhaps they also conform to a power law.[49] If the system of interest self-organizes, a new regime may take over. Future expectations and decision strategies change dramatically. So do future collective outcomes.

This seems to be the way of the world, the way we respond to the unexpected and accumulate experience. Experience is cumulative skill or judgment acquired through practice. They say that "practice makes perfect." But practice involves making mistakes, learning from them, and adapting future strategies accordingly. Experience can't be gained in isolation. It's accrued through an interactive, coevolutionary process. But now we've moved ahead of ourselves, skipping over some of our story. We know so little about the nature of knowledge and the mechanics of learning. How do creative entrepreneurs acquire the know-what and know-how to make innovative decisions? What does it mean to learn *adaptively*? Can adaptive learning cause an economy to self-organize? We'll begin to tackle these intriguing questions in the next chapter, where we look at the behavior of adaptive economic agents as they journey along the road to "know-ware."

two

On the Road to
Know-Ware

The heart has its reasons that reason does not know.

—Pascal

What Is Knowledge?

In a novel study of the American economy, Fritz Machlup claimed that the "knowledge industry" accounted for about 29 percent of the U.S. gross national product *by 1958.*[1] He also found that the growth rate of "knowledge-producing" occupations had exceeded all other job classes since the turn of the century. Studies elsewhere have confirmed that knowledge-producing occupations are growing rapidly. After subdividing the workforce into four occupations—knowledge-handling jobs, administration and information jobs, personal services, and goods-handling jobs—a Swedish study found that the share of knowledge-handling jobs grew from about 10 percent in 1960 to 18 percent in 1980 and was expected to reach about 30 percent by the turn of the millennium.[2]

Who are these knowledge producers? Machlup combined people who create new knowledge (e.g., research scientists) with those who communicate existing knowledge to others (e.g., teachers, managers, air traffic controllers). On reflection, this seems too generous. Why? Because the *creation* of new knowledge is a more complicated and demanding undertaking than routine tasks like passing on existing knowledge or information to others. Although all of us possess some degree of creative talent, the most creative knowledge producers are well known. They include researchers, inventors, entrepreneurs, authors, artists, and composers.

Some intriguing questions then arise. What kind of new knowledge do they create? How is this knowledge acquired and improved? Does it differ from information? One kind of new knowledge comes from scientific research. Scientific knowledge is produced by universities, research institutes, and other science-oriented organizations, where it often mixes with associated tasks (e.g., teaching, consulting). Much of this collective knowledge appears in books, scientific journals, and other technical publications. Some of it gets applied by industry in the design and production of new technology and products. Occasionally, it finds its way into the popular press.

Traditionally, most scientists used to work alone or in small groups led by a senior scientist. Today, however, there's a growing trend toward collaboration between researchers in many different locations.[3] Globalization, aided by the advent of the Internet and rapid advances in communication technology, seems to have spawned greater collaboration over longer distances. Nevertheless, there's also evidence that the frequency of research collaboration between researchers who speak the same first language decreases exponentially with the distance separating them.[4] Distance still matters, despite the information technology revolution.

The explanation for this frictional effect is that informal, face-to-face contact is thought to be an essential ingredient for generating new ideas by collaborating partners and that factors such as geographical proximity become significant because of the additional travel cost and time needed to bring the partners together. Thus researchers who are closer geographically can meet and exchange ideas more easily and more often than distant partners. The debatable point is that face-to-face meetings cannot be replaced by the use of telecommunications, the Internet, or related technologies when it comes to the generation of new knowledge.[5] One reason for this is that novel and surprising ideas tend to emerge more spontaneously from face-to-face exchanges than from other kinds of contacts. We'll return to the issue of face-to-face contacts later in this chapter, when we come to distinguish knowledge from information.

An increasing number of scientists work on research and development (R&D) in private sector corporations and public agencies.

This R&D leads to new products like pharmaceuticals, chemicals, airplanes, space products, instruments, electronics, and computer hardware and software. Because chance plays such a major part in the process of scientific discovery through R&D, once again we find ourselves plunged into the world of morphogenesis. Although knowledge producers can be found in all sectors of the economy, successful R&D is a crucial ingredient in the "get ahead, stay ahead" world of high technology. The potential payoffs are enormous for the winners. As we learned in the Chapter 1, high-tech scientists live in that very chancy world of increasing returns.

How do scientists and others acquire new knowledge? There's no magic elixir involved here. Like all of us, scientists must acquire their knowledge from learning. Yet for most of the twentieth century, economists have treated knowledge and learning as exogenous variables when it comes to explaining economic growth and development. Ironically, the idea that increasing returns could arise from the accumulation of knowledge is almost as old as economics itself. In his *Principles of Economics,* Alfred Marshall noted that an increase in "trade-knowledge" that cannot be kept secret is a form of external economy. Yet very few models of economic change adopted this suggestion.

Perhaps the foremost advocate of knowledge as the endogenous engine of growth and technological change is Paul Romer, an economist at the University of Chicago. Ever since the appearance of Kenneth Arrow's pioneering paper on "learning by doing," there's been a frantic rush to absorb learning into the main corpus of economic theory. Much of the discussion in this and later chapters will focus on learning as an adaptive process, drawing partly on the domain of psychology.

When we probe learning problems, we find that psychologists are no more in agreement than economists. But one empirical generalization seems to stand firm, having been accepted by all schools of thought: Learning is a product of *experience.* In other words, learning can occur only when we're attempting to *do* something—like reading a book, talking to someone, playing a game, or solving a problem. We already know that learning associated with repetition of the same problem is subject to diminishing returns. We're trapped in the world of stasis again. According to Arrow, the stimulus situations must themselves be steadily evolving rather than merely repeating, if we're to build on our experience and enjoy steadily increasing returns. This is a vital distinction because it means that learning belongs to the world of morphogenesis. And that makes it evolutionary.

Before we launch into a discussion of the evolutionary aspects of learning, let me round off this discussion with a few words about knowledge and information. Superficially, we tend to think of knowledge as data or facts that we can organize into predefined categories—compartments in the brain, if you like. For example, a financial analyst might notice that the rate of exchange between the yen and the dollar is running at 125. He stores this fact in the "yen-dollar" compartment in his memory bank; he now *knows* this. The next day he notices that the same exchange rate has dropped to 123. Therefore he revises this entry in his memory bank. Having updated his yen-dollar data string, he has *learned* something new.

Undoubtedly this is a kind of learning, but it's a very simple learning model. In fact, it's too simple. Knowing means nothing more than being aware of data and assigning them to the correct memory compartments. Learning means nothing more than revising these data in the light of fresh information from outside. Although this may be fine for some purposes, to understand what learning is really about we need to go deeper than this. Certainly the world of economic decisionmaking is not that shallow. Knowledge is not always spoon-fed to us in prepackaged forms. Rarely do we enjoy the luxury of infallible conceptual models that we can use to forecast, analyze, and act upon with absolute confidence. Our personal stock of knowledge is a very individual thing, being a unique product of our own experiences, constructs, and memories.

Like the empiricist philosophers before him, Immanuel Kant believed that our knowledge of the world comes from our sensations. But he also believed that *how* we see the world depends on the particular "glasses" we're wearing. We can never have certain knowledge of things "in themselves," just how things appear to us. Kant believed that there are clear limits to what we can know. Each mind's glasses set these limits. When we ask questions about totality, such as whether the universe is finite or infinite, we're asking about a totality of which we're but a small part. There's simply too much for a single person to handle, so we can never know this totality completely. We'll return to the issue of what may be knowable and unknowable in Chapter 8.

Knowledge becomes a much fuzzier concept in Kant's world. If there are clear limits to what we can know, then our ability to reach identical conclusions under similar conditions should not be taken for granted. Erwin Schrödinger sums it up nicely in his book *Mind and Matter:*

> The world is a *construct* of our sensations, perceptions, memories. It is convenient to regard it as existing objectively on its own. But it certainly does not become manifest by its mere existence. Its becoming manifest is conditional on very special goings-on in very special parts of this very world, namely on certain events that happen in a brain.[6]

Each of us is a unique product of our own brain and our uniquely individual experiences. Our personal knowledge is honed by the concepts, notions, and models that we choose to use to represent it. All of this has to be *created,* put together over time by us, as well as by others in society as a whole. Learning is a cumulative process that can be frustratingly slow, partly because some of us are stubbornly resistant to change. Thus some of our knowledge stocks turn out to be surprisingly durable.

An obvious distinction can be made between the simpler, more objective kinds of knowledge, such as the yen-dollar exchange rate, and the more complex, subjective kinds that result from our own mental "gymnastics" and contacts with others. We can usefully think of the simpler kinds as *information* and of our use of them as *information processing.* Basic information—like an exchange rate or the maximum daily temperature—is readily quantifiable. It's dispersed easily over geographical space and changes rather quickly over time. Most information has limited value, in the sense that its usefulness erodes rather quickly. Last Thursday's maximum temperature is of much less interest than today's high. Furthermore, this kind of information is *not* a product of our own thinking and experience. It's external to us, bestowed upon us like "manna from heaven." For this reason, information can be gathered and transferred in many different ways. Moreover, the exchange of information doesn't require face-to-face interaction (see Table 2.1).

Thus simpler tasks like information processing should be distinguished from the more complex processes that make up learning.

TABLE 2.1   Information and Knowledge

Characteristic	Information	Knowledge
Source	External	Internal
Nature	Weakly-interactive	Strongly-interactive
Primary exchange mode	Interface	Face-to-face
Learning rate	Fast	Slow
Usefulness	Temporary	Longlasting
Exchange process	Simple	Complex
Unit of measurement	Quantitative (e.g., bits)	Qualitative (e.g., deep)

Whereas information processing tends to be routine and repetitive, learning is more intuitive and adaptive. A key point is that learning cannot take place in a vacuum, isolated from others. It relies heavily on interactions between individuals, or between individuals and their environment. For example, individuals learn to make a living by creating and selling goods and services that make economic sense only in the niches afforded by other goods and services. As Stuart Kauffman suggests, an economy resembles an ecosystem because it consists of a web of coevolving agents. The learning effects of the interactions between agents can be beneficial to some, detrimental to others, or mutually beneficial. As we'll see shortly, the true story of technological evolution is actually one of adaptive coevolution.

Finding the Road to Know-Ware

Biological evolution teaches us that information is a relatively trivial concept in comparison with knowledge. For example, the divided cell or the fertilized egg possess a basic kind of *know-how*. Two fertilized eggs can have the same amount of information in terms of bits, but one knows how to make a hippopotamus and the other knows how to make a giraffe.[7] An ant or rat knows how to find its way to food in a maze. A trained racing pigeon knows how to find its way home from any distant origin. This special "sixth sense" or know-how is part of any living creature's behavioral repertoire. Furthermore, it gives the impression of being responsive, perhaps even *purposive.*

By giving the impression that it's purposive, know-how stretches the dimensions of knowledge beyond a simple information concept. The problem is that it's devilishly difficult to quantify. Because it's a multidimensional part of a person's knowledge stock, for example, it's more qualitative than quantitative. We can only measure know-how vaguely, using coarse measures like "little," "basic," or "extensive."

We run into a similar kind of problem in economics. Two different countries can have the same level of GNP, for example, but one knows how to make the world's best watches whereas the other knows only how to grow olives. One may have a fairly equal income distribution, the other a very unequal one. Yet they're given equal scores in comparative studies of economic performance! The problem doesn't go away by decomposing GNP into its constituent parts, such as firms and their employees. Although two watch-making firms may have the same output or earnings, one can make highly sophisticated watches using leading-edge technology, while the other knows only how to make old-fashioned faces with leather bands. Even at the microscopic level—say of individual watchmakers—the problem persists. No two individuals possess identical know-how.

Know-how is not the only component of human knowledge. There is also *know-what* and *know-that.* Returning to the biological example, a fertilized egg definitely has the know-how to make a hippopotamus, but it's unlikely to know *what* it's doing—*that* it's making a hippopotamus rather than a giraffe. Knowing how to reach food inside a maze does not mean that a rat knows *what* food is there, or even *that* there's food there. Knowing how to fly home does not imply that a pigeon knows *that* a particular path will get it home.

When it comes to economic agents, however, the nice thing is that we do have know-what and know-that. In fact, we use them to create know-how. By concentrating on know-what and know-that, for example, scientists have greatly increased our stocks of know-how.

Until science discovered the chemical elements and the periodic table, there could be never be a chemical industry. Until they discovered the silicon chip, developing the know-how to create integrated circuits was out of the question. Perhaps all we need to spawn some new know-how is a mixture of know-what and know-that, together with the added "spice" of a little contact with some other clever thinkers.[8]

Regrettably, it's not that simple. We must continue our little journey along this road to know-ware, going beyond know-what and know-how to *know-whether*. Human decisionmaking involves a series of choices. Know-whether involves evaluating the implications of alternative decisions in order to find out whether the chosen course of action was the best decision. Before choosing from among several alternative courses of action, we harbor expectations about the likely consequences of each different course. Once we've made our choice, however, we're "locked in" to it. Only at some later stage do we get additional feedback telling us about the wisdom of our choice. In other words, to know-whether requires feedback from the decision environment in which the choices are made.

This subjective ability is a more sophisticated part of the behavioral repertoire of humans. It's one of those instincts that seems to set us apart from other living species. Although rats and pigeons may act expectantly, they cannot explicitly state an expectancy. Nor do we believe that they can really think about it. Different environmental conditions lead us not only to act differently but also to think differently. For example, being caught up repeatedly in traffic jams not only encourages us to travel off-peak or take the train instead but also makes us think about the future of the whole traffic system and whether our politicians are doing enough to improve it.

Our economy needs science to develop know-what and know-that, primarily as ingredients for improving our know-how. Production always begins with know-how. There were no plastics one hundred years ago because we didn't know how to make them. Most managers and economic agents, however, rely on know-whether to make sound decisions. We'll reconfirm the need for careful distinctions between these elements of our personal know-ware when we look at an example of adaptive learning on networks, which we call *learning by circulating*. For the moment, though, let's return to some conventional wisdom: how knowledge and learning have been treated in traditional economic theory.

The Age of Deception

We've emphasized that the conventional world of economics is mostly confined to the world of stasis. What does this imply in terms of human reasoning and behavior? Nothing very sophisticated. Among the most popular set of simplifying assumptions, a particular one tends to proliferate. Most theoretical reasoning in economics assumes that economic agents behave in a perfectly rational manner; that is, they possess perfect, logical, deductive rationality.

Deduction is reasoning from the general to the particular.[9] A perfectly logical deduction yields a conclusion that must be true provided that its premises are true. Thus deduction involves specifying a set of axioms and proving consequences that can be derived from those premises. Sounds straightforward enough, doesn't it? The catch is that the premises must be complete, consistent, and well defined. As such, it's pretty easy to run into problems. Although deduction is handy for solving a host of theoretical problems, it's much less helpful for tackling practical problems. Why? Because for premises to be complete, consistent, and well defined, the problem must be relatively simple. In an economic setting, for example, the problem must be simple enough for agents to know what's in their self-interest, to act in their self-interest, and to perform the calculations needed to know the implications of alternative decisions. In other words, they need to have the brainpower to figure out the optimal decision.

A case in point is education. Farsighted parents plan ahead and deduce the amount of education that's economically feasible, both for their children and for themselves. Another example is housing. Potential buyers plan ahead and deduce the location, type, and amount of housing that they can afford. This is the kind of reasoning, deduction, and analysis that is assumed in most areas of economics. It certainly can help in family planning and house purchases. Also it's well researched. Psychologists have accumulated almost a century's worth of experiments based on deductive reasoning.[10] But is a deductive approach always sufficient to solve the full range of problems confronted in economics? To answer this question, let's see what's required in terms of know-ware.

To reason deductively, economic agents need to have a complete set of know-ware at their disposal. First, they need to know-what serves their best interest. Second, they need the know-how to act in their best interest. Third, they need know-whether in order to evaluate the implications of alternative decisions and be sure that they have chosen wisely. In brief, they must have perfect *know-what,* perfect *know-how,* and perfect *know-whether.* Their know-ware must be honed to perfection. This, of course, is a very demanding condition.

From the above, it's hardly surprising to find that deduction works well only on relatively simple problems. As Brian Arthur puts it, "If we were to imagine the vast collection of decision problems economic agents might conceivably deal with as a bottomless sea or ocean, with the easier ones on top and more complicated ones at increasing depth, then deductive rationality would describe human behavior only within a foot or two of the surface."[11] Before we tackle economic problems, let's visualize where various games might be found as we dive to various depths. Simple games—like tic-tac-toe—are readily solved by a deducible minimax solution. In everyday terms, this means that the human brain is quite capable of figuring out the "best" moves on a game board consisting of only nine squares. The best moves are the ones that leave your opponent in the worst possible situation. Thus a way of testing for goodness is to pretend you've made the move, then evaluate the board from your opponent's viewpoint. Meanwhile, your opponent is doing the same. He or she mentally runs through all possible moves and evaluates them from what he thinks is *your* viewpoint.

Note that we've defined our best move *recursively,* using the maxim that what's best for one side is worst for the other. It's recursive because it operates by trying a move and then calling on itself in the role of opponent. Since recursion can go on several moves ahead, it's possible to figure out the best strategy to adopt and the likely result in a game of tic-tac-toe. Each move generates its own "look-ahead tree," with the move itself as the trunk, your

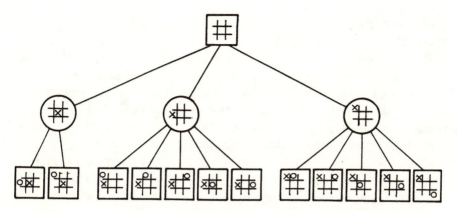

FIGURE 2.1 The branching tree of moves and responses in the game of tic-tac-toe.

opponent's responses as main branches, your counter-responses as subsidiary branches, and so on. In Figure 2.1, I've shown the look-ahead tree corresponding to the first few moves of a game.

Let's see how the minimax solution can be deduced. If you move first, your best move is to choose the central square, thus limiting your opponent's opportunities of scoring three noughts in a row to just four possibilities—two horizontally and two vertically. At the same time, you've secured four ways of winning in two additional moves. Choosing any other opening move offers your opponent more opportunities to win and secures fewer ways for you to win. Your opponent's best response to your opening move is to choose any one of the four corner squares. Then the game will finish in a draw. However. if your opponent doesn't choose a corner square, then you'll win the game.[12]

If each player always chooses their best move, the game's out-come can be deduced in advance. This is a rather pleasing result. In exchange for a well-defined decision problem, we get back a well-defined solution. The recursive solution invokes a logic that is re-lentless and consistent. It acts step by step on premises that are well defined. It's also self-consistent and self-enforcing, in the sense that if your opponent behaves according to the deductive solution (i.e., chooses his/her best move), then it would not be in your best inter-est to do otherwise. If the best moves are implemented properly, the drawn outcome confirms the deductions that went into it. It's a rational expectations equilibrium.

Because we can deduce the likely outcome to a game of tic-tac-toe after the first few moves, we can think of its logic as lurking just below the surface. We'd need to dig a little deeper, however, to catch a glimpse of games like checkers or Quads.13 Owing to larger board sizes (Quads = 36 squares; checkers = 64 squares), it takes longer to figure out the likely outcome. In other words, we can't deduce the perfectly rational solution. Not only are the choices of moves more numerous, but our best moves depend more and more on the moves of our opponent. Neither our best strategy nor the likely outcome are deducible in advance. There are simply too many possible branches in the corresponding look-ahead trees.

Deduction has no chance whatsoever when we finally reach the game of chess (see Figure 2.2). Something else is needed in even greater doses at these deeper levels. It's really an art to figure out how to avoid exploring every branch of a look-ahead tree out to its very tip. Good chess players seem to excel at this art. Or do they? The funny thing is that top-level players look ahead relatively little, especially if compared to chess programs. Until Deep Blue's success against Gary Kasparov, people were superior as chess strategists. We'll come back to the issue of the best chess strategy shortly.

Why, then, does deductive rationality fail us when we're faced with more complicated decision problems? Three reasons spring to mind. The obvious one is that beyond a certain degree of complicatedness, our logical apparatus ceases to cope. In other words, our rationality is *bounded*. Social scientists have been aware of this problem ever since Herbert Simon suggested "satisficing" as a way of describing less-than-logical behavior in some decision situations. But Simon's notion of satisficing is too vague to be adopted as a practical method for solving complicated problems. Of late, economists have joined the search for something to put in place of deductive rationality. When we look into the growing literature on bounded rationality, however, there seems to be little agreement on a suitable successor.

The second reason for the deductive mode to break down is more ominous. In *interactive* decision situations, where the rationality of one agent's decision is dependent on the strategy of other

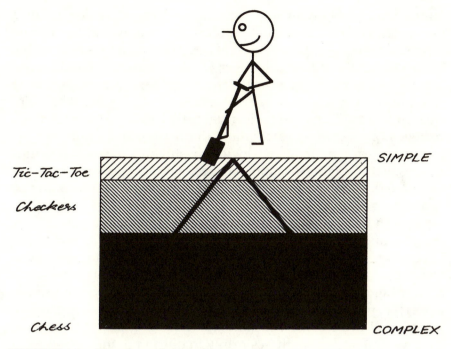

Tic-Tac-Toe

Checkers

SIMPLE

Chess

COMPLEX

FIGURE 2.2   Simple and complex games.

agents, there are no guarantees that each agent will toe the line, that is, behave with perfect rationality. Instead agents may be forced to guess the behavior of other agents. Suddenly they're plunged into a world of subjective beliefs, and subjective beliefs about subjective beliefs. Complete, consistent, well-defined premises are impossible under these conditions. Deductive reasoning breaks down for one very significant reason: The problem has become *ill defined*.

A third reason is just as devastating. Even if one agent guesses the behavior of others correctly at one point in time, there are no guarantees that this success will ever be repeated. In complex economic situations, agents learn and adapt differently. Thus future guesswork becomes more difficult. The evolutionary paths traced out by each agent are not familiar to other agents. Nevertheless, agents still make decisions in situations that are fuzzy or ill defined. What's even more surprising is that we seem to make them quite comfortably under such conditions. Perhaps we don't realize that the problem is ill defined. But it's clear that we no longer reason deductively. A different kind of decisionmaking process comes to the rescue. To find out what it is, we must return to psychology.

Let's begin with some basics from modern psychology that touch upon our area of interest. Aside from suggesting that we're creatures of habit, psychologists claim that we make use of three varieties of reasoning: calculation, deduction, and induction. As we've just learned, deductive logic is useful only in simple circumstances, like the family planning or residential choice examples we mentioned. What we're very good at, however, is recognizing or matching patterns.

When things get too complicated for our deductive powers, we seem to undergo a cognitive shift to the other side of our brain. Psychologists tell us that the right-hand side handles pattern recognition, as well as intuition, synthesis, and creative insights. By putting a combination of these processes to work, we use the perceived patterns to fashion temporary constructs in our mind. We can call these constructs *mental models* or *hypotheses*. Once we have a set of such hypotheses firmly in our mind, they assist us to carry out "localized" deductions and act upon them.

But the whole process doesn't finish there. Our observations and experiences provide us with feedback from the decision environment; feedback may alter the patterns we perceive, strengthening or weakening our confidence in our current set of hypotheses. What we're doing, of course, is trying to improve our ability to make prudent decisions; upgrading our know-whether, so to speak. We discard hypotheses that have proved to be unreliable, replacing them with new ones. We retain others. Wherever we lack full definition of the problem, we devise simple hypotheses to paper over the gaps in our understanding, and we act on the best of these. This kind of behavior is not deductive. It's *inductive.*[14]

If all of this sounds a little complicated, that's hardly surprising. Inductive reasoning *is* complicated. Even the psychologists don't fully understand it. Luckily, we can picture the inductive mind at work in a setting we've mentioned already: a chess game. In the 1940s, the Dutch psychologist Adrian de Groot studied how chess novices and grand masters perceive a chess situation. He found that grand masters don't simply look further ahead than novices.

Instead, they sharpen their intuition by studying the board's configuration and trying to discern chunks or patterns. In other words, they develop their own mental model of the board.[15] Then they use the perceived patterns and their mental model to form hypotheses about their opponent's likely motives and strategies.

Chess openings are definitive patterns of play formed in the first dozen or so moves.[16] The leading players can even recall their opponents' favorite openings from previous games. "He's offering me the Queen's Gambit again." "Isn't this the Catalan opening?" "That looks like the modern Dragon Variation of the Sicilian defense." Good players carry out local deductions based on these mental models, analyzing the implications of alternative moves and their subsequent responses. As play proceeds, they hold onto the most plausible hypotheses and toss away the others, replacing them with new ones as the state of the game dictates.

Clearly then, chess players engage in a sequence of reasoning that's inductive. This includes pattern formation, pattern recognition, hypothesis formation, deduction using the currently held hypotheses, and hypothesis replacement as dictated by the pattern of play that unfolds (see Figure 2.3). Seasoned players build on their experiences from earlier games. Chess is a strongly interactive game because players learn only *during the game* which of their hypotheses work best. It involves *adaptive learning* rather than information processing. Each player's strategy evolves partly in response to the evolutionary path chosen by his opponent. Neither player can afford to adopt a fixed strategy. They must be flexible and "roll with the punches," so to speak. In a word, strategies need to be *coevolutionary.*

It's interesting to note that Hermann Haken, founder of the field of *synergetics,* believes that the kinds of pattern recognition used in chess are closely associated with pattern formation. Synergetics is a general theory of self-organization. Although its generality comes from timescale separation and a slaving principle, the formalism of synergetics allows us to calculate evolving patterns, provided the microscopic laws for the formation of patterns are known.[17] Take another look at Figure 1.1 (near the start of the book). Interestingly, neither birds nor antelopes can be perceived all the time. After a while, one image fades away, allowing the brain to perceive the other interpretation. Some kind of oscillatory process sets in.

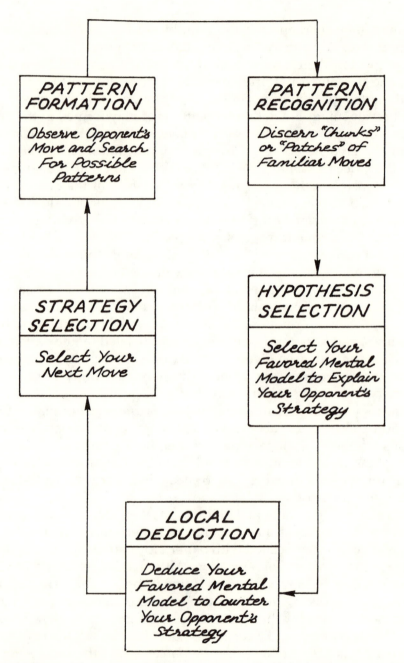

FIGURE 2.3   The game of chess as an exercise in inductive reasoning.

Haken believes that decisionmaking can be regarded as pattern recognition. Like grand masters staring at a chessboard, all of us search for a resemblance between a situation that we now confront and one that we have met before. To do this, we establish a "similarity measure" in our minds, which allows us to choose a course of action that is the best under the given information. Haken and his colleagues have mimicked this pattern formation process inside their "synergetic computer." Thus they're also adopting an inductive approach to decisionmaking.

Because it's closely connected with learning and adaptation, inductive behavior sits firmly in the world of morphogenesis. In economics, the popular interpretation of "rational" behavior connotes behavior that's sensible or sound-minded. Deductive reasoning is sensible or sound-minded only in fairly simple, well-defined problems. Once a situation gets too complicated or ill defined, like in a chess game, an intelligent person begins to reason inductively. Induction enters the scene whenever someone has to derive a whole solution from partial information. In the social sciences, for example, induction is widely used in the analysis of opinion surveys and macroeconomic data.

Surprisingly, there's now a third way of doing social science. It corresponds to the third mode of reasoning cited by psychologists: calculation. But the calculations are done by machines instead of humans. This growing focus on calculation goes by the name of *agent-based computer modeling* or *simulation*. Like deduction, agent-based simulation starts off with a set of assumptions. Unlike deduction, however, it doesn't prove theorems. Instead, an agent-based model generates simulated data that can be analyzed inductively. But the simulated data come from a rigorously specified set of rules rather than from direct measurements of the real world.

Whereas the purpose of deduction is to find consequences of assumptions, and that of induction is to find patterns in data or real-world experiences, agent-based modeling is a way of doing thought experiments that help to sharpen our intuition.[18] The examples to be discussed in this and later chapters have the same collective properties as those we found in Schelling's segregation model. Locally interacting agents can produce large-scale effects, most of which turn out to be far from obvious.

Economists have pushed the assumption of deductive reasoning beyond its limits. In doing so, they've locked most of us into the world of stasis. But this frozen world is only a tiny part of the whole universe of economic behavior. From an intellectual viewpoint, we've been trapped in an era of tomfoolery. We might even call it the "Age of Deception." Fortunately a new light is glowing in the distance. The source of this light is a group of social scientists who just happen to believe that human agents reason inductively and adaptively. Furthermore, they also believe that agent-based simulation represents a promising new way of doing social science, one that can help us to unravel some of the complexities of human behavior. The search for a new age of human enlightenment is now underway.

Seeing the Light at the El Farol

El Farol is a bar on Canyon Road in Santa Fe, which offered Irish music every Thursday evening. Having been born in Belfast, Brian Arthur was fond of going to hear the music and to enjoy a few beers in a relaxed atmosphere once a week. But soon he encountered a thorny problem. If the bar was too crowded, the chances of brushing up against a few too many pushing-and-shoving bar louts were high. This would spoil the night and cause him to think twice about going the following Thursday. Arthur realized that he needed a more reliable method of deciding whether the bar was likely to be overcrowded each coming Thursday night.

The reader might like to ponder this problem for a moment. As we'll see shortly, it turns out to be an instructive example of a complex adaptive system. To make it more concrete, let's suppose that there are one hundred people in Santa Fe who, like Arthur, are keen to go to the El Farol on Thursdays. Space is limited, and everyone enjoys themselves if the bar is not too crowded. A crowd beyond sixty is thought to be excessive. The tricky thing is that there's no way of telling beforehand how many will come. A person simply goes if he expects fewer than sixty to turn up or stays home if he expects more than sixty to show.

Arthur has highlighted two interesting aspects of this problem. First, if there were an obvious model that all agents could use to forecast bar attendance, then a deductive solution would be possible. But there's no such model. Irrespective of past attendance figures, a wide range of plausible hypotheses could be adopted to predict future attendance. This dastardly multiplicity of possibilities means that nobody can choose in a well-defined manner. The problem becomes ill defined and all the potential bar attendees are catapulted into a world of induction.

Second, any shared expectations will tend to be broken up. If all music lovers believe *most* will go, then *nobody* will go. But by all staying home, that common belief will be destroyed immediately. On the other hand, if all of them believe *few* will go, then *all* will go, thereby undermining that belief. The net result of this diabolical state of affairs is that expectations must differ.

Perplexed yet fascinated by this intractable problem, Arthur decided to turn his computer loose on it.[19] By creating a surrogate El Farol bar inside his machine to study how electronic music lovers would act in this situation, he stepped into the exciting new realm of agent-based computer simulation. All of his music-loving "agents" were given Thursdays' bar attendance over the past few months. For example, typical attendance figures might be:

. . . 44, 78, 56, 15, 23, 67, 84, 34, 45, 76, 40, 56, 22, 35

With this information at hand, each electronic agent has to keep track of a different subset of predictors (or hypotheses). He opts to go or stay home each Thursday according to the currently most accurate predictor in his set. Typical predictors might include the following:

- the same number as last week's (35)
- a mirror image around 50 of last week's (65)
- a rounded average of the last four weeks (38)
- the same as two weeks ago (22)

Once decisions have been taken, surrogates converge on the silicon bar and a new attendance figure is recorded. Each person reexamines the accuracy of his set of predictors, replacing the poorer ones with more reliable predictors. Then the whole decision process is repeated.

The set of predictors deemed most credible and acted upon by potential bar attendees—which Arthur calls the set of *active* predictors—determines the attendance. But the attendance history also determines the set of active predictors. This process of cumulative causation creates what John Holland has called an *ecology* of predictors. One of the aims of Arthur's computer experiments was to find out how this ecology evolves over time. So he created an "alphabetic soup" of several dozen predictors and randomly "ladled out" various mixes of these to each of the one hundred persons.

As long as the predictors are not too simplistic, the simulations show that the weekly attendance will fluctuate, but mean attendance always converges to sixty. The predictors self-organize themselves into an equilibrium "ecology" in which 40 percent of the active predictors forecast above sixty and 60 percent of them below sixty. This happens despite the fact that the population of active predictors keeps changing in membership forever. Such an emergent ecology is more like a forest whose contours do not change, but whose individual trees do.

But there's also another intriguing result. The computer-generated attendance results look more like the outcome of a random process rather than a deterministic one (see Figure 2.4). Yet there's no inherently random factor governing how many people show up. Weekly attendance is a purely deterministic function of the individual predictions, which themselves are deterministic functions of the past attendance figures. Curiously, the existence of a statistical regularity might be attributed to the deterministic nature of chaos. In other words, the time-series of attendance figures might well be a deterministically random (i.e., chaotic) process. The irritating thing is that we have no mathematical formalism with which to either prove or disprove this conjecture.

What does this kind of emergent simplicity tell us? It confirms that a system of interacting people (in this case, bar attendees) can "spontaneously" develop collective properties that aren't obvious from our knowledge of each of the individuals themselves. These statistical regularities are large-scale features that emerge purely from the microdynamics. As Jack Cohen and Ian Stewart have stressed, "Emergent simplicities collapse chaos; they bring order to a system that would otherwise appear to be wallowing hopelessly in a sea of random fluctuations."[20]

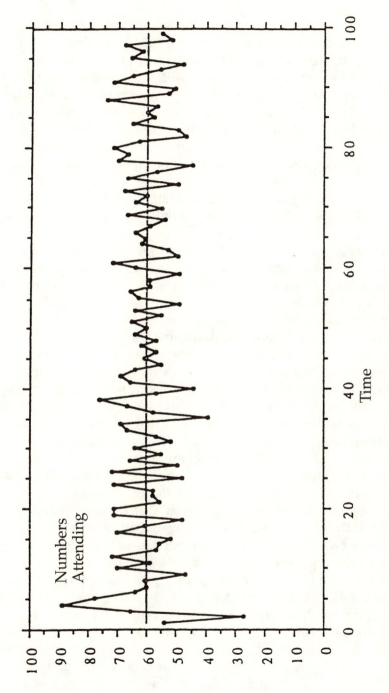

FIGURE 2.4   A simulated, 100-week record of attendance at El Farol.

The El Farol problem contains all the essential elements of a *complex adaptive system*. First, it involves a "largish" number of agents, where "largish" denotes a number too large for hand calculation or intuition but too small to call upon statistical methods applicable to very large populations. Second, it involves agents who are *adaptive* and *intelligent*. Such agents can make decisions on the basis of mental models (like the El Farol predictors) and are willing to modify these mental models or come up with new ones where necessary. In other words, they can reason *inductively*. Third, no single agent knows what all the others are thinking of doing, having access to only a limited amount of information. The El Farol case is extremely tight as each agent knows only what he or she is thinking of doing.

Conventional economic wisdom would tell us that these agents have only one reasoning skill: the ability to process the information available to them in a purely logical, deductive manner to arrive at the best decision in a given situation. But this is useless when the best thing to do—to go or not to go—depends on what everyone else is doing. There's no optimal predictor. The best each agent can do is to apply the predictor that has worked best so far, to be willing to reevaluate the effectiveness of his set of predictors, and to adopt better ones as new information about bar attendance becomes available. The latter is the inductive part of the decision process. This is the way that Arthur's surrogate music lovers behave in his silicon world, which is our world of morphogenesis.

Three results of the El Farol problem are significant. First, the computer experiments show that inductive reasoning can be modeled. Second, they show that agents' belief systems should be thought of as evolving and coevolving. Third, they suggest that under the influence of a sufficiently strong "attractor," individual expectations that are boundedly rational can self-organize to produce collectively "rational" behavior. But there's also an even stronger message for economists. Learning and adaptation should not be addenda to the central theory of economics. They should be at its core, especially in problems of high complexity.

What's more daunting is the idea that those silicon agents in Arthur's computer experiments may have developed superior intuition (i.e., know-whether) to the real bar lovers on which they're based. Ever since Deep Blue defeated Kasparov in their second round of chess games, the frightening idea that "calculative" reasoning might be able to outperform human reasoning (based on deduction or induction) in open-ended situations has been recognized.

One perplexing issue remains. How and why do the predictors self-organize so that sixty emerges as the mean attendance in the long run? Was it simply because Arthur picked sixty as the crowding threshold? If the threshold had been seventy instead of sixty, the simulations may have showed that the mean attendance would have converged to seventy. What would have happened if the assumption of a uniform crowding threshold had been dropped completely? After all, the heterogeneities of human thinking and decisionmaking suggest that music lovers could never agree on the same figure to define a bar's crowding threshold. Would sixty still emerge under these more realistic conditions?

Arthur's explanation for his result is that sixty may be a natural "attractor" for the microdynamics in this bar problem. If we view the problem as a pure prediction game, then a mixed strategy of forecasting above sixty with probability 0.4 and below it with probability 0.6 corresponds to what game theorists call a *Nash equilibrium.* Could this be the reason the forecasts split into a 60/40 ratio? Although this explanation illuminates the end of the journey, it fails to explain the means of achieving that end. Given each agent's subjective reasoning, it's still impossible to explain the collective outcome. In the next section, therefore, we'll look more closely at Nash equilibria in both a static *and* a dynamic context.

The Emergence of Cooperation

Life is literally teeming with perplexing problems, dilemmas, and paradoxes—not all of which are abstract and philosophical. Rather than being a source of frustration, some paradoxes are superbly enlightening. We savor the moment when the truth dawns upon us. One paradox that hinges on the quirks of human nature is the game theorist's favorite game, the Prisoner's Dilemma. This tantalizing puzzle was discovered in the 1950s by Merrill Flood and Melvin Drescher of the RAND Corporation, two early game theorists who were testing some bargaining theories with experimental games.[21]

Social scientists have become quite fond of the game, seeing Prisoner's Dilemma situations arising everywhere in socioeconomic interactions. It's a surprisingly ubiquitous metaphor. As Russell Hardin notes, if the dilemma had been called "exchange" originally, then everyone would've expected it to be ubiquitous.[22] In economics, we view exchange as a two-party affair. But exchange situations can involve more than two parties. Think of the bidding by competing parties at an auction, verbal exchanges between participants at a public meeting, or the debate between political parties leading up to an election. In its multiperson or collective guise, exchange is a very interesting problem. Although less tractable than the traditional two-party problem, it captures the perversity of the logic of collective action.[23] Under this logic, a group of people with a common interest that requires a common action can share an interest collectively but not individually.

Before we get immersed in a debate over collective versus individual behavior, it's worthwhile getting more closely acquainted with the Prisoner's Dilemma. Let's sidestep the original formulation about prisoners and jail terms because it can baffle the uninitiated. Instead we'll look at this puzzling paradox in the form of an economic metaphor: the "Trader's Dilemma." The scene for this metaphor is Medieval Europe. Imagine yourself as an enterprising merchant from Venice in the early days of Mediterranean trade. Venetian salt is what you have in abundance. Instead of trading it for grain and linen, on your next voyage you opt for something different. The latest rage is precious silk from Thebes (near Athens), so you stop there on your way from Venice to Constantinople.

You find a silk dealer whose terms are acceptable. But disappointment follows when you learn that he has a binding agreement with another Italian merchant. He's willing to trade, but only if the trade takes place secretly. He can't risk being seen dealing with you. So you agree to leave your salt consignment in bags at a well-concealed spot in a nearby forest and to pick up the bags of silk at the silk dealer's designated place. Of course, you'll have to leave more bags than him because salt has a much lower value than silk.

Given that the silk dealer is nervous about jeopardizing his existing agreement, it's pretty clear to both of you that this will be a one-time exchange. You're unlikely to meet again or have any further dealings with each other. Suddenly you realize that there's something for each of you to fear: namely that *the bags that you get could be empty.* Of course, there's no risk if you both leave full bags. But getting something for nothing would be even more rewarding. So you're tempted to leave empty bags.

Here's how you might think this through:

> If the silk dealer brings full bags, then I'll be better off leaving empty bags—because I'll get all the silk I want *and* keep all my salt. Even if the silk dealer brings empty bags, I'll still be better off leaving nothing—because that way I can never be cheated. *No matter what the silk dealer does,* my smartest move is to leave empty bags. So I'll leave empty bags.

By similar reasoning, however, the silk dealer reaches the same conclusion. So you both leave empty bags and come away empty-handed.

The result is obviously disappointing. In the jargon of the Prisoner's Dilemma, both of you chose *defection* over *cooperation.* If you'd both cooperated, you could have sailed away with precious silk and the silk dealer would own a cellar full of salt. There would have been smiles all around. Instead of that you have no silk. What went wrong? Why did logical reasoning rule out cooperation? This is the perplexing aspect of the Prisoner's Dilemma.

A revealing theorem by John Nash, an early pioneer in game theory, threw some light on this surprising outcome. He showed that there's always at least one "Nash" strategy for each player, with the property that if each player chooses that strategy, he or she will be better off than with any other strategy. But this situation holds only if all the other players opt for their Nash strategies. A choice of Nash strategies among all the players is called a Nash equilibrium. No doubt you've guessed the connection by now. The decision of both traders to leave empty bags corresponds to a Nash equilibrium.

To pinpoint a Nash equilibrium precisely, we need to assign some numbers to our problem. But how do we quantify it? According to game theory, we define a set of payoffs to each of the players. You and the silk dealer have a pair of strategies to choose from:

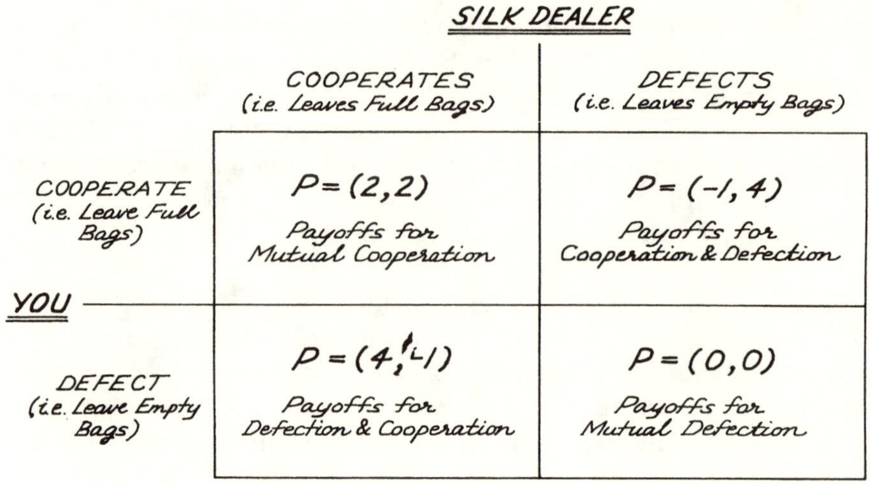

SILK DEALER

	COOPERATES (i.e. Leaves Full Bags)	DEFECTS (i.e. Leaves Empty Bags)
COOPERATE (i.e. Leave Full Bags)	$P = (2,2)$ Payoffs for Mutual Cooperation	$P = (-1, 4)$ Payoffs for Cooperation & Defection
DEFECT (i.e. Leave Empty Bags)	$P = (4, -1)$ Payoffs for Defection & Cooperation	$P = (0,0)$ Payoffs for Mutual Defection

YOU (label on left side, between rows)

FIGURE 2.5   Computing payoffs in the Trader's Dilemma game.

You can leave either full or empty bags. The payoff for each of you depends on the strategy chosen by the other. To display these various alternatives, we define a *payoff matrix* containing point values for the different pairs of strategies. Some typical point values are shown in Figure 2.5.

How do we interpret the figures? Payoff doesn't mean money since the exchange involves goods only. The numbers indicate the *degree of satisfaction* associated with each strategic outcome. For example, mutual cooperation scores two points to both of you. In this problem, two points means "quite happy." Both of you would be quite happy if all bags were full and you both got what you wanted. Mutual defection scores zero, and zero means you're "indifferent" to the idea of gaining and losing nothing.[24] If your worst fears were realized and you got empty bags after leaving full ones, then you'd score −1 and be "feeling upset," while the silk dealer would score 4 and be feeling "very happy." These scores would reverse if you found full bags after leaving empty ones.

The Nash equilibrium solution to this game lies at P = (0,0). But this means zero payoff to both of you. Why should you choose zero reward? Because defection risks at worst indifference (0), whereas cooperation could leave you upset (−1). No matter what the silk dealer does, your safest *individual* strategy is to defect. Note that the payoff for mutual defection is lower than for mutual cooperation. Thus your best *joint* strategy is to cooperate. Now you can see the dilemma. Because you're unlikely to meet again, the best solution is to defect—despite the seemingly paradoxical outcome that it would be *collectively* superior for you both to cooperate.

Stuart Kauffman sums up the Nash concept as a penetrating one: "The concept of Nash equilibria was a remarkable insight, for it offers an account of how independent selfish agents might coordinate their behavior without a master choreographer."[25] Despite its allure, however, a Nash equilibrium "solution" to the Trader's Dilemma has some major weaknesses. First, it sits stubbornly in the world of stasis. In the case where the Trader's Dilemma is played only once, a Nash solution is stable, predictable, and resistant to change. No other strategy can invade the strategy of pure defection. Second, it relies on all traders thinking and acting rationally and identically. Like the deductively rational economic agent we discussed earlier, traders are assumed to have the brainpower and enough information to figure out their optimal strategy. Third, it may not be the solution in which the payoff to traders is particularly good.

Even if these weaknesses could be overlooked (which they can't), there's still another problem. What happens in a large game with many players? How would you approach a market boasting a dozen or more silk traders and just as many salt merchants desperate to outperform you? There could be many more possible strategies and many more Nash equilibria. How would you find all these Nash strategies and then pick the best Nash equilibrium? Would this Nash payoff be worth pursuing in any case? Like Thursday nights at the El Farol bar, your problem quickly becomes complicated and ill defined.

Setting these problems aside for the moment, let's return to the scene of our Trader's Dilemma. By now your ship has been reloaded with the untraded salt. What have you learned from this abortive experience? What might you do next? You've discovered that for a *single* exchange conducted in secret, the temptation for both parties to cheat is irresistible. Now you recall your normal recipe for success: long-term, bilateral agreements. You go in search of another silk dealer who shares your desire for lifelong exchanges. Eventually you find a young dealer who accepts your long-term proposal. You agree to exchange fixed amounts every quarter but are unlikely to meet again face to face.

What do you do on the occasion of your first exchange? Leaving empty bags would hardly be a friendly way of fostering good will with a new trading partner. So you leave full bags. So does your silk dealer. What a relief! Three months pass and then you must go again. Empty or full? Every quarter you must make the decision whether to cooperate or defect. Two years later, the silk dealer defects unexpectedly. What will you do now? Can he ever be trusted again or will you call a halt to all future exchanges with him?

In the literature, the game you're now playing is known as the *iterated* Prisoner's Dilemma. Just as adding more players creates complications, so does allowing *repeated* exchanges. But it also adds more realism. The trading world has always featured long-term agreements, cartels, price-fixing, and other multilateral trading arrangements. Furthermore, traders engaging in repeated exchanges have always shown some degree of cooperation. And they also tend to review their strategies regularly over time. So it makes a lot of sense to study the iterated version of the Prisoner's Dilemma in order to understand the exact conditions under which cooperation might emerge.

The million-dollar question is: *Can cooperation ever evolve out of noncooperation?* Well, the answer turns out to be a resounding *yes.* Emergent cooperation has been demonstrated by a novel method: a computer tournament organized by Robert Axelrod, a political scientist at the University of Michigan. Cooperation won out among a diverse population of computer programs playing repeated games of the Prisoner's Dilemma with one another. After the tournament was over, Axelrod spotted the salient principles and proved theorems that could explain cooperation's rise from nowhere. His findings have been published in many papers and two thought-provoking books.[26]

Axelrod sent out invitations to game theorists in economics, sociology, political science, and mathematics. The rules implied a similar payoff matrix to the one shown earlier for the Trader's Dilemma. Submitted programs were designed to respond to the "cooperate" or "defect" decisions of other programs, taking into account the remembered history of previous interactions with that particular program. Fourteen entries duly arrived. Axelrod added another called RANDOM, which simply flipped a coin each time it met another program. Each program was made to engage other programs two hundred times.

Although some of the entries were quite sophisticated, the winning program turned out to be the *simplest* of all the strategies submitted. Known as TIT FOR TAT, it simply cooperates on the first move and then does whatever the other player did on the preceding move. That's all there is to it. TIT FOR TAT was written by the psychologist and philosopher Anatol Rapoport, who turns out to be an old hand at the Prisoner's Dilemma game.[27] Rapoport's program was also the shortest of all the programs submitted. Small is beautiful after all!

Given this surprising outcome, the full results were circulated and entries for a second tournament were solicited. Axelrod provided a few hints this time. He pointed out that many of the losing strategies suffered from self-punishment because such a possibility was not perceived by their decision rules. He also stressed that TIT FOR TAT was a strategy of cooperation based on reciprocity and that many of the other strategies were not forgiving enough.

This time Axelrod received sixty-two entries from six countries. Most came from computer hobbyists (including one ten-year-old). Rapoport's TIT FOR TAT was there again. So was a variation on the same theme called TIT FOR TWO TATS, which tolerates two defections before getting mad (but still only strikes back once). Axelrod already knew that TIT FOR TWO TATS would have won the first tournament if it had been in the lineup, so it was sure to be hard to beat. It was entered by one of the world's experts on game theory and evolution, John Maynard Smith, professor of biology at the University of Sussex.

Can you guess what happened? Amazingly, TIT FOR TAT won again. What a remarkable result! How on earth could such a simple decision strategy defeat so many other stratagems devised by all those whiz kids? Axelrod attributes TIT FOR TAT's success to its being

nice (not the first to defect);
provokable (responding to the other player's defection);
forgiving (punishing and then cooperating after a defection);
clear (easy for other players to understand).

So, nice guys, or more precisely, nice, provokable, forgiving, and clear guys, can indeed finish first. But success in two computer tournaments is hardly enough to prove that TIT FOR TAT would do well as an evolutionary strategy. To test this possibility, Axelrod conducted a series of *ecological* simulations, with various tournament entries and other strategies as his starting population. He found that TIT FOR TAT quickly became the most common strategy. Thus the conclusions seemed clear. A small cluster of players who opt for cooperation based upon reciprocity could establish themselves in a population of noncooperative players. Once established, they could become immune from re-invasion by any other strategies and could thus take over such a population.

The Prisoner's Dilemma game captures the tension between the advantages of selfishness in the short term versus the need to elicit cooperation to be successful in the long run. But the jury's still out on whether such voluntary cooperation is sustainable over the long run. Many analysts (like Axelrod) believe that TIT FOR TAT could be a robust and stable mutant; even an *evolutionarily stable strategy* under certain conditions. But others have challenged this idea. An article in the journal *Nature* showed that no pure strategy can be evolutionarily stable in the iterated Prisoner's Dilemma.[28] Another *Nature* article reported that the most successful strategy is one that repeats its previous choice when it gets one of the two highest payoffs.[29] This ongoing debate suggests that there's much more to be learned about the evolution of cooperation, especially under different socioeconomic conditions.

Nevertheless, it's nice to know that benign cooperation among selfish agents can emerge despite the constant temptation to defect. In Axelrod's words, "Mutual cooperation can emerge among a world of egoists without central control, by starting with a cluster of individuals who rely on reciprocity."[30] And in those of Hardin, "But coordination can come about without intent, without overcoming contrary incentives. It can just happen."[31] In other words, cooperation can *self-organize* within a population, despite its members' biologically determined egoism. This has ramifications for both the economic and political arenas.

Many of the challenging problems facing humanity relate to globalization and international relations, where independent nations often refuse to cooperate, instead exhibiting stark hostility.[32]

Such problems closely resemble the iterated Prisoner's Dilemma. In addition to trade negotiations, arms races, crisis bargaining, nuclear proliferation, and environmental pollution fall into this category. By understanding the process of mutual cooperation a little better, perhaps we could use our foresight to speed up its evolution.

There's another interesting message for economics from the TIT FOR TAT story. A strategy's success depends entirely on the environment in which it's swimming. At the beginning of Axelrod's ecological tournaments, poor programs *and* good programs were well represented. But as they "swam" through generation after generation of interactions, this environment changed. The poorer strategies began to drop out and the better ones flourished. So it is with technologies. Their rank order changes because their "goodness" is remeasured alongside a different field of competitors. Success breeds further success, but only when that success comes from interaction with other reasonably successful technologies.

Doesn't this ring a bell or two? Remember those high-tech firms we discussed in Chapter 1. In the economic world of morphogenesis, firms that get ahead get even further ahead. Like good strategies in the Prisoner's Dilemma, they're self-reinforcing. TIT FOR TAT didn't win all those tournaments by *beating* the other players, but by eliciting behavior from the others that allowed *both* to do well. This kind of mutual learning process isn't just evolutionary, it's *coevolutionary*.

Coevolution has been found in evolutionary versions of the Prisoner's Dilemma. Instead of starting like Axelrod did, with random selection from a rich set of strategies, Kristian Lindgren began with the simplest possible strategies. Using an extension of the genetic algorithm to evolve more and more complex possibilities, and allowing for the possibility of mistakes, he found that selection favors the evolution of cooperation and unexploitable strategies.[33] The result was long periods of stasis alternating with periods of instability, as one dominant pattern of strategies was invaded by another. Various kinds of evolutionary phenomena, like coexistence, punctuated equilibria, exploitation, the coevolution of mutualism, and evolutionarily stable strategies, were encountered in the model simulations.

Coevolutionary Learning

How stunning it was when biology revealed that organisms don't just evolve, they *coevolve*. Their adaptation over time isn't shaped merely by their encounters with other organisms; it's also honed by the environment in which they live. And this environment isn't fixed but is also adapting to the behavior of its changing inhabitants. What might this imply for agents in an economy? In behavioral terms, it suggests that what agents believe affects what happens to the economy, *and* in turn, what happens to the economy affects what agents believe. This, in fact, is the hypothesis explored in this book. The agents and goods and services in the economy coevolve, because those that are present must always make sense in the context of all the others that already exist. Diversity breeds more diversity, thereby fueling the growth of complexity.

There's another way of recognizing the fundamental difference between evolution and coevolution. Stuart Kauffman couches it in terms of fitness landscapes.[34] Evolution occurs on a fixed landscape where the attractors are local optima in the form of single points. This kind of landscape is a familiar one to economists, who are taught that optimization is a simple hill-climbing procedure. All that we thought we needed to know was the topography of the hill.

In a coevolutionary process, however, the landscape isn't fixed. Instead, it's adapting incessantly. In an economic environment, for example, we can picture the landscape of one agent heaving and deforming incessantly as other agents make their own adaptive moves. The resulting environment has a very unstable surface. In fact, it's more like a seascape than a landscape. Have you ever tried to surf on an incessantly choppy and undulating ocean surface? That's the kind of decision environment that exists when agents must adapt incessantly. Nobody quite knows where they're going next. It's even difficult to define the problem. For example, technological evolution is a process attempting to optimize a system riddled with conflicting constraints. In such an uncertain environment, the various behavioral regimes that may coevolve are mind-boggling. The likelihood of reaching local optima in the form of point attractors is very remote. *Coevolving systems may not be optimizing anything.*

What *are* they doing then? One insight comes from Axelrod's results. Sometimes coevolution allows TIT FOR TAT-style cooperation to emerge and thrive in a world full of treacherous defectors. The iterated Prisoner's Dilemma game simultaneously provides an abstract model for the evolution of cooperation and the setting for a very complex evolutionary landscape.[35] Another insight comes from Arthur's inductive economic models in which agents learn and adapt. Inductive agents, who persistently alter their mental models of other agents' behavior, will decide and behave differently. They're forever changing their mental images of others. These mental images are often nothing more than subjective expectations or half-hoped anticipations. They can be mutually cooperative or mutually competitive. They can arise, get a solid footing, gain prominence, fall back, and disappear. Arthur regards them as the DNA of an economy.

Whenever beliefs form a complex ocean of interacting, competing and cooperating, arising and decaying entities, it's possible that they may simplify into an ordered equilibrium now and then. But most of the time they'll be found in complex, unsettled, ever-changing states. Beliefs about beliefs are mostly volatile. There's no evidence to suggest that such adaptive behavior ever settles down into a steady, predictable pattern. This is a another signature of *coevolutionary learning.*

The light is beginning to shine at last! When economic agents interact, when they must think about what other agents might be thinking, their coevolving behavior can take a wide variety of forms. Sometimes it might look chaotic, sometimes it might appear to be ordered, but more often than not it will lie somewhere in between. At one distant end of the spectrum, chaotic behavior would correspond to *rapidly* changing models of other agents' beliefs. If beliefs change too quickly, however, there may be no clear pattern at all. Such a volatile state could simply appear to be random. At the other end of the spectrum, ordered behavior could emerge, but only if the ocean of beliefs happens to converge onto a mutually consistent set of models of one another. One familiar example is that classical pillar of the world of stasis, a state of equilibrium among a set of deductively rational agents.

For most of the time, however, we'd expect that mental models of each other's beliefs would be poised somewhere in between these two extremes, ready to unleash avalanches of small and large changes throughout the whole system of interacting agents. Why should we expect this? Given more data, we would expect each agent to improve his ability to generalize about the other agents' behavior by constructing *more complex* models of their behavior. These more complex models would also be more sensitive to small alterations in the other agents' behavior. Thus as agents develop more complex models to predict more accurately, the coevolving system of agents tends to be driven away from the ordered regime toward the chaotic regime. Near the chaotic regime, however, such complexity and changeability would leave each agent with very little reliable data about the other agents' behavior. Thus they would be forced to simplify, to build *less complex* models of the other agents' behavior. These less complex models are less sensitive to the behavior of others and live in calmer oceans.

Thus we can picture a constant struggle between the need to simplify and the need to "complexify" our thinking. This is tantamount to a struggle between the two halves of our brain. Being more objective, rational, and analytical, the left-hand side houses the simpler confines of convergent thinking. It's also responsible for the deductive metaphor among economic agents. By way of contrast, the right-hand side is more subjective, intuitive, and holistic. This kind of divergent thinking produces multiple outcomes and creative ideas. Thus the right-hand side is responsible for inductive reasoning among economic agents. We can picture these two modes of thought in constant interplay, driving the whole ocean of beliefs back and forward, from chaos to order and back again. In general, therefore, we might expect to find most economic agents hovering somewhere in between, poised, if you like, near "the edge of chaos."

Believe it or not, such poised states proliferate in our everyday world. Here's one example from my own backyard. For several years, my ten-year-old daughter, Sofie, and I have enjoyed the habit of cycling together on a bayside circuit near our Melbourne home. While pedaling around this predetermined circuit, we often play that simple guessing game that kids everywhere seem to adore: "I spy with my little eye, something beginning with . . . ." For the first few months, we played the standard game: We tried to guess each other's word given its first letter. Then Sofie began to ask for a clue if the word turned out to be elusive. A few months later, we allowed two clues under certain conditions. Then came a major "mutation." Our population of potentially guessable "things" expanded dramatically when we allowed two-word descriptions to join single words. First, it was just nouns needing two words to define them (e.g., ice cream). But very soon the set of possible words was expanded again. We included adjective-noun pairs (e.g., red car). Can you guess what was happening? Our little game of "I spy" was *coevolving* all the time. It seemed to be forever poised on the verge of an avalanche of smaller and larger changes. A bit like those sandpiles we discussed in Chapter 1.

Progress in science is a fertile example of coevolutionary learning. Scientists develop their own models or hypotheses about a particular phenomenon of interest. Then they test these ideas in a variety of ways: performing experiments in laboratories, discussing their results with colleagues, lecturing about them at seminars and conferences, and publishing them in journals and books. From each of these critical audiences, they get feedback. Usually they're obliged to revise their ideas in the light of this feedback, to discard some of their old models and replace them with new ones. Like chess players, scientists discern patterns, build temporary mental models, test them in a competitive environment, revise them in the light of new information, and come up with improved hypotheses. They're immersed in an ocean of ideas, where each one is evolving and coevolving. Scientists are experts at coevolutionary learning.

As we noted earlier, researchers understand the importance of oral communication when their own ideas are exposed for critical comment. One of the great advantages of face-to-face contact is that it fosters the unexpected! Unsolicited comments from thoughtful peers can be pearls of wisdom. Interestingly, face-to-face contact is dependent on the transportation system. And the world of transport is another arena where coevolutionary learning is hard at work. A traffic system supports a large number of interacting vehicles and drivers, and the behavior of both can be complex and unpredictable. As we shall learn in a later chapter, busy traffic may be poised near the edge of chaos.

three

Sheep, Explorers, and Phase Transitions

I have supposed a Human Being to be capable of various physical states, and varying degrees of consciousness, as follows:

(a) *the ordinary state, with no consciousness of the presence of Fairies;*

(b) *the eerie state, in which, while conscious of actual surroundings, he is also conscious of the presence of Fairies;*

(c) *a form of trance, in which, while unconscious of actual surroundings, and apparently asleep, he (i.e., his immaterial essence) migrates to other scenes in the actual world, or in Fairyland, and is conscious of the presence of Fairies.*

—**Lewis Carroll**

The Fallacy of Composition

In the previous chapter, we learned two important things about how the economy works. First, human decisionmaking reflects the *different* beliefs and expectations of individuals. Second, the *interactions* between these different individuals can produce unexpected collective outcomes. In turn, it's the evolution of these collective outcomes that shapes each agent's future behavior. *What agents believe affects what happens to the economy, and in turn, what happens to the economy affects what agents believe.* The impacts of this positive feedback loop are what this book is all about. We call it coevolutionary learning.

For the time being, we'll regard the first problem as a *psychological* one and the second as a *systems* problem.[1] Having looked at aspects of psychology in the previous chapter, our aim in this chapter is to look more deeply into the systems problem. This problem lies at the core of the complexity issue. It's not difficult to understand why. All of us have the feeling that our economy is complex . Why is it so complex? One reason is that it involves a very large number of elements. In a major city economy, for example, several million human agents can link together in a myriad of different ways. In a national economy, an even greater number of interactions can arise. Adopting this view of economic complexity is just one way of looking at the problem. It turns out to be a *combinatorial* view.

Most of us aren't expected to know very much about the whole economy and the way it works. What we often know (or can find out) are the prices of things we can buy or sell, the interest rates at which we can borrow or lend, and a little about the alternative ways we might earn our living and spend our money. Beyond these personal aspects, however, we tend to think of the rest of the economy as some giant accounting system, capable of balancing out all those transactions resulting from specific patterns of interaction between all the agents involved. Some of us believe we know more than this; others feel that they know even less. Most of us simply take our economy for granted, partly because we don't understand the way it really works.

What we tend to forget is that any specific pattern of transactions, whether in equilibrium or disequilibrium, is just one collective possibility. It's nothing more than one plausible set of agents' interactions from among many candidates. The magical thing is that, somehow, all of these chosen transactions seem to get coordinated. We have little idea of *how* this fantastically complex system selects this particular pattern of interactions, manages to balance them out, and then somehow decides where to go next. Because inductive agents learn and adapt, forever changing the ways they choose to interact, a coevolving economy is actually open-ended. There's simply no way we can know how each and every agent is going to behave, least of all what the economy as a whole will do under different conditions. Future outcomes depend on the historical trajectory of choices made along the way.

Most economists acknowledge that what seems to be true for individuals isn't always true for society as a whole. Conversely, what seems to be true for all may be quite false for any one individual. In stressing that things aren't always what they seem at first, Paul Samuelson provides some paradoxical examples in the form of the following *true* statements:

- If all farmers work hard and nature cooperates to produce a bumper crop, total income may fall, and probably will.
- One man may solve his own unemployment problem by great ingenuity in finding a job or by a willingness to work for less, but all cannot necessarily solve their job problems in this way.
- Higher prices for one industry may benefit its firms; but if the prices of everything bought and sold increased in the same proportion, no one would be better off.
- It may pay the United States to reduce tariffs charged on goods imported, even if other countries refuse to lower their tariff barriers.
- Attempts of individuals to save more in depression may lessen the total of the community's savings.
- What's prudent behavior for an individual may at times be folly for a nation.[2]

Many of the above paradoxes hinge upon a single confusion or fallacy. Logicians have dubbed it the "fallacy of composition." In books on logic, you can find the following definition:

Fallacy of Composition: A fallacy in which what is true of a part is, on that account alone, alleged to be also necessarily true of the whole.

The six statements mentioned above are typical of the many instances of the fallacy of composition that appear in economics texts. In the course of books like Samuelson's, these paradoxes are resolved. There are no magic formulas or hidden tricks. Each is explained in terms of standard economic principles. Some fallacies are due to comparative price or quantity changes at different levels of the economy, whereas others are due to structural properties of the whole economy. The interested reader might care to attempt an explanation of each.

Our view is that paradoxical statements typically chosen to illustrate the fallacy of composition (like the six mentioned above) hardly scratch the surface compared to the full set of paradoxes that can arise. Furthermore, they're a select group that *can* be resolved using the conventional static equilibrium view of the economy. In other words, most are traps that exist inside the world of stasis only. Although they're treated as if they're exceptions to the rule, what's overlooked is the fact that the more challenging economic paradoxes arise in that other world of economics: the world of morphogenesis. Many have nothing to do with equilibrium prices but are due to the positive feedback loop associated with learning from others and from collective experiences. In other words, they're governed by the coevolutionary learning processes in the economy.

A central difficulty in the economy, then, is one of *dynamic interdependencies*. How do we find a way of handling the huge variety of behavior—both individual and collective—that can arise when economic agents interact over space and time? Complexity arises, then, because of the numerous ways in which economic agents can choose to work together. Furthermore, unusual collective properties can arise if the agents choose to interact in particular ways. We caught a glimpse of some of these unexpected phenomena in Schelling's segregation model (Chapter 1) and Arthur's bar problem (Chapter 2). The point to remember is that we need to know what the economic agents are thinking and doing interactively over time, not simply what prices they're paying at specific points in time.

Before we probe the perplexing issue of dynamics more deeply, consider the following example of *how* the systems problem comes about. Instead of sandpiles, this simplifying illustration involves action on a billiard table. If you roll a billiard ball across such a table, any reasonable player can predict the path that it will follow. If you roll two balls across the table at the same time, it's still not difficult to calculate each ball's path individually. Once you add a few more balls, however, there's a strong chance that some balls will bump into others. The problem of keeping track of every ball's path and collision possibilities becomes more difficult. Now imagine what would happen if, with the help of friends, you rolled one hundred balls across the table at the same time! They'd be bumping into each other all the time. Predicting their individual paths would be impossible. The system as a whole would become unpredictable at the individual level.

If you happen to be a grand master at chess, you'd probably notice the pattern of behavior over the entire table. Oddly enough, the problem begins to simplify again at this macrolevel. The more balls you roll, the less important it is to trace every ball exactly. Once there are lots of balls rolling across the table, a new behavioral paradigm takes over. Individual interactions start to average out. Suddenly you can make reasonable predictions about the average speed and the average time between collisions. Macroscopic patterns form. A new kind of order has arisen. These collective properties emerge unexpectedly out of the countless number of individual interactions.

The billiard ball model turns out to be the starting point for the kinetic theory of gases.[3] In a container full of many particles, all whizzing around and bumping into each other at all sorts of speeds, one property is always stable with respect to all the other elements (such as type of gas, shape of container, and so on). In the case of gases, that property is temperature. A stable temperature is an emergent property because we would never have predicted it by looking at the individual particles themselves, or the shape of the container, or anything else that is part of the whole system. By now, you've probably got the message; emergence is one of the hallmarks of complexity in both physical and socioeconomic systems.

Certainly economic agents are more complicated than billiard balls. Nevertheless, the notions of interactive complexity and emergence are identical in both cases. Remember those music lovers at the El Farol bar. Nobody risked much chance of bumping into anyone else if the bar wasn't crowded. But as soon as the crowd grew to more than sixty, the chances of brushing up against one or two pushing-and-shoving bar louts were pretty high. From week to week, it was impossible to guess how many would turn up next Thursday evening. Despite all this uncertainty at the individual level, the mean attendance over time converged to a predictable value. Order emerged from seemingly random behavior.

Irreducible Interactions

There seems to be a consistent message here about simple and complex economic systems, at least in terms of two key properties. By and large, simple economic systems are *homogeneous* and *weakly interactive*. Individual beliefs and expectations must be sufficiently uniform, and the level of interactions sufficiently weak or trivial, for us to be able to predict collective patterns of behavior with any confidence. By way of comparison, complex economies are *heterogeneous* and *strongly interactive.* They lie beyond the point where individual behavior can be discerned with any degree of confidence (see Figure 3.1). Somehow, the whole economic system gets transformed into a qualitatively different behavioral state.

What we find is a high degree of irregularities together with heterogeneity of individual behavior. The surprising thing is that intrinsic unpredictability of individual behavior does not imply unpredictability of collective behavior. Furthermore, any failure to predict does not imply a failure to understand or explain. Not knowing the full details, we may nevertheless build theories that seek to explain the *generic properties.* Collective order may depend little on the details of structure and function. This was the point of the billiard ball example and the bar problem. Despite our ignorance of all the individual elements, we can still uncover interesting collective features like statistical averages.

Are such distinctions between simple and complex systems fundamentally important in economic life? I believe so. Plenty of examples can be found. Even when people appear to be doing very simple things—like driving a car, buying food, or going to the movies—their pattern of interactions can quickly add up to more complexity than we can handle. One example, familiar to all of us, is the unwelcome traffic jam. If the flow pattern of traffic on a roadway happens to approach a critical flow density, a qualitatively different kind of collective behavior appears. The traffic changes from a free-flowing state to one in which stop-start waves propagate back and disrupt the flow discontinuously. Which flow pattern you meet depends on what others are doing, not just on what you choose to do. Technically, this kind of unexpected change is known as a *phase transition.* But now we're getting ahead of ourselves again.

Suppose that you're planning to go to the movies. Which one do you see? Even if the reviews in the papers and magazines have kept you up to date with what's on—expanding your *know-what,* so to speak—you'll still want to get other opinions. So you talk to your family and friends, to find out what they thought of the ones they saw. Which movie you decide to see will depend on what you

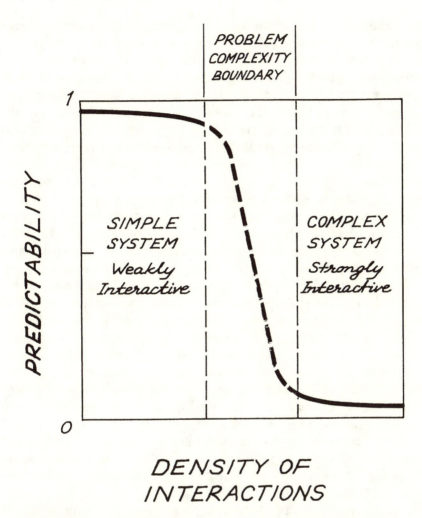

FIGURE 3.1 The difference between simple and complex systems.

learn from other people, people who've already gone through similar choice processes to the one in which you're engaged. Afterward, other people will ask you what film you saw and what you thought of it. Then you can boast a good degree of *know-whether*, that is, whether any of the ones you've seen are worthy of their attention.

If you also happen to follow the fortunes of the recent releases from the major studios, you may learn that one of the films you've elected to see has taken off like a rocket. Later, however, it loses its momentum. It ends up making a nice profit. Another starts more slowly but builds up an ever-increasing audience, doing well enough to earn a place on the all-time earners' list. Most of the others fizzle out, not even covering their production and distribution costs. You realize that you can't always pick the big winner beforehand. Because the movie selection business is strongly interactive, individual market shares at the macrolevel are hard to predict. There are many subtle and surprising ways in which agent characteristics and connectivity structure affect the market shares of competing products.[4] We'll return to the issue of connectivity shortly.

As noted earlier, the defining characteristic of a coevolving economy is that some of its collective properties can't be predicted from our knowledge of the agents involved or their likely interactions. Even if we could recognize and understand the implications of all the two-way interactions between pairs of agents, we would still be ignorant about three-way, four-way, and larger groups of interaction. This suggests a second way of distinguishing between simple and complex economic systems. A complex economy is *never additive*. It behaves quite differently from what we'd expect by simply adding up these pairs, trios, and quartets of interaction. Self-organizing economies are not additive; they're *emergent*. This is precisely why some of their collective behaviors can't be predicted in advance. There's simply no way of combining the parts into an aggregate when we're ignorant about the nature and extent of some of the interactions.

Aristotle may have been the first to recognize that the whole is something more than the sum of its parts. But it was the Scottish philosopher David Hume who impressed upon us the need to distinguish between the simple and the complex. Hume lived in the so-called Age of Enlightenment, along with such great French thinkers as Voltaire and Rousseau. His main work, *A Treatise of Human Nature,* was published when Hume was twenty-eight years old, though he claimed that the idea for the book came to him when he was only fifteen.

In Hume's day, there was a widespread belief in angels. Yes, we're talking about those human figures with wings. Many people of Hume's time also claimed that they had a very clear idea of heaven. According to Hume, however, "heaven" and "angels" are complex ideas. If we think about this for a moment, we quickly realize that our personal idea of "heaven" consists of a great many elements. It may include "pearly gates," "angels," "streets of gold," and so forth. Breaking heaven down into its various constituent parts doesn't solve the problem for us because each of the parts— pearly gates, angels, and streets of gold—are still complex ideas in themselves.

The prize for the most amusing illustration of Aristotle's view should go to the systems scientist John Casti. In recalling Mark Twain's tale about *Those Extraordinary Twins,* Siamese twins called Luigi and Angelo, Casti reminds us that the story was based on the lives of the first recorded Siamese twins in the real world.[5] These twins, Chang and Eng, were born in Siam in 1811 but ended up as American citizens. The truly fascinating thing was that both of them had an army of children: seven daughters and three sons for Chang, seven sons and five daughters for Eng. How they managed to be so productive is anyone's guess!

Hume and Casti were stressing the same point: If you want to study the behavior of a system composed of several parts, breaking it up into its constituent parts and studying each of them separately won't always help you to understand the whole thing. It's pretty clear that Mark Twain, for one, would not have been the least bit interested if Chang and Eng had been separated at birth. Siamese twins are very special because they're linked together in an unusual manner. It's the connection itself that makes them interesting and unique. The result is a system far more complicated than that of a typical human being. In trying to understand the whole system "Chang-and-Eng," it's essential to take this connectivity into account.

Connectivity is not just a fundamental feature of living systems. As we showed in the example of movie selection, it's also an important feature of products that we buy and sell in our everyday economic activities. A car is an excellent example of connectivity. If you'd lived all your life in the remotest jungles of Africa, chances are that you might never have seen a car. Then one day you come to town and happen to see this strange object, the purpose of which is unknown to you. The functions of each of its components are carefully explained to you in your native language—what the carburetor does, where the fuel is injected, how the wheels turn on axles, and so on. But imagine if the aim of the whole exercise is never revealed. Chances are high that you might never guess that this strange object sitting before you is designed for one simple purpose—to transport human beings from one place to another. A car's detailed structure is complex, but its overall purpose is behaviorally simple.

As you may have guessed already, the ability of a car to move is an emergent simplicity, an ordered outcome that the car can carry out by virtue of its overall organization. So is the ability of a clock to "tell" the time or of a fan to cool the surrounding air.[6] Many products that we buy and sell possess regularities of behavior that seem to transcend their own ingredients. We know what the emergent simplicities happen to be. But imagine if we didn't. Even after having all the intricate parts and mechanisms of a car or a clock or a fan explained to us in minute detail, we might never guess what the whole machine does.

Emergent simplicities can't be deduced by a reductionist approach, that is, reducing the apparent complicatedness of the problem by analyzing its constituent parts and then linking them together by relatively simple rules. Yet this is what much of economics attempts to do. Whole economies are subdivided into statistically convenient subclasses, like industries and households. These subclasses are often subdivided into even smaller parts, like jobs and persons. Then comes the problematical step. By making some simplifying assumptions about the behavior of these smaller parts, economists draw conclusions about collective outcomes.

The reductionist strategy—take it apart, see what the pieces are, understand how they fit together—does help with simpler economic systems. But it runs into major headaches when the system of interest is truly complex. Regrettably, we cannot use the reductionist philosophy to explain more than the very simplest interactions between or within human populations. It simply won't work on more complicated problems.

Obviously, it's difficult to predict the exact branchings of a complex coevolving system that involves living elements—like a human brain, a bustling city, or an expanding economy. The sheer complexity of some human systems is mind-boggling. For example, a brain is a collection of immensely many parts. Estimates of just how many vary from 10 billion to 100 billion neurons. These parts are hooked up to each other in incredibly complex ways, most neurons being connected to several hundred others. Some are connected to thousands of others! Having so many connecting wires, it's impossible to even imagine what an accurate circuit diagram would look like. It would need a gigantic computer system just for its storage. Although we do understand some basic features of how this gigantic neural telephone system works, we know virtually nothing about the meaning of the messages flowing through it.

Speaking metaphorically, we're left groping in the dark! Even an expert electronic engineer would have trouble understanding how a circuit worked if he didn't know what its components did or how they were linked together. This is precisely the situation in many parts of human society. Our cities are another example. Each of us knows very little about what other people and other organizations do and has limited knowledge of the circulatory patterns that the city generates. Yet, despite this uncertainty—or perhaps because of it—the city manages to survive! Most of the time it seems to be operating under the principle of "more of the same." Every now and then, however, it suffers abrupt and permanent change. The city's apparent equilibrium is suddenly punctuated by an avalanche of changes. To all intents and purposes, it undergoes a phase transition.

As mentioned earlier, phase transitions are quite commonplace in many physical systems. A lesser known fact is that they also occur in schools of fish, in human brains, and on city highways. When the interactions between the components of the system are sufficiently dense, and when those interactions add up in such a way as to make for large-scale correlations, then a different kind of entity emerges. Remember that sandpile behavior we discussed in Chapter 1. Self-organized criticality takes hold. The fascinating thing is that this new entity is on a higher level of organization than its constituents. It obeys certain laws of its own. These higher-level laws are sometimes very simple.

The collective behavior of crowds at a concert or voters at a meeting can undergo phase transitions. Before a public meeting starts, many of the individuals in the audience are unknown to each other. What can they possibly have in common? Perhaps only one thing, but one *important* thing. Once they begin to listen to the same performers, they begin to influence each other—by laughing, applauding, or interrupting. These interactive modes of behavior tend to get "locked in" very quickly. Their contagious nature creates *self-reinforcing* loops of interaction between performers and audience. The performers are aware of the interaction between themselves and the audience. They can sense the mood of the audience *as a whole.* In fact, their very success or failure relies heavily on the audience's collective psyche.

Such self-reinforcing feedback loops are of paramount importance in collective modes of behavior. They help to explain why a phase transition can arise. Once the density of interactions exceeds a critical threshold, then the collective character of the system can change unexpectedly. To further illustrate the pervasive nature of phase transitions, let's look at a toy experiment, one in which this kind of qualitative change is "catalyzed" at critical thresholds of interaction.

Getting Well Connected

Simpler toy problems are useful in science because they allow us to gain insight into more complicated, real-world ones. The toy problem of interest here involves *random graphs.* Before we launch into a discussion of random graphs, however, some introductory words about graph theory and modeling are in order.

Conventional economic modeling involves postulating causal relationships between known variables of the problem. These variables are often measured over aggregates of agents. Such models attempt to formalize relationships in the language of mathematics. As we learned in the previous section, and will find throughout the course of this book, it may be impossible to model a truly complex system in this way.[7] In many ecological and economic systems, there are simply far too many variables and far too many interactions to measure. Some of our forebears were well aware of this difficulty. For example, Joseph Schumpeter delivered a cautionary message about the use of economic models more than fifty years ago: "The process of social life is a function of so many variables, many of which are not amenable to anything like measurement, that even mere diagnosis of a given state of things becomes a doubtful matter quite apart from the formidable sources of error that open up as soon as we attempt prognosis."[8]

In many economic situations, the formulation and use of such conventional mathematical models is highly questionable. This is where graph theory can provide an alternative means of studying the relational processes involved. A graph is simply a set of vertices or *nodes* together with a set of edges or *links* connecting certain pairs of nodes. If each link also has a specific direction (i.e., a beginning and an end), then we call it a directed graph or *digraph.* Furthermore, if the strength of the causal relationship can be represented by a real number, the process results in a *weighted digraph.* This is simply a digraph in which every link has a real number associated with it.

We'll use a special kind of weighted digraph in this chapter. It's called a *signed digraph,* and it is simply a weighted digraph in which the weightings are either +1 or –1. It usually corresponds to a situation where we can identify possible interactions or relationships between pairs of socioeconomic variables, but only to the extent of deciding whether they're positive or negative for the pairs involved. We simply don't know enough about the strength of the various interactions to assign real numbers to them. Even if we can measure the strength of an interaction at one point in time, we can't be sure that the same relationship will prevail at another point in time.

Take a look at Figure 3.2. It's a signed digraph representing the causal linkages in a key subsystem of an urban economy: a waste disposal system. The arrows indicate the direction of influences. A plus sign indicates that the changes occur in the same direction, but not necessarily positively. For example, the plus sign between P and G indicates that an *increase* in the population of the city causes an *increase* in the amount of garbage per unit area. At the same time, it also indicates that a *decrease* in the population of the city causes a *decrease* in the amount of garbage per unit area. The minus sign between S and D indicates that an *increase* in sanitation facilities causes a *decrease* in the number of diseases. At the same time, it also indicates that a *decrease* in sanitation facilities causes an *increase* in the number of diseases.

Note how some of the arrows form loops. For example, there's a loop of arrows from P to M, M to C, and then from C back to P. A

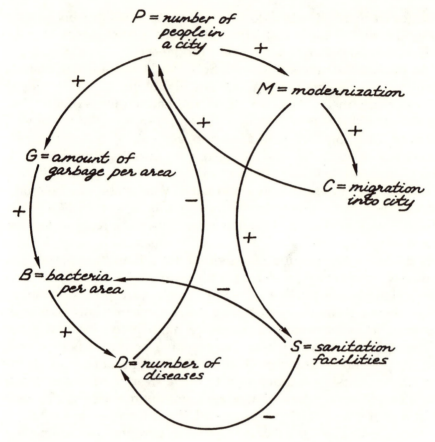

FIGURE 3.2   Causal linkages in an urban waste disposal system.

loop indicates a mutual causal relationship. By this we mean that
an initial influence on an element comes back to amplify itself by
way of other elements. For example, in the loop P-M-C-P, an increase in the city's population causes an increase in modernization,
which in turn increases migration into the city, which in turn increases the population in the city. In short, an increase in population causes a further increase in population through modernization and migration. On the other hand, a decrease in population
causes a further decrease in population through decreased modernization and decreased migration.

In such a loop, therefore, each element has a positive influence on all other elements, either directly or indirectly, and therefore each element influences itself positively through other elements. The thing that distinguishes this approach from typical closed-form modeling is that there's no hierarchical causal priority in any of the elements. That's why the loop depicts a *mutual* causal relationship. None of the elements are assumed to be the principal causal element affecting the others. The resulting mutual causal relationship in this loop is *deviation-amplifying*. For simplicity, we'll refer to it as a positive feedback loop.

Now look at the loop P-G-B-D-P. This loop contains a negative influence from D to P. An *increase* in population causes an *increase* in the amount of garbage per unit area, which in turn causes an *increase* in the number of bacteria per unit area, which in turn causes an *increase* in the number of diseases, which in turn causes a *decrease* in population. In short, an increase in population causes a decrease in population through garbage, bacteria, and diseases. On the other hand, a decrease in population causes a decrease in garbage, bacteria, and diseases, and thus causes an increase in population. In this loop, therefore, any change in population is counteracted by itself. The mutual causal relationship in this loop is *deviation-counteracting*.[9] Such a deviation-counteracting process may result in stabilization or oscillation, depending on the time lag involved. We'll refer to it as a negative feedback loop.

The loop P-M-S-D-P has two negative influences. An increase in population causes an increase in modernization, which in turn causes an increase in sanitation facilities, which in turn causes a decrease in the number of bacteria per unit area, which in turn causes a decrease in the number of diseases, which in turn causes an increase in population. This is therefore a deviation-amplifying or positive feedback loop. The two negative influences cancel each other out and become positive overall. In general, any feedback loop with an *even* number of negative influences is positive, and any feedback loop with an *odd* number of negative influences is negative. An economy contains many positive as well as negative feedback loops. What matters most is that all the pertinent loops affecting the system of interest be identified and their influences considered.

Now that we're familiar with the idea, let's see how digraphs can be used to gain deeper insights into some economic complexities.

Our next example focuses on a controversial issue in the global arena: fixing the terms of trade between nations. Appropriate tariff and quota levels have been debated vigorously for decades, especially for agricultural products. During the 1990s, for example, American newspapers were full of criticism of Japan's restrictive policy on beef imports from the United States. There's little doubt that the Japanese do play by different rules when it comes to agricultural goods. In the case of beef, they try to protect their cattle farmers and promote the "home-grown" product. In today's "borderless" world, however, it's not that easy to figure out what's really in a nation's best interest.[10] Who stands to gain most from increased beef exports from the United States to Japan? Let's try to work through the arguments, visualizing the relationships between the key factors in the form of a digraph.

Conventional economic wisdom—like the Hecksher-Ohlin theory—attributes international trade to underlying differences between countries. The key idea is that each country produces and exports goods that reflect that country's comparative advantage over other countries. In determining the volume of beef exports from the United States to Japan, for example, four variables seem to be important: consumption levels of comparable beef in Japan (B), the size of Japan's cattle herds (J), exports of American beef to Japan (A), and the dollar/yen exchange rate (X). These causal linkages are depicted in Figure 3.3. Having witnessed rising family incomes in Japan, the Americans reasoned that growing demand for beef in Japan could be satisfied by expanding American beef shipments to the Japanese. This is indicated by the positive sign on the arrow from B to A.

Although this reasoning is sound, it merely scratches the surface. In their desperation to get American beef onto Japan's dinner tables, the U.S. government failed to consider some related issues of fundamental importance. First, is beef that's grown in America "American"? For that matter, are the cattle raised in Japan really "Japanese"? The answers may seem obvious. But they're not obvious. Why? One complicating factor is that Japanese cattle are raised almost entirely on American grain. If more Japanese beef is eaten in Japan, then more American grain will be consumed there. Although an increase in the size of Japan's herds may have a negative impact on imports of beef from America, almost certainly it

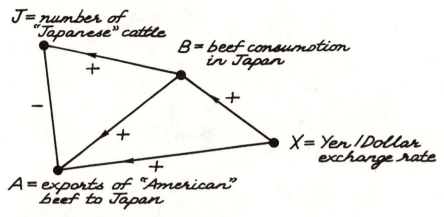

FIGURE 3.3   The Beef Story, Part I.

will have a positive impact on imports of American grain. Furthermore, grain agriculture has much higher levels of productivity in the United States than does cattle raising. Thus the Americans are more likely to be able to win the grain race. Competition from the Australians and the Argentinians makes the beef race much tougher.

Another complication is the issue of ownership. Who owns the ranches, feedlots, and packing plants that make up the lion's share of the beef industry in the United States? Japanese importers like Zenchiku Ltd. own many of them, mainly because it's easier for the Japanese to invest in U.S. industry than for Americans to invest in Japan. They and others will soon be shipping more beef from the United States than Americans do today. Japanese owners can control all stages of cattle raising and handling to meet their own market's requirements. They can also use Japanese know-how and repatriate profits back to Japan.

As Paul Krugman suggests, whenever a Japanese firm buys an American firm, we need to know whether that firm will be run differently, and if so, whether the U.S. economy will be hurt or helped by the difference.[11] It's not at all clear in what sense the beef shipped by Zenchiku from the United States to Japan represents a net increase in American exports. Not only does growing Japanese ownership in the United States make it difficult to answer the two earlier questions. More importantly, it points to the growing

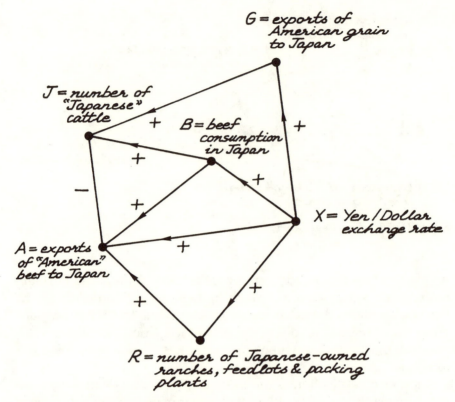

FIGURE 3.4   The Beef Story, Part II.

interdependencies between the Americans and the rest of the world. Rising levels of trade and foreign ownership mean that the U.S. economy is becoming increasingly multinational and inter-dependent. In other words, the U.S.-led global economy is rapidly becoming a *strongly interactive* economy.

Now let's return to our main question: Will an increase in beef exports from the United States to Japan be of net benefit to the U.S. economy? The answer is far from obvious. Less obvious linkages and relationships need to be factored in when an issue like this is debated. What we're seeing in Figure 3.4 is just a small sample of the full range of economic interdependencies affecting beef exports between the two countries. When a change occurs in one part of this interlinked economy, it can lead to a myriad of chain reactions elsewhere. A handful of these responses are large and direct, but many others are small and indirect. Their "global" repercussions may be unpredictable. Shades of Schelling's segregation model and Bak's sandpile avalanches spring to mind.

It's time to move on to the topic of random graphs. A random graph is similar to the graphs discussed earlier, except that the nodes are connected *at random* by a set of links. Although we know how the network graph looks at one point in time—that is, which pairs of nodes are already connected—we've no way of knowing which pair of unconnected nodes may be connected at the next point in time. Thus we're less concerned with the direction and strength of particular links (like those shown in Figure 3.4) and more concerned with the overall pattern of connectivity that develops.[12]

This is the starting point for the toy problem we wish to discuss. To put it in an everyday context, Stuart Kauffman visualized the nodes as "buttons" and the links as "threads." Imagine that an assortment of buttons lie scattered on a wooden floor. Choose any two buttons at random, pick them up, and connect them with a thread. After putting this pair down, randomly choose two more buttons and do the same. As you continue to do this, at first you'll mostly pick up buttons that you haven't threaded earlier. Sooner or later, however, you're likely to pick up a pair of buttons and find that you've already threaded one of them. When you thread that button again, you'll have linked together three buttons. As you go on choosing pairs of buttons randomly to link together with threads, you'll find that some of the buttons soon become interconnected into larger clusters. To put Kauffman's toy problem into an economic context, think of the buttons as places—towns and cities—and the threads as transport links, such as roads and railroads. An important part of economic development is the level of investment in network infrastructure linking various towns and cities. We could approximate early investment patterns by randomly choosing two places from twenty towns and cities within a nation and linking them directly by road. Gradually we could choose more pairs of places and do the same. Eventually we'll pick a pair of places and find that one of them is already connected to another place (see Figure 3.5a). At this early stage, however, it would be correct to say that the collection of towns and cities is only *weakly interactive,* in the sense that the spatial scale of interaction possibilities is relatively small (see Figure 3.5b).

Take a look at the pattern of interconnections shown in Figure 3.5c. As our random number generator continues to do its work, we find that a majority of towns and cities have become interlinked within one giant cluster. Only seven of the twenty places remain outside this giant cluster by the time the ratio of roads to places reaches 0.75 (i.e., 15/20). Denoting the ratio of roads to places by R, the interesting thing is that random graphs exhibit very regular statistical behavior as one tunes this ratio. Once R passes the 0.5 mark, something seemingly magical occurs. Suddenly most of the clusters become cross-connected into one giant cluster![13] When this giant web forms, the majority of places are directly or indirectly connected to each other. As R approaches one, virtually all the remaining isolated towns and cities become cross-connected into the same giant web (see Figure 3.5d). Note how closely the situation resembles the sudden transformation of a weakly connected social group into a strongly connected one once

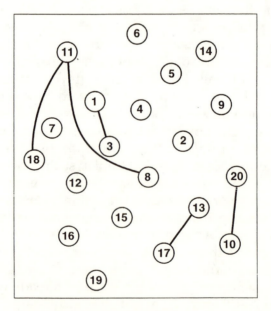

FIGURE 3.5a   The crystallization of connected webs (R=0.25).

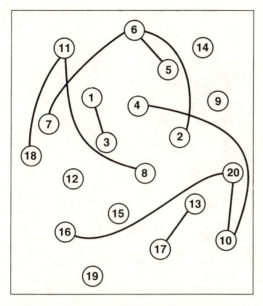

FIGURE 3.5b   The crystallization of connected webs (R=0.5).

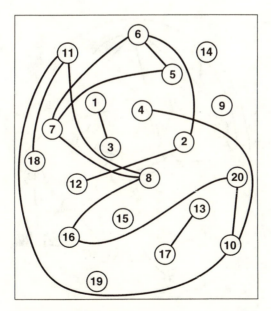

FIGURE 3.5c   The crystallization of connected webs (R-0.75).

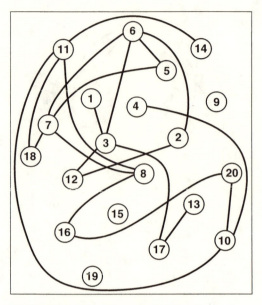

FIGURE 3.5d   The crystallization of connected webs (R=1.0)

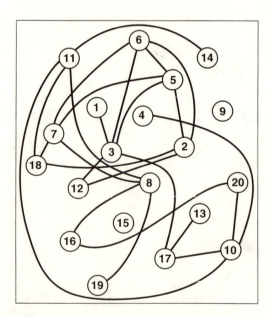

FIGURE 3.5e   The crystillization of connected webs (R=1.25).

there's unanimous acknowledgment of a common accord. It's the sandpile effect again!

This sudden and unexpected change in the size of the largest cluster, as R passes 0.5, is the signature of a nonlinear process we met in Chapter 1. It resembles a phase transition. The size of the largest cluster of places increases slowly at first, then rapidly, then slows again as the value of R increases further (see Figure 3.6). If there were an infinite number of buttons or places, then the size of the largest web would jump discontinuously from tiny to enormous as R passed 0.5. The steep part of the curve would become more vertical than it is in the figure. Such abruptness is typical of a phase transition, just like when separate water molecules freeze to form a block of ice.

The point of this toy example is to highlight the nonlinear nature of transitions from a weakly interactive to a strongly interactive state. Technically speaking, an isotropic random graph crosses a threshold when the system passes from "nearly unconnected" to "nearly connected." Such threshold transitions are rampant in graph theory. Suddenly, many small clusters are cross-linked to

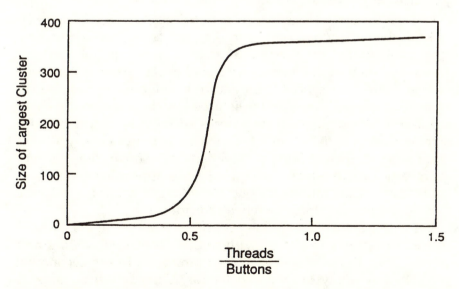

FIGURE 3.6 **A phase transition in the size of the largest cluster as the ratio of links to nodes changes.**

form one large cluster. But it's also reminiscent of Bak's sandpile experiment and Schelling's segregation model. A state of self-organized criticality is reached once local interactions between individual elements are replaced by global communication throughout the whole system. Could this be some kind of universal law when it comes to the dynamics of complex systems? Does it apply to socioeconomic systems?

The argument for universality is strengthened by insights into random behavior stemming from another field, known as *percolation theory*. In a random medium like a porous stone, large scale penetration of water depends on the proportion of passages that are broad enough to allow water to pass along them. We'll call this proportion R. By simulating the stone's porous structure as a sequence of open and closed edges (or connected and unconnected links) on a square grid, large-scale water penetration is seen to be related to the existence of strongly (i.e., infinitely) connected clusters of open edges. When R = 0.25, the connected clusters of open edges are isolated and rather small. As R increases, however, the sizes of clusters increases. There's a critical value of R at which a "super cluster" forms, pervading the entire grid. As we throw in more and more open edges, suddenly we reach a threshold when large-scale connections emerge.

Just like the onset of self-organized criticality, the occurrence of a critical phenomenon is central to the process of percolation. One may surmise that the wetting of a stone is only a "local effect" when R is small, but becomes a "global effect" when R reaches a critical value. Drinkers of Pernod acknowledge such phase transitions. Transparent Pernod is undisturbed by the addition of a small amount of water, but as more water is added drop by drop, an instant suddenly arrives when the mixture becomes cloudy. Recent simulation studies of bond percolation have shown that the random value of R at which such global paths appear is very close to 0.5.[14] It's the same ratio as the one that emerged in our toy example of random graphs. Is this merely a coincidence?

The physical theory of phase transitions and critical phenomena is well developed, together with multidimensional scaling and power laws. But what about phase transitions in socioeconomic life? Do they apply to human behavior? Consider what happens when a bunch of urban residents meet frequently to discuss an issue of common interest. As the intensity of their interaction increases, clusters of "like-minded" residents begin to emerge spontaneously. Like-minded residents don't know in advance that they're like-minded. They don't even know who their closest allies may be. These kinships emerge spontaneously during the meetings. Such like-minded clusters may do more than simply interact among themselves. To pursue their common interests more widely, eventually they may link up with other like-minded clusters, creating even larger clusters. Sounds familiar, doesn't it? People behaving like nodes and links or grains of sand! It's precisely how the weak may grow strong.

In fact, the socialization processes by which performers enchant an audience, politicians sway voters, or common interest groups gain support are analogous to the toy problem depicted in Figure 3.5. People form clusters (e.g., political parties, unions, clubs) in order to pursue their joint interests. These weakly interactive clusters can gather strength unexpectedly, especially with the help of a key catalyst or persuasive argument. The latter can play a powerful role in the shaping of society as a whole. Electoral outcomes can be swayed spontaneously by charismatic or forceful arguments from one of the protagonists. The collective outcomes can be quite different from those intended or expected at the outset by other individuals. Such unpredictable outcomes are further examples of emergent behavior.

As we'll learn in Chapter 6, traffic jams on city highways are another form of emergent behavior, springing from the collective interactions of a bunch of drivers on a road network. Once the critical flow density has been exceeded, smooth laminar flow changes abruptly to stop-start waves. Emergent phenomena can arise in many other socioeconomic situations. Their common bond is that the population of interacting individuals "spontaneously" develops collective properties that were neither intended nor expected by individuals a priori. Order through fluctuations again!

Sheep and Explorers

Granted that strongly interactive systems display self-organized criticality, an obvious question arises. Who triggers these phase transitions? Who are the architects of strongly interactive socioeconomic systems? The answer is pretty obvious. We all are. We, the interactors. But "we" aren't identical. Quite the opposite, in fact. As we learned in the previous chapter, our expectations, decisions, and experiences vary greatly, even under identical circumstances. Because we're forced to reason inductively in situations where information is limited, and such reasoning is open-ended, our chosen behavior usually differs.

Inductive reasoning places different demands on us as thinking individuals than the deductive metaphor. We're all constrained by our personal stock of know-ware and the cognitive abilities within us. Inductive reasoning involves pattern formation and pattern recognition, aided by intuition and creativity. Clearly some people are more intuitive or creative than others. They're better at seeking and discovering novel solutions to problems. They're willing to experiment, adapt, and instigate change. Others merely follow existing patterns, often resisting change under almost any circumstances. It's pretty clear that we don't possess the same catalytic potential to create novel solutions or adapt to changing circumstances. Like the spectrum of light, cognitive equipment consists of a range of cognitive skills of varying intensities. Some of us are strongly creative, others only weakly creative; some of us are strongly adaptive, others only weakly adaptive.

For convenience, we'll classify economic agents on a scale delimited by two extreme forms of behavior (Figure 3.7). We'll call those who actively search for new possibilities *explorers* and those who prefer to remain with the status quo *sheep*.[15] This spectrum of cognitive skills implies that we all possess sheep and explorer qualities, albeit in different doses. Pure explorers tend to be imaginative, creative, highly strung individuals who constantly search for better solutions to the problems they face. They're more inclined to reason inductively, to learn quickly, and to adapt willingly to changing circumstances. Sheep are more placid, patient, and resigned than explorers. Preferring to reason deductively, they're prone to choosing a well-established pattern. They mostly cling to particular beliefs because they've worked well in the past. Sheep are slow learners who must accumulate a record of failure before discarding their favorite beliefs.

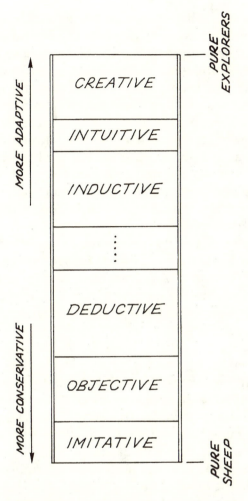

FIGURE 3.7   A spectrum of cognitive skills.

Success in the economic world, as in life itself, requires both of these facets of behavior. Yet the two traits are almost contradictory. The first trait is an ability to organize one's behavior so as to exploit the available information to the fullest extent possible. In short, sheep like to think deductively and act predictably. The second trait is an ability to ignore the available information to some extent and to "explore" beyond the boundaries of current knowledge. Explorers tend to think inductively and their decisions are unpredictable. Both kinds of behavior can be found in all walks of economic life. For example, sheep and explorer strategies have been observed among fishing fleets searching for profitable fishing zones. The only difference is one of nomenclature. Nonequilibrium systems scientists like Peter Allen, who've studied the behavior of fishing fleets, call the sheep "Cartesians" and the explorers "Stochasts." As Allen notes, the first group makes good use of information, but the second generates it! At the root of all creative activity lies an explorer, punctuating the restful equilibrium of the sheep with unexpected change.

Because they're driven by a constant struggle between creative (explorers) and conservative (sheep) forces, economies evolve in an unpredictable way. Over short time horizons, the deductive agent may outperform the inductive one. Deductively optimal behavior can rule supreme in a world of stasis. Sheep can strut about with confidence in a frozen world that isn't doing anything or going anywhere. But not in that dynamic world of morphogenesis. Invariably, sheep will be found lacking in the long run. Unfortunately for them, the best performance doesn't follow optimization principles. Instead it amounts to an adaptive compromise. Remember our findings from the Trader's Dilemma game in the last chapter. If the game's played once only, the best strategy for each trader is to defect (i.e., leave empty bags). But a Nash equilibrium is only imperturbable because it compels all traders to think and act rationally. In the iterated version of the game, however, the best strategy is to cooperate. Emergent cooperation evolves out of noncooperation in the long run. Order for free again!

And the long run is where our main interest lies. To the extent that the real "laws" of economics exist at all, the key point to remember is that they can't be fully understood by studying economic change within a time frame that is short compared with the economy's overall evolution. It's remarkable that the fallacy of a simple supply-demand equilibrium has persisted for so long. In the medium to long run, supply and demand functions cannot be specified in isolation of one another. They're not independent functions of price. Each depends crucially on chance events in history—

like the way in which fads start, rumors spread, and choices reinforce one another. Supply and demand affect each other, as well as being subject to common factors like the media.

If we look at the key economic agents who control technology in the world of morphogenesis, such fallacies become more transparent. Once again, sheep and explorers can be found under different names. This time they're called *imitators* and *innovators.* Innovation is the domain of creative explorers. Whenever their exploratory search uncovers an area where positive feedback outweighs negative, then new growth-inducing development can occur. It's only when we wish to rationalize about what's happening that we insist there must have been some "pent-up" demand that justified the supply. We allow ourselves to slide back into the world of stasis. *There's really no static hill to climb.* The economic landscape's too complex for that. It's heaving and deforming incessantly because it's formed by the interacting agents themselves. All the agents are coevolving continuously, learning by interacting. Some are innovative explorers, others are imitative sheep. Once we admit even to just the presence of innovative or imitative mechanisms, then the potential demand for something becomes a *dynamic* variable, which itself depends on the unfolding of events.

A small, growing band of economists have begun to treat technological change as an evolutionary process. Work carried out by Richard Nelson, Sidney Winter, and others has emphasized the role of innovations and analyzed conditions under which firms should invest in innovations or imitate others. Some firms invest huge sums in innovation, thereby climbing up the learning curve of a technological trajectory. Others simply copy the innovator. IBM invested in innovation; Compaq cloned, selling IBM imitations. Sheep follow explorers, just as long periods of relative stasis follow short periods of morphogenesis.

Research into technological evolution sometimes ignores the fact that evolution is actually *coevolution.*[16] Just as agents change their minds when they interact with other agents and explorers are constantly learning by interacting, so are technologies. They live in the niches afforded by other technologies. For example, the arrival of the automobile technology put the smithy's hammer out of business. But it also spawned new markets for traffic lights, gas stations, motels, and drive-in food chains. We're all hustling our wares, creating and destroying niches for one another. Many of the goods and services in our economy are *intermediate* goods and services; they're used in the creation of other goods and services that are finally consumed by households.

Searching for new possibilities among this vast web of goods and services is essentially a stochastic activity. Multiple possibilities abound, but few choices or solutions are uniquely superior. New ideas, products, or methods are mostly recombinations of old ones. Schumpeter recognized that recombination is a valid way of defining economic development. He argued that the carrying out of new combinations meant the different employment of the economic system's existing supplies of productive means, thereby providing a second definition of development.[17] In the chapters that follow, we'll look at several examples of how and when the recombination of old ideas takes place, what's recombined, and what's actually created.

How do we, as economic agents, trade off economic necessity against the elements of chance? Should we behave like low-risk sheep or dare to enter the domain of the high-rolling explorers? Putting it in more explicit economic terms, how do we decide between the certain prospect of earning modest profits now as against the uncertain prospect of earning far higher profits in an unknown future? Once again, this parallels the Traders' Dilemma game played once against the iterated version played many times. Perhaps the outcome of the iterated game can provide a clue to the answer. Over the longer term, we search not only for novel solutions but also for long-lasting cooperative strategies with those agents whose custom we learn to value most. To soften the impacts of an uncertain trading environment, for example, merchants seek to develop bilateral trading agreements with their principal trading partners. These long-term agreements are designed to hedge against the volatility of a series of one-time transactions with different partners. Wherever the continuity of shipment and quality are important, supplier loyalty is likely to prevail.

There's another important reason for seeking bilateral trading agreements. Our choice of preferred partners is based on personal experience—what we've learned about our potential trading partners. Once we've spent time and money identifying suitable partners, bilateral agreements enable us to "lock in" the benefits of what we've learned. Mutual advantages accrue to the partners. Our cooperative network grows. Learning by interacting proves to be an adaptive process out of which a desire for cooperation emerges. We can capitalize jointly on what we've learned. And capitalizing on what we've learned is the key attribute of an explorer. In the next section, we'll look at an example of how we capitalize on what we've learned. Whether consciously or unconsciously, each of us behaves like sheep or explorers in our everyday activities.

Are You an Inductive Graph Theorist?

Most people use graph theory in their daily lives without ever realizing it. I don't mean that they're unsuspecting designers of signed digraphs, like the waste disposal system and the beef story we discussed earlier.[18] Instead, people use a much simpler kind of graph theory as they move about conducting their daily business. We all travel on networks of various kinds. For example, the London Underground map is a network graph used by millions of commuters each year (see Figure 3.8).[19] Although it shows only the rail connections between stations, that information helps Londoners to make informed decisions about the journeys they can make. For example, if the stations of embarkation and disembarkation are on the same line, then the journey can be made without changing trains. Alternative routes can also be compared in terms of the number of intermediate stops between points of embarkation and disembarkation.

The London Underground system has several hundred stations. There are literally millions of possible ways of traveling between them all. It looks like a very big combinatorial headache for most commuters. Despite the network's apparent complexity, the map and a few simple rules are sufficient to allow most commuters to select reasonable routes at a glance. Let's see how it works.

Suppose that you, the reader, want to use the Loop for the very first time. You wish to catch a train from Victoria (near the bottom center of the map) to Notting Hill Gate (at the left center). First you must search the map for routes or sequences of stations that will allow you to do this. You find two that are feasible. One sequence is Victoria–Sloane Square–South Kensington–Gloucester Road–High

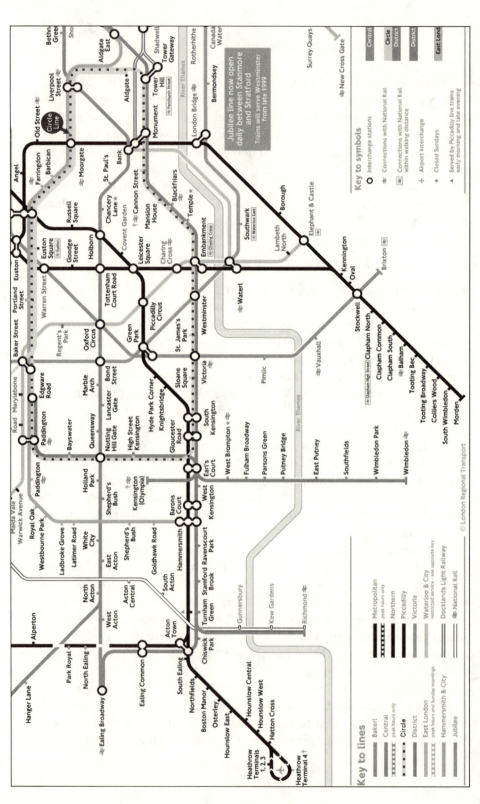

FIGURE 3.8 Map of the London Underground.

Street Kensington–Notting Hill Gate. The other is Victoria–Green Park–Oxford Circus–Bond Street–Marble Arch–Lancaster Gate–Queensway–Notting Hill Gate.

Choosing between these two possibilities turns out to be a relatively simple task. You opt for the Sloane Square route for three reasons. First, you can make the whole journey on one line without changing trains. You'll simply get on a westbound Circle Line train at Victoria and duly arrive at Notting Hill Gate. If you took the second route, you'd need to change trains twice—at Green Park and again at Bond Street. Second, there are only four intervening stations on the first route compared to five on the second route. Third, you've been told that trains on the Circle Line are invariably more frequent than those on the Victoria and Jubilee Lines.

Because the problem is well defined, you're able to deduce the optimal solution. Moreover, you feel confident about your choice. You have all the information you need to make an objectively rational decision. And you're absolutely correct! Most London commuters do take the Circle Line train to reach Notting Hill Gate from Victoria. Commuters have no need to resort to intuition or fancy guesswork. The problem is simple enough to be solved by deduction.

Now suppose that you've been making the journey from Victoria to Notting Hill Gate on a daily basis for several months. In fact, you've been using the Loop for some other journeys as well, most of them on a single line. From these commuting experiences, gradually you've formed a picture of the Loop system in your mind. Let's call it a "mental model." It's your own mental impression of how the Loop operates in time terms—trip times, delay times, line frequencies, and so forth. Of course, this model's only a crude, partial approximation to reality. It may even be flawed. But it's helped you to select routes for several months now and you've been satisfied with the resulting travel times. You begin to wonder if the commuting life of a London Loop traveler is always so simple!

I'm willing to bet that your mental model turns out to be rule-based.[20] By this I mean that your mental representation of the Loop system is formed and altered by the application of condition-action rules, which take the general form, IF (condition 1, condition 2, . . . condition n), THEN (action). In choosing between alternative route possibilities, for example, experience has taught you that there is an important rule to observe:

IF you can make your whole journey on one line
THEN choose that line.

Another rule, which you may apply, is:

IF trains run more frequently on one line
THEN choose that line.

A third rule, which may form part of your mental model, is:

IF one route has fewer intervening stations
THEN choose that route.

Undoubtedly, your mental model will consist of more than just a set of IF/THEN rules. For example, experience may have taught you to apply the above rules in a different order on weekdays than on weekends. The key point is that you're reasonably happy with the overall result. Travel times experienced have fallen within your expectations. You feel confident that you understand how the Loop system operates and that you can estimate travel times, albeit roughly.

Then, one day, you find the need to commute between a pair of stations that you haven't visited before. You must get from Baker Street to St. James's Park. Searching the map for feasible routes, you find a direct link (westbound) between these two stations on the Circle Line, with eleven intervening stations. There's a second route that goes via Bond Street, Green Park, and Victoria. Although there are only three intervening stations on this route, you'll have to change trains at two of them (Green Park and Victoria). There's a third route via Regent's Park, Oxford Circus, Green Park, and Victoria. This time there are four intervening stations, but again you'll have to change trains at two of them (Oxford Circus and Victoria). As well as these three possibilities, several additional routes could also be contemplated.

If you apply your favored mental model, the direct route via the Circle Line is the obvious choice. But will it be the quickest? Suddenly you realize that you're facing a more complicated decision problem. Diabolically, you lack some key information. You've no way of knowing what the likely delays will be if you choose either of the indirect routes. How long will you have to wait when you change trains? The two indirect routes certainly *look* much shorter on the map, because there's only a few intervening stations. Should you relinquish familiar determinism (the direct route approach) and test the elements of chance (unknown waiting times)? In other words, should you behave as a sheep or as an explorer?

The truth of the matter is that you simply don't have sufficient information to make a rational choice between these alternatives. Having never traveled on the Loop between St. Baker Street and St. James's Park before, you're forced to rely on intuition and an ounce of luck. But once you've made this journey several times, you can begin to form a more accurate picture of the relative merits of each alternative. If you're an explorer at heart, you'll test all feasible routes. Only by trying out the indirect routes can you hope to estimate the relative frequency of trains on different lines and the average delays incurred by changing trains. Sheep tend to resist this kind of experimentation. They favor the certainty of familiarity, that is, the direct option. By way of contrast, explorers are keen to learn incessantly from their own experiments. Gradually they begin to form a more accurate impression of the typical behavioral patterns of the Loop system. Then they adapt and change routes accordingly.

In summary, explorers are adept at *learning by circulating*. They believe in testing and updating their own mental models of the Loop system on a regular basis. This means judging how well their favored rules work when applied to the reality of their day-to-day experiences. They also compare these experiences with their prior expectations. If this experimentation suggests that their favored mental model may be unreliable, then they discard some old rules and add some new ones in order to improve it. Then they repeat the experiments. Testing, adapting, testing, adapting. This is the way of an inductive explorer. And this is how to travel on the road to know-ware.

four

The Ancient Art of Learning by Circulating

If everything occurred at the same time, there would be no development. If everything existed in the same place, there could be no particularity. Only space makes possible the particular, which then unfolds in time.

—August Lösch

Pirenne's Hypothesis

European history has always been a touchy subject. But few historians can match the stormy heights reached by the Belgian Henri Pirenne. At the heart of this enduring controversy are some of Pirenne's ideas concerning the transition of Europe from classical antiquity to medieval civilization.[1] One fertile thought sparking widespread criticism was his explanation for the revival of medieval towns in Middle Europe during the tenth and eleventh centuries. Another dealt with a broader issue: the general relationship between Roman antiquity and the First Europe.

To see why Pirenne upset the tranquillity of the historian's world, we need only examine his first idea. Instead of agreeing with the popular view that the rebirth of urban Europe was triggered by technological change, or by the transfer of political authority from the feudal lords to the communities, Pirenne steered a very different course. He claimed that the impact of Islamic forces in the seventh and eighth centuries destroyed the commercial unity of the Mediterranean, thereby ending the Roman world in economic terms and ushering in a strikingly different civilization

117

in the Carolingian era. Also, he asserted that the unusually fast growth of population and human settlements that followed in the High Middle Ages (1000–1300) was triggered by an expansion of trade over longer distances.

You may be wondering how Pirenne's idea relates to our discussion of adaptive learning and complex economies. The first point to note is that the linchpin of his idea about economic revival was the pursuit of profits by trading in scarce goods at novel locations. In other words, his theory of revival was based on exchanges of goods and ideas. Trade over very long distances was possible only after key transportation routes were opened up again and the safety of travelers could be guaranteed. Only then could merchants circulate freely, promote new products, and expand their trading area. The incentive for such an expansion of trade must have been great, since potential profits were enormous.

A second key factor is that Pirenne saw the revival of urban Europe as a direct response to an *external* stimulus—trade with distant places scattered around the Mediterranean. By way of contrast, the bevy of scholars who opposed him chose to focus almost exclusively upon noninteractive factors internal to European society. Pirenne sensed the importance of circulation and interaction as catalysts of change. His main critics did not.

The third point to note is that Pirenne's explanation was a *qualitative* one. It focused on the phase transition from a weakly interactive to a strongly interactive economic system. By arguing that European settlements were transformed by an escalation in trade over longer distances, perhaps unwittingly he stepped into the realm of nonlinear analysis. His thesis was one of positive feedback: more merchants generated more circulation, more exchange, and higher profits, which, in turn, attracted even more merchants. There's a fascinating saga of coevolution to be unveiled in this chapter. Like today's apostles of complexity and self-organization, Henri Pirenne seems to have sensed the importance of phase transitions associated with the sudden interlinking of many small, isolated clusters to form a larger, well-connected cluster.

Can we be sure that Europe was in a weakly interactive state prior to this transition? There's plenty of evidence to suggest that the high risks and costs of transporting goods during the Carolingian period contributed to urban stagnation across western Europe. Norseman controlled the Baltic and the North Sea, making it dangerous even to live near any waterways. Moslems and Magyars invaded frequently. The dangers of travel by sea or land forced Europeans to refrain from exchanging goods over longer distances. Although it's difficult to confirm the number of European inhabitants at that time, the plagues of the sixth and seventh centuries caused great loss of life. What we do know is that population levels dropped significantly between the sixth and the ninth centuries (see Table 4.1). Carolingian Europe was thus a sparsely populated continent.

This doesn't mean that people lived alone or far away from one another. Rather it meant that the villages, or groups of villages, were mostly self-contained, small oases of cultivated land in a largely uncultivated continent. Carolingian Europe was a primitive agrarian society, relatively isolated and underdeveloped. Towns were contained within castle walls and self-sufficient manors, mostly willing to make do with the fruits of their surrounding land and forests. They were populated mainly by farmers and townspeople, the former tilling the land and the latter crafting or distributing simple products from the forests and elsewhere. Given the risks of travel over land, there wouldn't have

TABLE 4.1   Population Growth in Europe

Date	European Population in Millions	Margin of Error (%)
200	48	35
500	36	30
800	32	30
1000	39	20
1300	75	20
1500	76	10
1700	102	8

been much opportunity for different villages to exchange goods over long distances. We can conclude that Carolingian Europe was indeed a weakly interactive economic system.

Such a feudal state could hardly remain forever. Popular goods like salt, metals, and wine were not produced locally and had to be found. If such things could not be obtained by war and plunder, the last resort was to engage in trade over longer distances. Some trade was carried on continuously by the oriental merchants, who sailed their ships on the Mediterranean (as they had done in Roman times) or traveled by boat up and down the great western and central European rivers—from the Loire to the Rhine and the Elbe. Together with their countless tributaries, these rivers were key transport links rather than barriers. Many "would-be" entrepreneurs of the day must have seen the potential for greater trade over longer distances.

At a time when long-distance commerce was insignificant and money still a rarity, suddenly the circulation of goods and merchants intensified. All forms of trade rose significantly, but that over longer distances grew most of all. Interestingly, this sudden expansion of trade occurred at the same time as large increases in the urban population. Were these two factors intimately related, as Pirenne would have us believe? We know now that the potential gains from trade attracted more people into the riskier but potentially more rewarding mercantile activity. Was this why many larger towns grew suddenly and explosively? Convincing answers to these questions would certainly help to resolve the debate surrounding Pirenne's hypothesis once and for all.

The Mees Analysis

A fascinating analytical sketch that shed some light on these questions was devised by the mathematician Alistair Mees.[2] He analyzed the effect of increasing trade opportunities on urban and rural populations. Mees's central idea was that each person knows whether the city or the countryside is more attractive as a place to live and work. Then people tend to move between the two according to their preferences. Although his analysis was far from the economic mainstream at the time, his model of employment dynamics illustrates some qualitative features of the world of morphogenesis, our principal area of interest throughout this book. Without delving too deeply into the mathematical intricacies, it's worthwhile exploring some key features of his analysis.

As we mentioned earlier, medieval Europe's regional populations consisted mostly of farmers and city merchants. Let's call the farmers group f and the city merchants group c. Also there were a few landowners and traveling merchants (the "orientals"), but they were vastly outnumbered by farmers and city merchants. Furthermore, the self-sufficient nature of most towns and villages in the Carolingian era meant that each region's total population (farmers plus city merchants) remained about constant.

Mees's fundamental idea was that the attractiveness of belonging to either group f or group c could change quite rapidly. Over a period of several years, people would naturally try to move from a less attractive situation to a more attractive one.[3] In an isolated region, the farmers and city merchants depend solely on each other for their needs. Thus the attractiveness of both groups at any time depends only on the size of each group in relation to the demand for their products. Simple economics dictates that when only a few people are producing a *popular* commodity, there'll be excess demand for this commodity. Thus its producers can charge higher prices and earn a higher income. For example, if there are very few city merchants but strong demand for city goods, then it's worthwhile becoming a city merchant.

The dynamics of this situation have been illustrated in Figure 4.1. We'll call the point E_m a stable equilibrium point, corresponding to a mixed region employing both farmers and city merchants. It's stable because on either side of this point, small changes in each group's working population will not alter markedly the relative attractiveness of either group. You can think of E_m as a fulcrum, where the relative attractiveness of choosing farming ahead of being a city merchant is zero. You're equally happy with either choice.

The points E_c and E_f are unstable. For example, a pure farming population puts us at the point E_f. Any small decrease in the farming population sets in motion a self-perpetuating decline in the population of farmers. Because there's demand for both products, complete specialization in farming (point E_f) or city merchandising (point E_c) will always be inferior to a balanced mix of farmers and city merchants (point E_m).

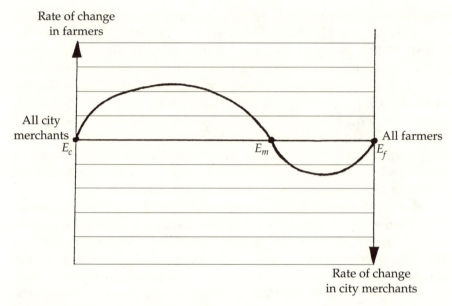

FIGURE 4.1   The dynamics with no trade: stable and unstable equilibria.

From this simple dynamic analysis, we can see how a stable and self-sufficient economy could be attained—with a balanced mix of farmers and city merchants. Such an isolated state of affairs would have been typical of the autarkic, manor-bound economies dotted across the Carolingian landscape. To retain this delicate state of balance, however, the region in question must remain isolated from other regions. If, for any reason, trading opportunities with other towns become easier, the balanced mix of farmers and city merchants could quickly disappear.

How might trading opportunities become easier? Safer trans-portation routes would be one possibility, because they improve the likelihood of successful passage and thus lower transportation costs. If they felt that the risks and costs of travel over longer dis-tances were reasonable, some enterprising city merchants might try to visit a few more distant places where they could sell their goods at higher prices. Such a quest for distant markets would be even more compelling once local demand had been satisfied. If the more adventurous merchants reported profitable trading ventures, then other merchants would surely follow in their footsteps. A positive feedback loop could be set in motion. Suddenly we're confronted with the carrot of an increasing returns economy.

What would happen to our stable, self-sufficient, economy under such conditions? In graphical terms, a rise in the relative attractiveness of being a city merchant vis-à-vis farming can be seen as a change in the shape of the curve between E_c and E_m. It begins to flatten out as the attractions of farming diminish and the appeal of long-distance trading grows. Eventually a stage is reached where the curve between E_c and E_f drops below the axis. This heralds a major qualitative change, leading to an entirely different kind of economy. Our stable equilibrium point E_m disappears, and the previously unstable E_c becomes stable. Everyone moves from the country to the city, farming dies out and the region then specializes in city activities.

The above analysis is hardly textbook economics. Most of the inspiration for this kind of dynamic analysis comes from outside the social sciences.[4] In a dynamic world, one learns to expect the

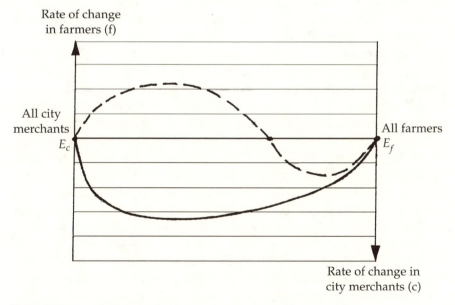

FIGURE 4.2   Catastrophic change as trade costs increase.

unexpected. Phenomena like disequilibria, nonlinearity, and instability are commonplace. It's something of an exaggeration of course, since farming in and around the key trading centers of Europe never died out completely. Nevertheless, Mees's illustration is fascinating because it shows us that abrupt changes are not just curiosities of the modern world. Sudden, unexpected structural changes to the economy have been going on since the Middle Ages, if not earlier.

The point to grasp is that a change in the relative attractiveness of one economic activity in comparison with another can have unexpected consequences. The economy may self-organize. If conditions had been different—for example, if farming had been particularly profitable in comparison with city activities—then the line between E_c and E_f could have shifted above the axis and a pure farming economy would have emerged. On the other hand, if the city merchants' interest in long-distance trade had been minimal, then the original weakly interactive (mixed) economy might have remained. Simplicity and predictability might have endured forever.

At the height of the feudal period, the difficulties and dangers of travel in Europe meant that transport costs were relatively high in comparison with the value of most agricultural goods. Thus Mees reasoned that farmers were less likely to engage in trade than city merchants, and the catastrophic shift depicted in his analysis was more likely to occur. In places where the population of city merchants was small, the mixed-economy equilibrium E_m would have prevailed. By way of contrast, cities much larger than the norm could have appeared rather suddenly as trade costs reduced through a critical range and trade flows grew accordingly.

Mees's explanation for the simultaneity of urban growth and the escalation of trade endorses Pirenne's hypothesis. Slow improvements to the transport system led to greater circulation by merchants, more specialization, and more trade. A growing band of interacting merchants created a qualitatively different economic landscape. Suddenly some regions specialized in city goods, others in agricultural commodities. Europe's economy self-organized. A shift away from self-sufficiency toward greater specialization and trade undermined the efficiency of the old feudal and manorial system, setting in motion an explosive positive feedback loop (see Figure 4.3).

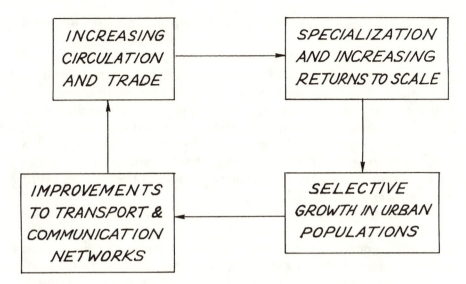

FIGURE 4.3   Some positive feedback loops in Europe's medieval economy.

If each region's population is also assumed to vary with its attractiveness, Mees argued that overall growth can also be explained.[5] Additional arguments based on increasing returns to scale and agglomeration can be drawn upon to show why cities expanded much more rapidly than their rural surroundings. Some of these arguments were discussed in Chapter 1, so we'll bypass them here.

Learning by Circulating

The city merchant seemed to be the key architect of this dramatic change in the economic landscape, so let's take a closer look at his decision problem. Like any good entrepreneur, he sought to profit by buying goods in places where supply was abundant and prices relatively low, with the aim of selling them in places where demand was strong and higher prices could be charged. To decide on the viability of such an undertaking for each tradable product, he would need to know or estimate (1) the purchase price and the selling price in various places, and (2) all the additional costs to transport and protect the product between the two places involved.

The periodic peddling of goods by the oriental traders was slanted toward the silks of Constantinople and the spices of the Indies. This is hardly surprising since only goods of great rarity and profitability could withstand the burden of the high transportation costs and risks of loss that must have beset the early merchants. The Venetians, on the other hand, were quick to realize that trade could be profitable for a variety of goods in various places. Slaves, in particular, could be sold profitably in Constantinople. Then a host of luxury goods could be brought back from the East. Further profits might accrue if various Italian goods could be sold for profit in the East and elsewhere.

Why did the Venetians excel as merchants? Unique topographical conditions, outstanding seafaring skills, and plenty of innovative entrepreneurship may have been the answer. For the typical Carolingian town, their protected area of cultivated land surrounding the manor meant everything. But commerce stood for nothing. Venice was a striking exception. Bereft of arable land, its very survival rested purely on commerce. The early fish-eating, marsh-dwelling Veneti gathered and processed salt, then sought other markets where it might be sold for profit. One such market was found in Constantinople.

The search for new markets, where a product is unfamiliar, is not just an act of courage. Nor is it simply revealing a natural talent for sniffing out entrepreneurial profit. A rare, unfamiliar product is valued by purchasers much as gifts of nature or pictures by old masters.[6] Often its price is determined without regard to the actual cost. Monopolistic profit potentials can be enormous. Despite the innumerable difficulties of the trading venture, the Venetian merchants realized that the rewards could be exceptional.

As the final decade of the tenth century began, Venice prospered under the strong hand of the statesman, warrior, and diplomatic genius, Pietro Orseolo II. In less than a year, he negotiated commercial terms with Basil II in Constantinople that guaranteed admittance of Venetian goods at tariffs far lower than those imposed on foreign merchandise in general. By reducing the total transaction costs for Venetian goods sold in Constantinople, the Doge established a major comparative advantage for Venetians trading in the Greek city. Among the bevy of trading centers dotted around the Mediterranean, Venice stood out as a key node, second in status only to Constantinople.

Imagine the thoughts of an enterprising Venetian merchant. Foremost in his mind might have been the idea of trading in a bundle of goods that guaranteed profitability regardless of the trading route traversed. Venetian salt was highly regarded by both Muslim and Christian alike. Constantinople supplied many luxury goods such as silk cloth, gold and silver plate, carved ivory, jewelry, and semiprecious stones. It also produced more pedestrian commodities such as linen, cotton cloth, and armaments. Sicilian grain could be bought in Palermo and sold for profit in many other ports.

From a host of possibilities, this enterprising merchant decided (1) to buy salt in Venice for sale in Constantinople, (2) to buy a few luxury goods in Constantinople for sale in Palermo or Venice, and (3) to buy grain in Palermo for sale in Venice. In view of the risks associated with each leg of his journey, how could the merchant ensure that such a voyage would be profitable? He couldn't. But he would have tried to estimate it. How? The longer the journey, the greater the prospect of profit in an era when prices were largely dependent on the rarity of the imported goods. But how could economic determinism prevail when rarity and insecurity increased with distance? Surely the outcome must have been at the mercy of some unwelcome chance events.

Imagine for a moment that you, the reader, are this merchant. You've studied a map of the area and realize that the three cities form a simple *network economy* (see Figure 4.4). Each city is a "node" in this network and each leg of your journey serves as a "link" between a pair of nodes. You've also realized that you're searching for a profitable compromise between economic necessities and elements of chance. Setting off on your maiden voyage to Constantinople, your spirits and profit expectations are high, perhaps even a little unrealistic. You see yourself as an enterprising explorer venturing into uncharted territory. Admittedly your cost calculations and price estimates are crude and approximate, but you sense that your mercantile skills will carry you through. Thanks to good fortune at sea and the temporary monopoly enjoyed by early entrants in a new market, you manage to earn a healthy profit on your first voyage.

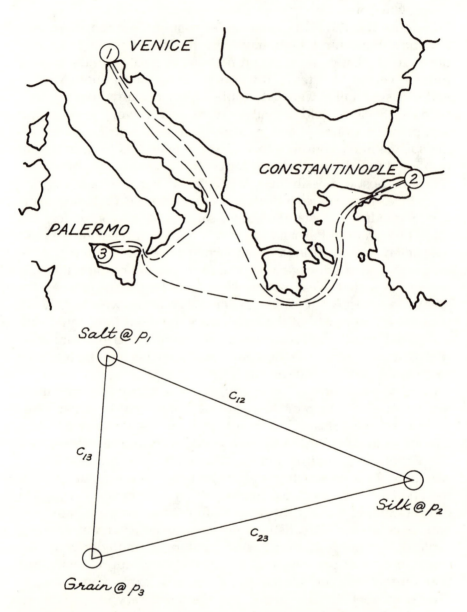

FIGURE 4.4 The network economy of Venice, Palermo, and Constantinople.

On this maiden voyage, intuition was your guide. But now you have the benefit of a little hindsight. Upon comparing your cost and price expectations with those realized on your first voyage, you realize just how wide of the mark they were. So you decide to record all this economic information in a diary. Your mind is set on developing an accounting system that will enhance your ability to estimate costs, prices, and profitability more accurately in the future.[7] A detailed record could even help you to become an expert on each of the economic links: Venice-Constantinople, Constantinople-Palermo, and Palermo-Venice.

Your diary records the historical prices, $p_i(t)$, prevailing in each city i on a particular date t, but only for the goods forming part of your chosen bundle of tradable goods—say salt, silks, spices, and grain. It also records the transaction costs, $c_{ij}(t)$, of transporting and protecting them between cities i and j, as well as other data pertaining to the reliability of each leg of your journey. The profitability of each leg, i-j, as well as overall profitability, can now be calculated. All information is based on your own trading experiences in each city. It's your personal diary.

The diary provides enough information to convince you to alter your bundle of goods before your next voyage. Upon checking the profit achieved on each leg of your latest journey, for example, you see that spices produced your most profitable return. So you decide next time to buy more spices in Constantinople. By way of contrast, you note that the profit from selling Sicilian grain in Venice was marginal. Yet grain could be sold at a much higher price in Constantinople. So you decide to call in at Palermo on your way to Constantinople to buy grain. Each of the entries in your diary provides "food for thought" in terms of setting the agenda for your next journey.

But the real value of your diary lies in the fact that it helps you to build a crude mental model of this three-city network economy. Your mental model is relatively simple. It consists of a few basic rules. For example, experience has taught you to apply the following two rules for profitable trade:

IF p_j (sell) > p_i (buy) + c_{ij} (trade), for a marketable product,
THEN that product should be traded.
IF p_j (sell) > p_i (buy) + c_{ij} (trade), summed over all products chosen,
THEN that bundle of products should be traded.

In other words, since you know that you can sell Venetian salt in Constantinople or Palermo at a price, p_j (sell), that covers all the costs incurred—namely the purchase price, p_i (buy), plus all transaction costs, c_{ij} (trade)—then salt should be traded. If you can sell your bundle of different goods at prices that cover the total costs of purchasing and transporting them to their point of sale, then your chosen bundle of goods can be profitable over the whole journey and should be traded.[8] Applying these rules to various combinations of goods enables you to form a picture in your mind of those goods that can be traded most profitably between various nodes of the network.

These aren't the only condition-action rules that form part of your mental model. You've also learned to rank the goods in terms of their contribution to overall profitability. For example, you invoke the following rules:

IF unit profits from one product exceed those of another product,
THEN increase your share of trade in the first product.
and
IF unit profits on leg i-j of your journey exceed those on leg i-k,
THEN increase your share of trade on leg i-j.

Furthermore, you've also learnt to chart the safest course in order to reduce the risks of inclement weather or piracy. This leads to a set of rules of a different kind:[9]

IF my ship sails too close to the Adriatic coastline,
THEN there's a risk of attack by Dalmatian pirates.
and
IF my ship joins in convoy with other ships,
THEN the risks of piracy will be reduced.
and
IF my ship sets sail in winter,
THEN the winds may destroy it completely.

Satisfaction of each of the above rules depends on the sophistication of your know-ware. Earlier voyages have taught you to apply these rules in a certain order. If trading profits are large, you're happy with your decisionmaking skills. Gradually you build up confidence in your ability to select goods, vessels, and routes wisely. You even acquire the know-how to estimate potential profits on each link.

After a few more voyages, you find that your cost and price estimates are much closer to the mark on each link. Improved risk assessment has also followed from the experience accumulated during each voyage. With the benefit of this additional hindsight, your deductive abilities can now come into play more reliably. But you will always need to display adaptive behavior on certain occasions. For example, your know-whether skills may cause you to modify your chosen route in response to news of piracy or inclement weather on a particular leg of a journey.

Eventually, your cumulative know-ware allows you to expand your "rule-of-thumb" hypotheses for the profitability of pair-wise trades on each link into a crude mental model of the profitability and risk associated with trading across the whole three-city economy. Then you find that certain combinations of goods, city pairs, voyage, and sailing dates consistently turn out to be the most profitable. Because you've gathered this knowledge during your own voyages, only you and the members of your *hanse* or *gild* have access to it. It's privileged know-ware, the fruits of *learning by circulating*. This inside knowledge allows you to decide more confidently on a preferred strategy for future trading ventures.

The medieval merchant gained valuable feedback from his experiences during each voyage: the swiftness and riskiness of his chosen route, the wisdom of his chosen bundle of goods, and the profitability of his whole trading strategy. This feedback would have strengthened or weakened his belief in any crude mental model of the three-city economy that he may have developed. Sometimes he would have altered his preferred route if it proved to be too risky or if he happened to hear of a safer or quicker route from other merchants. Naturally he would have altered his bundle of goods if some of them failed to achieve his profit expectations, replacing them with more popular or profitable ones.

There's little doubt that seafaring merchants lacked information about the prevailing economic circumstances. Faced with these uncertainties, they would have been obliged to take a "seat-of-the-pants" approach. For example, they may have simply "papered over" the gaps in their own knowledge. By this we mean that they may have acted like crude economic statisticians, guessing and testing and discarding simple expectational models to fill these gaps. In this way, they could have imagined a more general possibility from their own partial picture of the state of affairs. As logic, this kind of behavior is inductive.

But the inductive process of learning by circulating was never a purely *individual* experience. The diverse perils by which merchants were threatened compelled them to travel in armed convoys. Security could be had only at the price of force, and force was to be obtained only by union. Whatever these unions were called—*frairies, charites, compagnies, gilds,* or *hanses,* the reality was the same.[10] Troops of merchants banded together, usually bound by an oath of fidelity. A spirit of close solidarity and unity of purpose prevailed. Often the merchandise was bought and sold in common and the profits divided *pro rata* according to each man's share. The same thing happened in both Italy and the Low Countries, the two regions where commerce was developing most rapidly.

Thus the seeds of coevolutionary learning were sown. A number of specialized *hanses* soon emerged.[11] Merchants' beliefs and hypotheses about trading conditions were constantly formulated, tested, and refined amidst the collective experiences of each hanse. As time went on, this learning process led to better-educated merchants, who eventually were able to conduct much of their affairs by correspondence. The need to convoy merchandise grew less urgent, and commercial life became more stationary. Merchants could then turn their attention to local issues. In many Italian and German towns, the gilds and hanses had secured a share of urban government by the thirteenth and fourteenth centuries.

According to Pirenne, most merchants possessed a more or less advanced degree of instruction.[12] It was this initiative that led to Latin replacing the vulgar tongues used in earlier dealings. In Italy, the practice of writing was so much a part of commercial life that the keeping of books was widespread in the thirteenth century. Soon after, it was adopted throughout Europe. Leading scholars wrote works designed to assist the merchants in their endeavors. For example, Leonardo Fibonacci of Pisa composed a treatise on arithmetic for the use of merchants. We'll return to his fascinating work in Chapter 7.

Small wonder that the status of merchants grew remarkably quickly. Out of the ashes of the Carolingian economy, this new class of economic power mongers arose. Entrepreneurial merchants became the economic leaders of the medieval period. They became aristocrats and formed powerful patriciates to govern the great trading cities. Even the higher nobility eventually "turned merchant," as the great trading cities grew and prospered to an unprecedented extent. At the start of the eleventh century, who could have possibly foreseen that long-distance merchants would become the doyen of society?

As Pirenne suggested, "a state of mind was being gradually created which was particularly favourable to the progress of international trade and labour."[13] Founded on learning by circulating, long-distance trading proved to be handsomely rewarding, especially for the pioneering gilds and hanses—the ultimate explorers, in our terminology. They carved out a new niche for themselves and their cities. They also "locked in" competitive advantages by dint of their personal experiences and accrued knowledge. Theirs was an increasing returns economy. But most important of all was the fact that their learning by circulating contributed to the emergence of a new urban hierarchy in Europe. Like self-starting nodes in a random graph, the leading mercantile towns of Venice, Genoa, and Bruges catapulted up the urban hierarchy (see Table 4.2).

TABLE 4.2   The Ten Largest Cities in Europe

1000	1100	1200	1300	1400
Cordova	Constantinople	Constantinople	Paris	Paris
Constantinople	Fez	Palermo	Granada	Bruges
Seville	Seville	Seville	Constantinople	Milan
Palermo	Palermo	Paris	Venice	Venice
Kiev	Cordova	Venice	Genoa	Genoa
Venice	Granada	Cordova	Milan	Granada
Thessalonika	Venice	Granada	Sarai	Prague
Ratisbon	Kiev	Milan	Seville	Constantinople
Amalfi	Salerno	Cologne	Florence	Rouen
Rome	Milan	London	Cologne	Seville

Big Buttons and a Critical Thread

During the eleventh and twelfth centuries, the towns of northern Italy, central Germany, and Flanders became thriving centers of commerce, as population and trade continued to grow. As if part of an autocatalytic network, two "clusters of buttons" began to emerge as the "threads" between them materialized. Surprisingly enough, trade in northern Europe received a major stimulus from the Vikings. Pirenne suggested that "the Vikings, in fact, were pirates, and piracy is the first stage of commerce."[14] These Norsemen were so well versed in the construction of seaworthy ships and their navigation in distant waters that when their raids ceased, they simply became merchants.

By dint of its strategic role as a center for the medieval cloth trade, together with its convenient coastal location, Flanders became the key trading web in northern Europe. Some merchants threaded their way to Flanders from the interior parts of Europe, along the valleys of the Rhine, the Meuse, and the Scheldt. Others threaded a path across from the British Isles. Still others (mainly German merchants) used Flanders as the entrepôt between east and west. Bruges fulfilled a similar role in northern Europe to that of Venice in the south. It was even nicknamed "the Venice of the North"!

Thus emerged two great European clusters of commercial activity—one in the north on the shores of the Baltic and the North Seas, the other in the south on the shores of the Mediterranean and Adriatic Seas (see Figure 4.5). In between lay a central landmass mostly in the grip of feudalism. But commerce is nothing if not contagious. There's a craving for adventure and the love of profit. The incentive for threading a continuous link between these two vibrant trading areas could hardly have been stronger. Could one giant trading web emerge? Self-organization then lent a hand and wove its now familiar spell.

The final thread in this giant web of commerce started in Flanders, ran through Champagne and the Rhineland, down the Rhone Valley to Liguria and Lombardy. From there the Pisans, Genoese, and Venetians sailed to the eastern Mediterranean. Later the German plains boomed while Baltic and North Sea trade peaked under the direction of the German Hanse. The key threads of Europe's network economy were woven into a vibrant new tapestry.

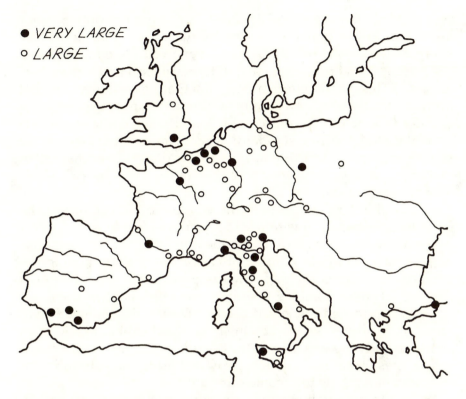

FIGURE 4.5   The "buttons" of Europe's medieval network economy.

Nestled centrally within this giant web of commerce, one particular "button" stood out as the meeting place between north and
south. What better place for the Flemish cloth to meet the buyers
from Lombardy and Tuscany than at the famous fairs of Champagne? Fairs emphasized the episodic character of trade over
longer distances. Each country sought its own.[15] But above all they
prospered in France. Two great French centers were universally famous in this respect: the Ile-de-France and Champagne-Brie. But
the patterns of circulation threaded by long-distance merchants
meant that only the Champagne fairs in the twelfth and thirteenth
centuries attracted merchants from the whole of Europe.

The Champagne fairs became the "embryonic clearinghouses" of
the European economy. Four towns in the area developed a rotating

system of six fairs each year.[16] These fairs were not only a major market for international trade but also the center of an embryonic international capital market. A market evolved there for exchanging currencies, with ratios quoted in terms of local and foreign currencies.[17] This was, in effect, a freely fluctuating exchange rate that mirrored the demand and supply of different European currencies. Trading volume was so considerable that the coin of the district became the model for the standard currency in much of Italy in the second half of the twelfth century. An early prototype of the "bill of exchange" also helped to lower the transaction costs of international trade at the fairs.

We shouldn't underestimate the economic importance of the fairs' institutional innovations. The manorial world of relatively isolated, weakly interactive economic units did not have continuous information about relative prices or the underlying supply-demand conditions for their own regions, let alone for foreign dealings. Transactions were simply too infrequent in time and space to support an organized market. During the thirteenth century, this vacuum was filled by the fairs, which embodied huge institutional advances. Along with the improvements in communication, these true marketplaces provided additional stimulus for circulation and trade to become self-reinforcing.

As their trading volume grew, the fairs provided general knowledge of prices for an international market. The transaction cost *per merchant* declined as the information was disseminated among increasing numbers, thereby simplifying the costly search by merchants for market information. Learning by circulating was centralized, thus removing much of the uncertainty of earlier days. With the Champagne fairs as a major hub, other fairs and markets were programmed to avoid clashes and encourage circulation. Thus carriers, merchants, and artisans could travel from one fair or market to another, selling their goods and absorbing vital economic information from the markets' transactions. Fernand Braudel refers to this circle of fairs as a sort of "perpetuum mobile."[18] It was also a coevolutionary circuit.

By exercising an incomparable power of attraction, the fairs marked one of the key stages in the advance of Western commerce. They brought classes and nations together, fostered a spirit of enterprise, stimulated cultural exchanges, and created a more peaceful Europe. But above all, they provided a meeting place for circulating merchants to ply their trade and compare notes. More than any other single activity, the fairs did most to bring about an end to the economic isolation that the West had suffered during the Middle Ages. Yet none of the fair sites developed into manufacturing centers, nor did any evolve into cities. Today they're all deader than Troy. Even their names have been forgotten.

Ephemeral Entrepôts

Why did the fairs prove to be ephemeral? For much the same reason as other entrepôts before them. Something new replaced something old. While the fairs were prospering, goods, coins, and credit were all part of the circulation process. Because it was simplest to arrange credit from a central point, single centers came to dominate the European system of payments. In the thirteenth century, it was the larger fairs like those in Champagne. The irony was that by encouraging trade over longer distances, the fairs themselves helped to catalyze a sequence of network changes that ushered in entirely new ways of circulation and means of transaction in Europe.

Four factors conspired to turn positive feedback loops into negative ones. The first was a new thread between north and south, a direct sea connection between Bruges and the towns of the Mediterranean using large Genoese vessels of the late thirteenth century. The second was the introduction of a regular mail system for Dutch and Italian merchants. Third came the absorption of the Champagne district into the kingdom of France, thus subjecting the fairs to heavy royal taxation. The final nail in the fairs' coffin was the introduction of more novel payment systems, bringing greater flexibility and frequency than they could offer.

Although each change affected the tapestry of trade and movement, the last was perhaps the most influential in the long run.[19] The Swedish economist Åke Andersson points to progressive improvements in the transaction system as the catalyst of a second "logistical revolution."[20] The merchants' desire for risk reduction, commercial credit, and reliable currencies spawned a growing interest in banking and insurance activities among the merchants, monarchs, and speculators alike. As the volume of trade grew, banking, insurance, and commercial law became in urgent need of more explicit instruments. Italian cities led in the formalization of legal forms. Urban markets like Bruges welcomed the opportunity to provide these commercial needs on a grander scale.

First to respond to the need for reliable banking was Amsterdam. By establishing an officially guaranteed central bank, the governors of that city set in motion a spate of central bank openings that were the forerunners of our modern banking system today. But the history of banking is not our principal concern. It suffices to note that this steady improvement in the system of transactions was a key factor in the growth and expansion of long-distance trade. It also contributed to the demise of the fairs.

The emerging industrial center of Flanders, the ports of Genoa, Venice, and Bruges, the fairs in Champagne and Flanders, the Italian colonies in the Levant, and the German Hanseatic towns can be viewed collectively as the principal "buttons" or entrepôts of medieval Europe's reviving network economy. In each market center, and along the routes threaded between them, the use of credit became more extensive; towns grew and became more active; and industry for distant markets took on a new lease of life. Progress was not slow and steady. It was abrupt and unexpected. Long spurts of growth alternated with times of stagnation and decline. Yet again, the picture is one of punctuated equilibria.

Surprisingly, none of the places mentioned above rank with the urban powerhouses of today. Yet the coevolutionary web of links threaded catalytically between them still remains. Such ephemerality is difficult to understand. Part of the explanation can be found in earlier chapters, where we saw that entrepreneurial learning is an adaptive process. Self-organizing networks make prediction nearly impossible. New nodes rise while old ones fall. But another explanation comes from the ingredients that are needed to make a city great in the first place. This intriguing question is addressed in the next chapter.

five

Networks, Boosters, and Self-Organized Cities

The shortest path between two truths in the real domain passes through the complex domain.

—Jacques Hadamard

The Shortest Network Problem

In January 1989, *Scientific American* published an article with the brief title "The Shortest Network Problem." The question seemed straightforward enough: "*What is the shortest network of line segments interconnecting an arbitrary set of, say, 100 points?* First popularized in the 1940s, the solution to the shortest network problem has eluded not only the sharpest mathematical minds but also the fastest computers. Why? Because it happens to belong to a class of problem that is tantalizingly difficult to solve. For starters, you cannot simply draw a series of lines between the given points. Additional points are needed. Known as Steiner points, these extra nodes serve as junctions in the shortest network. Scientists have developed a number of sophisticated algorithms to determine the location and number of Steiner points.[1] But even the best of these, running on the fastest computers, can't find the optimal solution because the time it would take is unacceptably long.

What makes the Shortest Network Problem so tricky? The difficulty is that the number of ways of connecting a given set of points to form a network grows very quickly with the size of the problem. In mathematical terms, it grows *geometrically*. Although there are

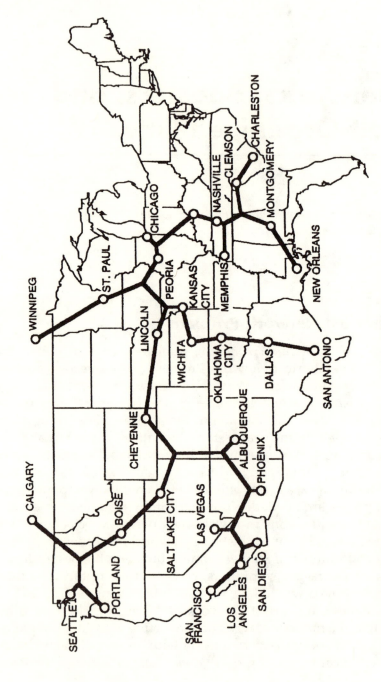

FIGURE 5.1   The shortest network of lines connecting 29 American cities.

only 4 ways of linking 3 points, this number jumps to 360 for 5-point networks, and to almost 3 million for 8-point networks! Mathematicians tell us that the introduction of additional intermediate (i.e., Steiner) points makes the problem "NP-hard."

In this ball game, a relatively easy problem is one whose solution time grows as a *polynomial* function of the size of the problem. For example, the problem of multiplying two N-digit numbers together usually takes an amount of time that's proportional to N^k, that is, N raised to the power of k where k is fixed. We call this polynomial time, or simply a P problem.

Problems like jigsaw puzzles—where the challenge is to fit pieces of different shapes into a given space—belong to a class of "nondeterministic polynomial," or NP problems. Jigsaw puzzles would be much easier if we knew the order in which the pieces should be inserted into the puzzle. Fitting the pieces and checking the solution could then be done in polynomial time. Because we don't know the order, we normally have to resort to some kind of "trial-and-error" method to solve the puzzle. That's why the problem is nondeterministic. There are many different ways of fitting the pieces together at each step. It's something of an intuitive nightmare for even the most ardent explorers.

A similar kind of problem plagues us when we come to deal with self-organizing human systems. As we mentioned in Chapter 1, changing patterns of residential location in a city would be much easier to understand if we knew the order in which the moves might occur. As well as many different size classes, there are different *ways* in which an avalanche of moves can be started. The same is true of commuting patterns and migration flows over longer distances. Because we don't know the order of moves, we're forced to resort to some simple heuristic model, or deal with average statistics instead. That's why these strongly interactive processes of socioeconomic change are so poorly understood.

If you think NP problems are difficult, you're in for a shock when you meet an NP-hard problem. Finding a polynomial-time solution for this class of problem would require one to find a polynomial-time solution for all problems in the corresponding class NP! This simply takes too long. Thus it's very easy to understand why the 100-point network problem described in the *Scientific American* article lies beyond the current limit of our computational capabilities. When that article first appeared, a 29-point problem (like in Figure 5.1) was close to the limit.[2]

You might be saying, so what? Surely the Shortest Network Problem is purely of scientific interest? Definitely not. What makes this kind of problem so intriguing is that it has dozens of real-world applications. Furthermore, many are of economic significance. Think of those situations where we want to minimize the cost of materials used to build networks of various kinds: telephone networks, pipelines, railway grids and roadways, to name a few. Shortest networks are also of growing importance in aircraft routing and scheduling. In fact, the solution to Steiner's problem is of interest whenever we wish to link up nodes in a network in a cost-efficient manner.[3] But the clear message to be learned is that building networks in an efficient manner is no simple task. Larger networks are very complex systems. Paradoxical behavior abounds. In the next chapter, for example, we'll learn that the addition of a new link between two existing nodes in a network can make everyone worse off!

Like the cognitive skills of humans, ground transportation networks must strike a balance between two extremes. At one end of the scale is the cost-minimizing Steiner solution, often preferred when the availability of capital is limited. Such a solution can be expensive to find. At the opposite end of the spectrum lies the utility-maximizing solution, which corresponds to the most convenient network for users. The utility-maximizing solution requires each city to be connected directly to the other. Such a solution can be expensive to construct. Chance and necessity both have an input to the final compromise solution.

The American geographer William Bunge pointed out that the evolution of North America's railroad network could be partly understood in these terms.[4] The utility-maximizing network was characteristic of the Northeast and Midwest, where the larger metropolitan centers are clustered more closely together and where the demands for transportation are greater. Elsewhere, urban centers generate smaller intercity traffic volumes because they're scattered farther apart. The cost-minimizing Steiner solution tends to prevail under these conditions. This kind of pattern shows up if we look at a detailed configuration depicting the density of rail traffic across

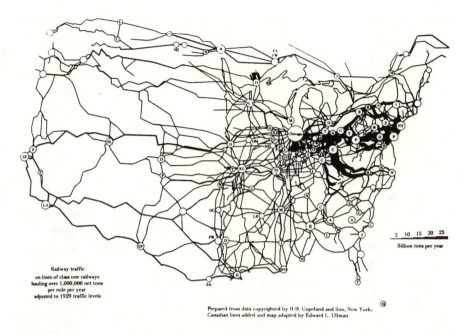

FIGURE 5.2   Traffic densities on the American rail network of the 1950s.

the United States. The density pattern of this historical network is shown in Figure 5.2.

In reality, of course, transportation networks aren't as simple as Bunge suggests. Historically, variations in physical geography have tempted many geographers to explain the location of particular transportation routes almost entirely in terms of the prevailing topographical conditions. Mountain ranges like the Sierra Nevadas clearly illustrate that natural barriers do influence the chosen network. But variations in the natural landscape may not be as influential as invisible factors, particularly chance events. Growth of cities, for example, may not be guaranteed by a gateway location. Unpredictable events, like capital investments engineered by enterprising entrepreneurs or astute politicians, can be crucial.

Like the economy it supports, a transportation network is a complex adaptive system. Its spatial form, connectivity, and flow capacity depend on a variety of factors—some topographical, some technological, some economic, and some political. To illustrate the growing importance of networks in economic development, and gain a deeper understanding of their inherent complexity, let's look at some geographical developments prior to and during the era of the American railroad.

Pirenne Again?

You've probably seen that majestic mountain range in the United States within a few hundred miles of the Atlantic Coast. How imposing the Appalachians must have looked to the would-be traveler of the late eighteenth century. In the absence of any cheap overland transportation, however, they must have loomed like an impenetrable barrier dividing the new territory west of the mountains from the old territory east of them.

Some well-respected scholars of American history have claimed that construction of the trans-Appalachian railway was the critical link that ignited the growth of American cities, thereby catapulting the United States into the cherished status of an industrial nation.[5] Underpinning this hypothesis was the argument that the railroad meshed the Atlantic Coast economy with the Ohio Valley–Great Lakes complex to form an integrated network economy in the Northeast. Strangely enough, this hypothesis has all the trappings of the one in the previous chapter, namely Pirenne's explanation for Europe's urban revival in the Middle Ages. In both instances, improvements to the transportation network seem to have served as the catalyst of selective, unexpectedly rapid urban growth.

Was it accidental that this period of frenetic railroad construction coincided with the era of greatest urban growth in the history of the United States?[6] Most observers would rule out chance alone. Plenty of historical evidence points to the potency of the railroad. Between 1830 and 1890, the total length of the U.S. railroad track increased by about 16 percent per year. There was a very sharp increase (from 6,000 miles in 1848 to 30,600 miles in 1860) that marked the completion of the basic railroad network east of the Mississippi River. The timing of this spurt in railroad growth coincided perfectly with accelerated urbanization. It also coincided with Walt Rostow's designated "takeoff" period for the U.S. economy—between 1843 and 1860.[7]

Despite the apparent nexus between rail infrastructure and urban growth, quite a few historians remained unconvinced. They claimed that the catalyst for American industrialization was the completion of the Erie Canal in 1825. Certainly freight costs using the Erie Canal were at least ten times cheaper than the National Road (the next best alternative before the railroads), revealing the extent of the canal's superiority at that time.[8] But neither the railroad nor the Erie Canal were good enough for some observers. They showed their historical bent, claiming that the true catalysts were unleashed well before the advent of the Erie Canal. For historians like Robert Fogel, the accelerating economic development resulted from the knowledge acquired in the course of the scientific revolution of the seventeenth, eighteenth, and early part of the nineteenth centuries.[9]

We're now confronted with a thorny problem every bit as challenging as the controversial issue of medieval Europe's revival. What really did catalyze such a selective growth spurt among the U.S. city economies? Was it the construction of the Erie Canal or the trans-Appalachian railway? Or were some earlier events just as important? Because aggregate American data yield conflicting insights, the views of analysts differ.

Who should we believe? Obviously it's difficult, nearly impossible, to pin down the key causal factors involved. But one thing's abundantly clear. It's impossible to reach any sound conclusions if we base our analysis on the aggregate behavior of the American settlement system as a whole. We must descend to the microlevel in order to build up a synthetic picture of how an urban economy works. Urban growth is selective and uneven. Thus it's a serious mistake to generalize. Some cities and their surroundings underwent much more dramatic structural change, compressed within shorter time spans, than others.

In the light of the lessons learned from Champagne's ephemeral role, it's important to ascertain the specific fate of each of America's entrepôt cities if we want to gain a deeper understanding of how the American economy works. To achieve this, we must probe changes over space at particular points in time and changes over time at particular points in space. For example, Figure 5.3 makes it clear that seaport cities like New York and Philadelphia were propelled upward much earlier than inland cities like Cincinnati and

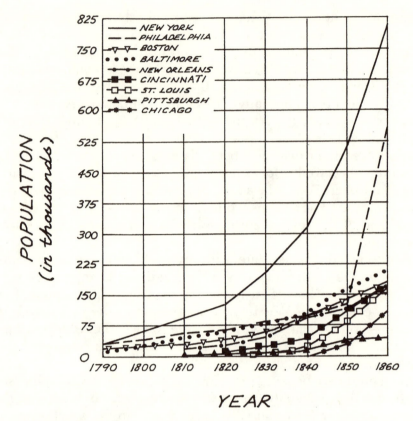

FIGURE 5.3   Stages of takeoff for selected American cities.

Chicago. What we find in this picture also reinforces our view that sharp discontinuities in the process of urbanization are not that unusual. Look at Philadelphia, for example. Sudden, dramatic takeoffs seem to be commonplace. Perhaps the world of morphogenesis guarantees that.

Selective Urban Growth

One way of recognizing the selective complexity of urban growth, and the path-dependent character of each city's evolution, is to look at how an urban hierarchy changes over time. Table 5.1 charts changes in rank—measured in population terms—between 1810

TABLE 5.1   Changes in Rank of Selected American Cities

City	-------------Rank in-------------		
	1810	1860	1910
New York	1	1	1
Philadelphia	2	2	3
Baltimore	3	3	7
Boston	4	4	5
New Orleans	6	5	14
Cincinnati	42	6	13
St. Louis	-	7	4
Chicago	-	8	2
Buffalo	-	9	10
Louisville	-	10	22
Albany	17	11	44
Washington	12	12	16
San Francisco	-	13	11
Providence	8	14	21
Pittsburgh	28	15	8
Rochester	-	16	23
Detroit	-	17	9
Milwaukee	-	18	12
Cleveland	-	19	6
Charleston	5	20	77

and 1910. It hints at which inland cities might have stood to gain most from the coming of the railroad era. I wonder which city would have got your vote as the likely leading gateway city back in 1810? With the aid of a map of America's West, it's not hard to come up with a plausible group of candidates. Potential gateway cities at that time included Buffalo, Chicago, Cincinnati, Pittsburgh, St. Louis, and a few others. Without the benefit of hindsight, however, how could we possibly decide between this handful of candidates? The truth is that the correct answer is unknowable. Even as late as 1860, nobody could be sure.

A keen observer of American history, William Cronon, tells a fascinating story of the race to become the principal gateway city linking the American east to its west.[10] It's a tale of economic dynamism fueled by speculation, the mid-1830s witnessing the most intense land speculation in American history. But it's also a story about the "boosters," as they came to be known, people who expounded serious theories of economic growth that dominated nineteenth-century thinking about frontier development.[11] The fascinating thing about booster theories was that no one person could claim sole authorship. Instead, according to Cronon, the theories quickly became the intellectual property of a much larger group—speculators, newspaper editors, merchants, and chambers of commerce throughout the West. Here, once again, was the blueprint of a familiar process: coevolutionary learning.

The hidden strength of booster theories was that they provided a surprisingly coherent "mental model" of urban and regional growth. They saw the engine of western development as the "symbiotic relationship between cities and their surrounding countrysides."[12] In those pioneering days, boosters believed that the growth of cities had its roots in natural phenomena, but that cities ultimately grew because people chose to migrate to them for various reasons. The natural advantages fell into three broad categories: (1) the natural resources of the region, which would help to generate trade for the city, (2) the transportation routes, which would guide these resources to their natural marketplaces, and (3) global climatic forces, which had historically created great urban civilizations elsewhere in the world.

But natural advantages represented only the potential for economic development and urban growth. Something or someone else had to make it happen. This the boosters saw in migration. Some of them argued that the demographic attraction of cities provided a sound basis for predicting urban growth. This group thought of cities as stars or planets, with gravitational fields that attracted people and trade like miniature solar systems. They even thought of using Newtonian mechanics to further understand the reach and influence of a city.[13]

Note how closely these self-reinforcing booster theories of city growth corresponded to the Pirenne-Mees hypothesis of urban revival in medieval Europe. In the case of the boosters, improvements to the transportation networks also provided greater access to nearby natural resources. These resources, together with a positive climate, were the forces generating migration and trade for a city. More migration and trade led to more specialization, increasing returns to scale, and thus further in-migration and growth in the urban population. Thus the positive feedback loops envisaged by the boosters bore a strikingly close resemblance to those underpinning Pirenne's analysis. Pirenne's feedback loop is enclosed by the dotted line in Figure 5.4.

According to Cronon, the strongest advocate of the "gravitational" theory of cities was an obscure figure in Cincinnati named S. H. Goodin. As we shall see shortly, Goodin's remarkable essay on Cincinnati's destiny anticipated the central place model of

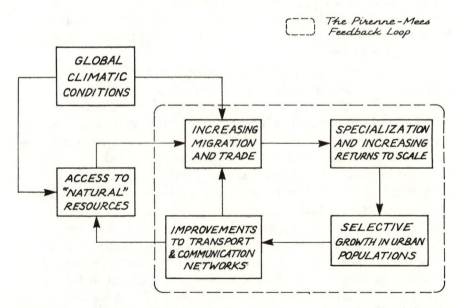

FIGURE 5.4   **Booster theories of city growth—positive feedback loops again.**

urban development. "The law of gravitation or centralization is known to be one of the laws of nature," wrote Goodin.[14] This "serial law" predicted that frontier migrants would displace Indian communities in the West, generating new villages to serve the surrounding territory and thereby attracting a larger share of population and trade. Goodin called these villages "the first circle in the serial law." They were to be followed by subsequent circles, each marking a higher stage of urban progress.

Goodin's argument saw rural populations clustered around small villages, which clustered in turn around larger towns, which clustered in turn around still larger cities. Road connections reinforced this hierarchical constellation of human settlements. Goodin's serial law bears a striking resemblance to central place theory, a body of literature that has exerted a powerful influence on 'twentieth-century research into economic development patterns over geographical space. The roots of central place theory can be traced to a contemporary of the boosters, who wrote in Germany at much the same time. Johann Heinrich von Thünen, a well-educated gentleman farmer in Mecklenburg, published the first edition of his book on the "Isolated State" in 1826. He attempted a rigorous mathematical description of the spatial relationships and economic linkages between city and country, but the boosters seem to have been blissfully unaware of it.

Von Thünen's theory grappled with the question of how the economy organizes its use of space. Surprisingly, this isn't a question that seems to engross the economics profession. I find it weird that most of the profession have turned a blind eye to all those interesting things that have something to do with *where* economic activities occur. As Paul Krugman has noted, hardly any of the popular economics textbooks contain any references to "cities," "location," or "space" in their indexes.[15] Considering how much time commuters waste in traffic jams, how much of their income families spend on housing and residential location, and how much capital firms spend on location decisions, this neglect of spatial economics is nothing short of mind-boggling. Perhaps the lack of attention is attributable in part to the issues raised in this book, namely the inherent complexity of economic changes and disequilibrium phenomena.

In any event, a brief explanation of von Thünen's idea can help to put the boosters' spatial problem into perspective. Imagine an isolated world, where a single town sits in the midst of an endless, fertile plain. As crops differ in their yield per acre and their transportation costs to town, a fundamental question arises: How should we allocate the land among the various competing landowners and farmers, each of whom acts in his or her self-interest? Von Thünen reasoned that each farmer faces a trade-off between land rents and transportation costs. What farmers could grow or raise profitably at any given location depends on how much people in the city are willing to pay for it and how much it would cost to transport it to the marketplace. "With increasing distance from the Town," he wrote, "the land will be given up progressively to products cheap to transport in relation to their value."[16]

The geographical consequences of von Thünen's idea are quite striking. A series of concentric agricultural circles form around the town, each of which defines the land areas that can afford to support certain kinds of economic activity. Heavier crops, like fruit, vegetables, and dairy products, are produced nearest the town. Since the price of land in this inner zone is too high for crops like wheat or corn, they are produced further out. Cattle and other livestock graze even further out from the town. Eventually a zone is reached where nobody would buy land at any price, because nothing it produced would be valuable enough to cover the prohibitive cost of transporting it to market.

Figure 5.5 illustrates von Thünen's schema. The top part of the figure shows four "bid-rent" curves (shown here as straight lines). Each line shows the rent that farmers would be willing to pay, at any given distance from the town, for a particular crop. Once growers have sorted out the rent gradient, one gets concentric circles of cultivation. This land-use pattern is shown in the bottom part of the figure. The funny thing is that this unplanned outcome is also efficient. Unplanned competition will allocate agricultural activities to land in a way that minimizes the total cost of producing and transporting the fruits of those activities.

This is quite a startling result. We might even dare to suggest that this pattern of concentric rings is an *emergent* property of the

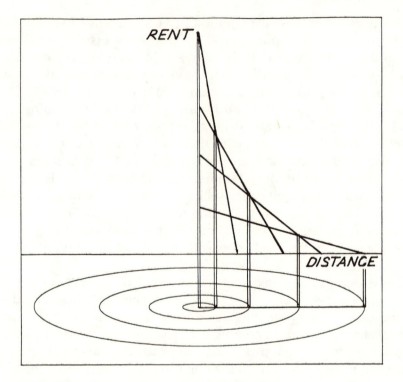

FIGURE 5.5   Von Thünen's isolated state.

economic system described. It's hardly something that's evident
from looking into the individual minds of all the farmers. Such circles will form even if no farmer knows what the other farmers are
growing. Yet von Thünen himself acknowledged that his abstract
thought experiment departed starkly from reality. No city would
ever be as isolated as his was. All are surrounded by a variety of
smaller towns and villages. No region would be as uniformly fertile as his hypothetical plain. All feature towns along rivers
or canals and natural resources clustered in seemingly random
patterns.

   Although such realities complicate the hinterland picture, none
of them destroy the descriptive validity of von Thünen's basic
idea. The vision that von Thünen and the boosters shared was that

urban markets made rural development possible.[17] Wherever agents organize their economy around market exchange, trade between city and country will be among the most powerful forces shaping economic geography and environmental change. Markets will organize themselves according to rent gradients and other competitive factors. Such rent gradients remain key features of a modern urban economy, shaping residential and commercial land markets as well as agricultural ones. But the problem for us is that von Thünen's model doesn't help to explain the existence of the town in the first place.

Central place theory put back some of the realism missing from von Thünen's landscape by linking cities, towns, and villages together in an orderly system of networks and subnetworks. The idea was that human settlements arrange themselves in hierarchical relationships with one another. Hinterland towns served as local marketplaces, selling their food and clothing to the nearby rural villages. Medium-sized cities sold more specialized retail products to the towns and villages that surrounded them. But all bought their main supplies, such as key equipment and inputs to their own production, from the wholesale markets in the central city. Any map of human settlements reflects this hidden network of markets within markets, lowly ranked places within the catchment area of highly ranked ones.

Classical central place theorists, like Walter Christaller and August Lösch, provided elaborate formal geometries to describe these nested urban hinterlands, with intricate layers of large and small hexagons delineating the honeycomb-like market areas for highly and lowly ranked goods in highly and lowly ranked places.[18] Reading the works of these German theorists, one is deeply impressed by the abstract neatness of their economic geography. Nested hexagons belie the uneven patterns observed in real places and landscapes. By allowing the fantasy of a flat, featureless plain, which the central place theorists shared with von Thünen, population grows until small village centers begin to appear with the expansion of market demand. They, in turn, eventually create a market for medium-sized towns; medium-sized towns, in turn, create larger cities; larger cities, in turn, create a giant metropolis. Just like the Cincinnati booster S. H. Goodin had proclaimed.

One Great Metropolis

But which great metropolis would be the central star around which all other town and country satellites would come to orbit? For Goodin, cities such as Buffalo, Chicago, Cincinnati, Pittsburgh, and St. Louis were all "competing cities of the same grade of circles." One more stage was still beckoning. "The next circle beyond," he prophesied, "is a central city—a city which shall have all these cities as satellites or outposts. Where shall that city stand?"[19] According to Cronon, no single question more excited booster imaginations. It was discussed incessantly and everyone had their own prophecies.

Surely the elegant mathematical simplicity of central place theory could supply an answer. Alas, like von Thünen's agricultural zones, central place theory suffers from one insurmountable flaw. It's profoundly static and ahistorical. What seems to be organic and evolutionary, like Darwin's model, with clusters of smaller hexagonal cells nested within and nurtured by larger cells, turns out to be a system locked in the world of stasis. Hierarchies of central places look almost lifelike, but they're not actually growing at all. At best, central place theory is a description rather than an explanation. Its static character couldn't answer the burning question on every booster's lips: Where will that great central metropolis of the West be?

With the benefit of hindsight, the answer comes easily, of course. A glance at the network of American railroads operating by 1860 reveals that only two cities were perfectly located to serve as gateways to both east and west: Chicago and St. Louis. If waterway geography had been the key determinant of urban growth, the major inland city would surely have been St. Louis. Located at the confluence of two of the continent's greatest rivers, the Mississippi and the Missouri, St. Louis could reasonably expect to draw resources from the entire country to its north and west. Chicago's modest claim to waterway advantages lay principally in its harbor and canal corridor, neither of which extended very far to the west.[20]

Then came the railroads and Chicago's meteoric rise. The story is a familiar one, but perhaps one that's not always told correctly. Cronon speaks of two different landscapes. One, the original landscape, is natural: mountain ranges, rivers, lakes, and all the other "givens" of the environment. The second is the created landscape of railroad lines, canals, farming patterns, and cities. This second landscape results from human decisionmaking. A key difference between the two landscapes is that the first one is relatively static, whereas the second landscape is inherently dynamic.

Being more dynamic, the created landscape became far more important as a determinant of location than the natural landscape in which it was embedded. For example, Chicago's role as a Great Lakes port was quickly overshadowed by its role as a rail hub. Furthermore, the second landscape is often self-reinforcing: Railroads aimed at Chicago because it was the economic center of its region, and this, in turn, reinforced its centrality even more. Once again, we must look to positive feedback loops and an increasing returns economy for hints of likely things to come.

The first railroad to reach the Mississippi in 1852 put Chicago and St. Louis in competition by rail without actually connecting them. This intensified the rivalry triggered earlier by the opening of the Illinois and Michigan Canal in 1848. Other railroads soon followed. Rather than face the risks and uncertainties of buying and selling via St. Louis and the river, upriver residents began to reorient trade east toward Chicago. Like modern commuters on the London Loop, these traders were learning by circulating. Their "mental models" of efficient trade were warming to the idea that the railroad was safer and cheaper. Finally, the emerging advantages of rail over water—greater speed, predictable schedules, and year-round movement—pulled other goods in Chicago's direction as well.

But transport alone doesn't fully explain the shifting importance of the two towns. Regional hierarchies were also changing. St. Louis had traditionally looked to New Orleans as its chief trading partner in the southward movement of farm products, and to Philadelphia wholesalers for the merchandise it purchased from the east. Both of these older cities were in relative decline by mid-century, thus retarding St. Louis in its rivalry with Chicago. With the railroads came bridges across the Mississippi, rendering navigation by water even more hazardous and drawing more commerce away from the river. But the final blow to St. Louis's dreams of greatness was yet another chance event: the Civil War and the blockade of New Orleans by Union forces in 1862. The river's blockade reduced the whole business turnover of St. Louis to about one-third of its former amount.

In the 1830s, Chicago was nothing more than an old trading post and garrison fort. It had fewer than one hundred residents as late as 1832. Yet, in just three or four years, this tiny village suddenly increased its population twentyfold, the value of its land grew by a factor of three thousand, and boosters began to speak of it as a future metropolis.[21] By 1840, land speculation and the prospect of a key canal had propelled the population of this small, bustling town to almost 5,000.[22] Capitalists from leading cities in Europe and America raced to invest in the "would-be-great" city. Neither von Thünen's rings nor central place theory could shed any light on the city's explosive growth during the 1830s. To understand these dramatic events, we must turn again to the boosters and their methods of mental persuasion.

Where the boosters had it over central place theorists was in the *dynamic* nature of the booster models of urban growth. Some were even Darwinian in character. "I shall assume that a city is an organism," wrote Jesup W. Scott, "springing from natural laws as inevitably as any other organism, and governed, invariably, in its origin and growth by these laws."[23] But others were dynamic in a visionary sense. They championed their beliefs with skill and perspicacity and sought the support of wealthy investors to turn predictions of urban greatness into self-fulfilling prophecies. Their mental models of urban prosperity made sound theories, so sound that they convinced New Yorkers to invest huge sums to help make Chicago's urban dream come true. As depicted earlier, such grand schemes were the catalysts of potential positive feedback loops. They were also coevolutionary.

Chicago's population exploded after 1833, seemingly oblivious to the need for a pastoral stage, or a settlement of pioneering subsistence farmers, or even an agricultural community of any kind.[24] Instead, the town's speculators gambled on an urban future. They staked fortunes on land they hoped would soon lie at the heart of a great city. Meanwhile, each booster had refined his own mental model of how this immense city would spring into being. Once the boosters had convinced the out-of-town investors, who then invested in land, prices rose quickly, thereby attracting more investors and inflating booster confidence further. And so the process of growth became self-reinforcing and the prophecy self-fulfilling. The positive feedback loop of a new, increasing returns, city economy was set in vigorous motion.

In the terminology of previous chapters, the boosters were explorers. They were risk takers who "all believed that cities were the key to the Great West," said Cronon. "And since their reasons for this belief were anything but academic, they sought to discover why some cities grew and not others, so that intelligent investors could profit accordingly."[25] Chicago was a place "pregnant with certainty." The boosters sought to make their visionary mental models come true by conveying just this certainty to investors and merchants who might set up shop there. They knew that capital was the most important key needed to unlock the gates to their metropolitan empire. Movements of people and capital helped link Chicago to the international system of cities, thereby creating an urban market that drove the surrounding region's growth.

Networking Futures

Chicago became the critical link that meshed the different American worlds of east and west into a single system. As the region to the west was settled, surplus produce was routed via Chicago for shipment eastward through the Great Lakes to the Northeast and Europe; and the city became the key entrepôt for eastern products going further west. In a truly literal sense, from 1848 to the end of the nineteenth century, it was where the West began.[26] The isolation that had hitherto constrained the trade and production of frontier areas would disappear in the face of what Karl Marx called "the annihilation of space by time."[27]

But this newfound gateway status did not create the city by itself. Goods and people rode the trains to get to the market, where together buyers and sellers from city and country priced the products. Like Champagne half a millennium earlier, Chicago became the site of a grand country fair. Its radius of attraction was to stretch so far that only New York could match its markets in terms of reach and power. A new geography of capitalism was in the making. By 1848, it was the leading primary market in the country. And in that same year, the city took a seemingly modest step in organization that was to guarantee its future as a commercial hub and gateway market to the world.

When eighty-two grain merchants met on South Water Street in 1848 to open the Chicago Board of Trade, few, if any, had heard of the Tokugawa era in Japanese history. Fewer still would have known that in forming America's first commodity exchange, they were repeating what their Japanese predecessors had done in Osaka two centuries earlier. Like the Japanese rice merchants of the mid-1600s, the Chicago grain merchants were hoping to alleviate the economic havoc that resulted from the wild price swings of the agricultural production cycle. By buying and selling forward contracts, which eventually were standardized as "futures," the merchants could lock in prices and reduce the dramatic swings between winter shortages, when cold weather blocked access to and from Chicago's grain elevators, and summer harvests, when so much corn, oats, and wheat flooded the market that boxcar loads of worthless grain were dumped into the waters of Lake Michigan.[28]

To put the Board of Trade's influential role into historical perspective, a few words about grain elevator technology are in order. Before the advent of the railroad, shippers loaded their grain into sacks before sending it on its journey by water to the mill for grinding into flour. Each sack remained unique and intact, being unmixed with grain from other farms. Ownership stayed with the original shipper until it reached the point of sale. In a manner akin to the uncertainties borne by Venetian merchants in the medieval era, the grain shipper bore all the risks of damage in transit. If the grain became waterlogged, if it spoiled in warm weather, if prices collapsed before it reached market, or if the ship sank, the resulting losses accrued to the original shipper.

The railroads brought a dramatic explosion in Chicago's receipts of grain. With whole freight cars carrying nothing but corn or wheat, freight traffic congestion became a problem. Rapid unloading of grain cars was imperative. The invention that made this possible was the steam-powered grain elevator. This unheralded innovation in grain handling bestowed on Chicago the potential to handle more grain more quickly than any other city in the world.[29] But this increasing scale and efficiency of Chicago's grain-handling technology depended on two conditions: moving grain without recourse to old-fashioned sacks, and severing the bond of ownership between each shipper and his individual consignment. Only then could corn or wheat cease to act like solid objects and begin to behave more like liquids: golden streams that could flow like water.

Change proved to be inevitable. As the scale of Chicago's grain trade grew, elevator operators began objecting to keeping small amounts of different owners' grain in separate bins that were only partially filled. They sought to mix grain in common bins. Crops from dozens of different farms could then mingle, and the reduced cost of handling the grain would earn the elevator operator higher profits. The only obstacle preventing this greater efficiency was the small matter of the shipper's legal ownership of the grain.

The organization that eventually solved this problem was the Chicago Board of Trade. At its outset, it had no special focus on grain. It simply sought to represent the collective voice of business interests in the city, enjoying very limited success. Not until European demand for grain expanded during the Crimean War did the Board of Trade's fortunes begin to change. In the space of three short years (between 1853 and 1856), the total amount of grain shipped from Chicago more than trebled.[30] Traders began to find it more convenient to do their business centrally, bringing samples, bickering over prices, and arranging contracts between buyers and sellers at the board's meeting rooms. As more traders gathered, that single marketplace quickly became more efficient and attractive. Yet another positive feedback loop was set in motion. Soon the advantages of this centralized market were so great that no serious grain merchant could afford not to belong.

The Board of Trade began to regulate the city's grain trade for the first time in 1856, restructuring Chicago's market in a way that would forever transform the grain trade of the world. First, it introduced a grading system to set standards of quality for each type of grain. This solved the elevator operators' problem. Grain from one producer could now be mixed with grain from another producer if it was of the same grade. For their shipment of grain, traders were given a receipt that they, or anyone else, could redeem at will. A person who owned grain could conveniently sell it to a buyer simply by selling the elevator receipt. Anyone who gave the receipt back to the elevator then received an equal quantity of equally graded grain. This was a fundamental change.

It wasn't long before Chicagoans discovered that a grain elevator had much in common with a bank. After depositing his grain in an elevator operator's bin, the original owner received a receipt that could be redeemed for grain, just as a check or banknote could be redeemed for gold. Such transactions could be completed and repeated many times, without a single grain of wheat moving from the bin. The elevators had effectively created a new form of money, secured not by gold but by grain.

Then chance intervened again. In 1848, the same year that Chicago merchants founded the Board of Trade, the first telegraph lines reached the city. Since commodity prices were among the most important bits of information that traveled the wires, those with the best access to telegraph news were usually in the best position to gauge future movements of prices. Although the telegraph dispersed prices far more widely, it also concentrated the sources of such information in a few key markets. The dense flow of news in cities such as Chicago and New York allowed their prices to reflect trade conditions for the local, the national, and even the global economy.

As Cronon argues, by acquiring the three key institutions that defined the future of its grain trade—the elevator warehouse, the grading system, and linking them through telegraph at a central market governed by the Board of Trade—Chicago underwent another revolution.[31] The new communications technology ushered in what traders called "to arrive" contracts for grain, whereby a seller promised to deliver grain by some specified date in the future. Such contracts, together with standardized elevator receipts, made possible Chicago's greatest innovation in grain trade: the futures market. "To arrive" contracts solved grain shippers' anxieties by ending their uncertainty about future price changes, while also opening up new opportunities for speculators who were willing to absorb risk themselves. If one was willing to gamble on the direction of future price movements, one could even contract to sell grain one didn't own, "selling short" so to speak.

By the second half of the 1860s, there was a growing market in contracts for the future delivery of grain that perhaps did not even exist yet. This second market coexisted with the older, more familiar one that traded elevator receipts for grain actually present in the city. Futures contracts were interchangeable and could be bought and sold independently of the movement in physical grain. As the historian Morton Rothstein has aptly stated, when viewed in the most cynical terms, the futures market was a place where "men who don't own something are selling that something to men who don't really want it."[32] The Chicago futures market was a market not in grain but in the price of grain.

The speed with which futures trading surpassed cash trading at the Board of Trade was quite astonishing. In 1875, the *Chicago Tribune* estimated that the city's cash grain business amounted to about $200 million; the trade in futures, on the other hand, was ten times greater, with a volume of $2 billion.[33] A decade later, the futures market had grown to a point where its volume was probably fifteen to twenty times greater than the city's trade in physical grain. One trembles to even imagine what the scale difference might be today. The unpredictable behavior of stock and futures markets are examined again in Chapter 7.

In summary, a location favorable for the expansion of trade was an essential factor in the rise of America's largest cities. Just as Pirenne observed about trade in medieval Europe, people engaged in other pursuits are drawn to locate in great trading centers to supply the needs of the trading population or to take advantage of the facilities for trade that these centers offered. In the case of Chicago, positive feedback loops abounded. Access to an expanding hinterland was merely one of a number of factors stimulating the city's explosive growth and change. Land speculation was the initial catalyst. Then came the railroads and improved communications. Factories also multiplied rapidly. By reinforcing one another, these and other factors helped to bring about the boosters' self-fulfilling prophecies. This is the way an increasing returns economy works.

In 1860, America's center of manufacturing—as defined by the U.S. census—was just east of Pittsburgh. Thereafter it began to move westward. By 1920, it was a little northwest of Columbus, Ohio; and by 1940, it was very close to Chicago. Yet the most unexpected, trailblazing factor was the Chicago Board of Trade, conducting a market within a market: boxes within boxes within boxes, all mediating between the commodified world inside and the physical world outside.

The message to be learned from Chicago's unbridled growth in the second half of the nineteenth century is that each city is a *complex adaptive system.* Its collective behavior cannot be predicted merely from our knowledge of its population alone. The myriad of interactions are mind-boggling. New collective possibilities emerge unexpectedly. Who could have foreseen that the boosters' visions of a great city would have been so influential and prophetic? Who could have foreseen the emergence of the Chicago Board of Trade as such a powerful instrument of economic exchange? Who could have foreseen the scale of the development of futures trading itself? As a complex adaptive system, the macrobehavior of an urban system transcends all of its parts! Some collective outcomes emerge only as aftermaths of the collective experience. And so it was with Chicago.

City-Size Distributions Obey Power Laws

Great cities like Chicago never thrive in isolation. They feed continuously on many other places. Cities interact with other towns and cities to form systems of settlement. They're but a small part of a complex network economy that synthesizes from the coevolutionary interactions between them. Such interactive urban systems are never static. They're constantly reorganizing themselves into a different order if we compare them purely on the basis of size.

By 1890, Chicago had leapfrogged ahead of Philadelphia to become the second-largest metropolis in the United States. No other city in America had ever grown so large so quickly. At that time, there were only 3 cities with populations of more than 1 million. Below the top three were 25 cities with populations less than 1 million but more than 100,000. Another 326 cities had populations below 100,000 but above 10,000. Beneath them were the more than 994 towns with fewer than 10,000 inhabitants, and the 6,490 villages and rural areas with fewer than 2,500 people.

Most economic geographers know what happens if we plot this size distribution of settlements on double logarithmic paper. Figure 5.6 shows the resulting distribution. I've ranked the cities in descending order, beginning with the most populated and ending with the least populated. The downward-sloping curve is pretty close to a straight line. What this tells us is that the population distribution of U.S. cities in 1890 conformed roughly to a *rank-size rule*. This rule says that the population of a city is inversely proportional

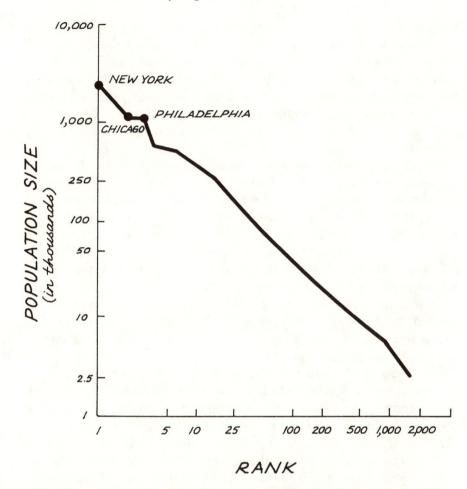

FIGURE 5.6   Rank-size distribution of cities in the United States, 1890.

to its rank. As we'll see shortly, a familiar principle is at work. You've probably guessed its identity already. It's yet another power law!

In the 1940s, George Kingsley Zipf produced dozens of plots of this kind, finding the same kind of regularity.[34] Subsequent research by Brian Berry, a geographer at the University of Chicago, showed that such macroscopic order also holds for many systems of cities outside the United States.[35] But not every nation conforms to the rule. Some countries display a primate pattern, meaning that the first-ranking city may be much bigger than twice the size of the second-ranking city. For example, the French, English, and Argentinian distributions do not conform to the rank-size rule. Paris, London, and Buenos Aires dwarf their nearest neighbors in their respective distributions. Other nations, such as Australia, display "kinks" or horizontal segments, indicating that some top-ranking cities are closer in size to one another than the rank-size rule suggests.

Obviously the rank-size rule doesn't hold *perfectly.* In fact it seems to work best in large countries with mostly self-sufficient economies, as measured by the ratio of their external trade to total trade. If this ratio is less than 10 percent, as it is for the United States and Russia, the rule fits well. It also works well in large countries with long urban traditions—like China and India.

Comparative work suggests that deviations from the rule can often be explained by two factors: (1) improper specification of the complete settlement system, or (2) different qualitative stages of development. For example, Portugal's distribution may conform to the rank-size rule once it's recognized that Lisbon heads a larger-than-national urban system.[36] If Singapore and Malaysia are lumped together—as history demands—then their combined distribution conforms approximately to the rank-size rule.[37] The primacy displayed by Japan's city-size distribution also disappears once Tokyo's chief rival is seen to be the multicentered Kansai or Keihanshin conurbation.[38] These examples show that quite different results can be achieved by taking cultural or political issues into account. Once again, history matters in the world of morphogenesis.

Austria is another interesting case. During the years of the Austro-Hungarian empire, Vienna and Budapest dominated the urban hierarchy. No rank-size rule prevailed then. Nor did it in the ensuing days of "Brave Little Austria." But after Austria was annexed to Germany and the Sudetenland in 1939, Zipf showed that their combined distribution roughly conformed to the rank-size rule.[39] Perhaps the linguistic element should also be respected. In any event, a historical analysis of flows and interaction patterns between all candidate towns and cities is a more reliable way of defining a truly interactive system of cities.

Since our primary interest is in dynamics, let's take a look at how well the rank-size rule has withstood the test of time. The United

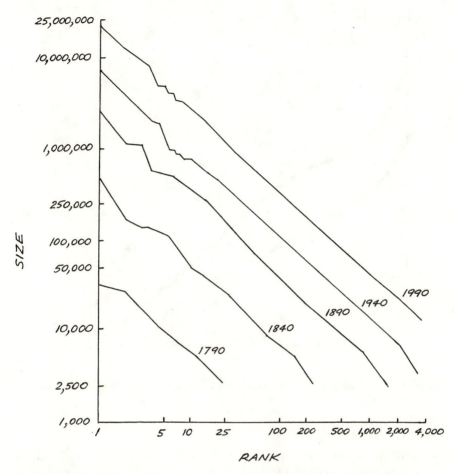

FIGURE 5.7 Rank-size distribution of cities in the United States, 1790–1990.

States can serve as our first laboratory. Remarkably, the American rank-size relationship has been stable for a very long time. Despite tumultuous changes to its urban system during the past two centuries, Figure 5.7 confirms that the rule has applied continuously. Neighboring lines are almost straight and roughly parallel. What incredible stability! Overall growth is depicted by the gradual shift upward and to the right. A similar story can be found in Europe. There's a high degree of macrostability in the French urban system,

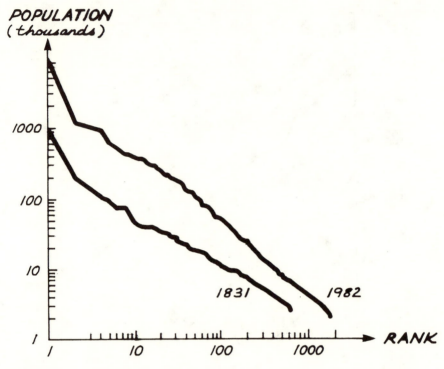

FIGURE 5.8   Rank-size distribution of French cities, 1831 and 1982.

for example, despite the fact that the relative position of individual cities has varied considerably. This state of collective order is shown in Figure 5.8.

What's the explanation for this remarkable stability over time? Could there be something like a universal law of city sizes? Very few economists or geographers have tried to answer this fascinating question. Those that have usually argue that it reflects some kind of hierarchy of central places.[40] After all, a power law distribution like the rank-size rule seems to be consistent with a simple hierarchy. Yet the hierarchical story relies on the constancy of some parameters that we can't really assume to be constant over time. Furthermore, central place theory is a static theory. How can a static theory possibly hope to explain something that results from a decidedly dynamic chain of events?

Brian Berry was perhaps the first to offer an explanation in terms that complexologists would applaud. He argued that as the economic, political, and social life of a country grows more complex, its city-size distribution evolves toward a rank-size pattern, because this represents the *steady state* of the whole urban system.[41] In other words, economic development will move an immature system of cities closer and closer to a rank-size distribution over time. This suggests that there's a scale from primate distribution to rank-size distribution, which is somehow tied to the maturity and complexity of the interactive forces affecting a nation's urban structure. When few strong forces prevail, primacy results. When many strong forces prevail, the rank-size rule results.

In view of what we learned earlier about complex adaptive systems, perhaps we can be more explicit about the coevolutionary process involved. The rank-size distribution seems to be an *attractor* in the phase space of all possible dynamics governing urban change. This suggests, but falls short of proving, that individual towns and cities may *self-organize* in such a way that they preserve this rank-size pattern over time. Indeed there's evidence to support the idea that the rank-size pattern is an attractor.[42] The macrostability of the American and French urban systems has persisted despite the changing position of individual cities in each nation's urban hierarchy. There's no sign of proportionate growth in these systems.

Can we visualize what such a rank-size attractor might look like? A possible metaphor is the upper canopy of a forest, containing trees of various heights and ages. As the different trees mature, the profile (or contour) of the canopy shifts upward over time, just like the rank-size distributions. But its shape never seems to alter, despite the fact that individual trees change markedly. Some grow quickly, others grow slowly; some die, others are born. Could it be that towns and cities in the U.S. system self-organize into a kind of equilibrium pattern like trees in a forest? If so, then it's a special kind of dynamic equilibrium. We might even think of it as a rank-size *ecology.* Although some cities grow and others decline, the overall ecology, or the profile of the aggregate city-size distribution, doesn't change.

Speaking of ecologies, the rank-size distribution looks like one of those emergent properties of a complex, socioeconomic system. It's a higher-level "simplicity" that emerges from the interactive mix of individual cities and their coevolution. Such an unexpected result collapses the apparent chaos of a highly interactive system into a very simple rule. As we've stressed already, the urban hierarchy of the United States is not the only nation to exhibit this kind of macrostability. A similar order can be found in Asia. Indonesia, Japan, Malaysia-Singapore, South Korea, and Taiwan have more or less preserved their rank-size distributions over the past fifty years, despite many individual towns and cities "jumping rank" dramatically.[43]

Perhaps the most important feature of the mysterious regularity inherent in the rank-size rule is that it's not unique to urban economies. I referred to the ubiquitous character of power laws in Chapter 1. The analogy with sandpile avalanches is a powerful one. Instead of plotting how many avalanches there are of each size, we might plot how many cities there are of each size. It would appear that power laws can arise in an urban context when three criteria are satisfied. First, the system of cities under scrutiny must be subject to substantial growth over time. Second, the growth rate of any individual city must be (viewed as) random, so that you get a diversity of sizes over time. Third, and most important, the expected rate of city growth must be independent of scale. In other words, larger cities will grow (on average) neither faster nor slower than smaller cities.

The rectilinearity of rank-size plots has been shown to rephrase an underlying scaling distribution.[44] Zipf put forward the bold claim that scaling is the "norm" for all social phenomena. Mandelbrot's work has added weight to Zipf's claim. A special feature of all these coupled dissipative systems is that they evolve naturally toward a self-organized critical state. The rank-size condition may correspond to a state of self-organized criticality, where cities are formed by avalanches of human migration. In this critical state, there's plenty of communication between each and every part of the urban system. Even the most peripheral settlements communicate with the central cities. Just like a self-organizing sandpile.

Remember how a sandpile reaches a critical state in which there's communication between the grains at the center and at the edge of the pile. Space scales suddenly jump from microscopic to macroscopic. A new organizing mechanism takes over, one that's not confined to local interactions. In the case of an urban system, the emergence of this new order manifests itself in the form of a rank-size distribution, a stable macrostate in a heterogeneous and dynamic system of people and cities. The emergence of this stable state, with its unique rank-size property, could not be anticipated from the various properties of the individual cities involved. It's an *emergent* property.

Zipf reasoned that the rank-size condition was a special kind of equilibrium state, balancing two opposing forces. Man's dual role as a producer and a consumer posed a profound conflict in the economy of his location.[45] Two extreme outcomes could result. One course of action involved moving the people close to the sources of raw materials to save on transporting materials to the people. The effect of this economy, which he called the *Force of Diversification,* was to split the whole population into a large number of small, widely scattered, autarkical communities, having virtually no communications or trade with one another. Sounds very much like medieval Europe's self-sufficient, agrarian economy, doesn't it?

The other course of action, which he called the *Force of Unification,* moves the materials to the population. All production and consumption would take place in one big city, where the entire population would live.[46] In practice, of course, neither extreme occurs. Zipf argued that the actual location of the population depends on the comparative magnitudes of both forces in question, that is, on the extent to which persons are moved to materials and materials to persons in a given system of cities. One force makes for a larger number of communities of smaller size, and the other makes for a smaller number of communities of larger size, so the realized outcome must balance these forces, leading to a rank-size distribution of cities.

What's fascinating about these opposing forces is that one produces a *simple,* weakly interactive economy, but the other produces a *complex* economy that's strongly interactive. Putting all the population in just one city is certainly an extremely interactive solution, bordering on the chaotic. We might even think of it as an economy that's too strongly interactive! Most nations' settlement systems lie between these two extremes. Developed economies are more strongly interactive, whereas many developing economies are only weakly interactive. Some are dynamically stable, others are potentially unstable.

The thing to note is that these two extreme conditions correspond to states that we've met before in earlier chapters. In our discussion of coevolutionary learning in Chapter 2, for example, we discussed how mental models get caught between two extremes—the simple and the chaotic. Like our old friend, the sandpile, they're poised to unleash an avalanche of small, medium, and large changes throughout an economic system of interacting agents. The result is that a coevolving economy gets driven away from the ordered regime toward the chaotic regime, but soon gets driven right back again. Order to chaos, then chaos to order, forever adaptive. Thus its most probable state is somewhere in between. Near the edge of chaos, if you like.

Since a relevant notion for the analysis of coevolving urban systems is that of dynamic stability, the rank-size distribution corresponds to that special kind of dynamic equilibrium we met in Chapter 1: self-organized criticality. Rather than being a surprising result, this seems to be a favored outcome under conditions found in a mature, strongly interacting system of cities. A necessary, though hardly sufficient, condition for the survival of a system of cities is that the life cycle of the system be dynamically stable in a particular environment. To achieve this dynamic stability might require a constant struggle between the forces of diversification and unification, much as Zipf suggested. Our tendencies to simplify and "complexify" are powerful forces that shape much of our behavior, so it's very likely that they've shaped our residential landscapes as well.

Artificial Cities

In this chapter, we've learned that some cities grow abruptly, whereas others can wither just as quickly. Yet groups of cities also form surprisingly regular structures collectively. Order springs from random growth, if you like. Urban theory and economics have largely failed in their quest to model and explain such outcomes. Recently, the multifractal dimension of rank-size distributions has been established.[47] For many urban analysts, however, the rank-size rule remains a quaint curiosity, and their understanding of how a city self-organizes over time is modest at best. This final section of our chapter on the urban economy surveys an exciting new means of exploring socioeconomic dynamics: *agent-based simulations of evolving urban processes.*

Simulation games that deal with urban problems have gained in popularity. The success of software packages such as *Sim City* are proof of that. We'll restrict ourselves here to simulations using cellular automata (CA), because this breed of simulation boasts two advantages over other methods of urban analysis. First, a CA-based approach is explicitly dynamic. Second, it links macrobehavior to microdecisions. In Chapter 1, we stated that Schelling's chessboard model (the one that led to segregated neighborhoods) has some features of a two-dimensional CA. In the same issue of the *Journal of Mathematical Sociology* that published Schelling's famous model, there's a lesser-known article by James Sakoda titled "The Checkerboard Model of Social Interaction." After describing a similar model to Schelling's, Sakoda stresses that the main purpose of cell-based modeling is not a predictive one, but clarification of concepts and "insight into basic principles of behavior."[48] These are the insights that make CA and checkerboard modeling promising when it comes to deepening our primitive understanding of socioeconomic dynamics.

A two-dimensional CA consists of the following: (1) a two-dimensional grid; (2) at each grid site, there's a cell, which is in one of a *finite* number of possible states; (3) time advances in *discrete* steps; (4) cells change their states according to *local* rules, so that the state of a cell in the next period depends upon the states of neighboring cells in past periods; (5) the transition rules are mostly *deterministic,* although nondeterministic rules are also possible; (6) the system is *homogeneous* in the sense that the set of possible states is the same for each cell and the same transition rule applies to each cell; and (7) the updating procedure usually consists of applying the transition rule *synchronously* or selecting cells *randomly.*[49]

Although not as hard to solve as the Shortest Network Problem, the number of different transition states in a CA can quickly go through the roof. Consider a two-dimensional CA with just two possible cell states, a neighborhood of one cell and its four orthogonally adjacent neighbors, and with only the last period having an influence on the next period. In such a seemingly simple case, the

TABLE 5.2   Similarities Between CAs and Socioeconomic Dynamics

	Cellular Automata	Socio-Economic Dynamics
Basic elements	Cells are the basic units or "atoms" of a CA	Individual agents are the basic units of an economy
Possible states	Cells assume one of a set of alternative states	Agents form mental models which enable them to make choices from alternatives
Interdependence	The state of a cell affects the state of its closest neighbors	The choices made by an agent affect the choices made by other agents
Applications and tasks	Modeling the emergence of order, macro outcomes explained by micro rules, and the path dependence of dynamic processes	Important tasks include: understanding the emergence of order, macro to micro relationships, and economic dynamics

number of different transition states is $2^{32} = 4,294,967,296$! No wonder we need a computer to implement a CA-based approach to simulation. The fortunate thing is that the kinds of problems tackled successfully in some of the physical sciences using CA just happen to be among the most urgent, unsolved problems in the social sciences. Economics is a case in point. Table 5.2 provides a comparative overview.

Using the simplest CA, it's easy to show that complex global patterns can emerge from the application of local rules. Schelling's zones of segregation are a perfect example of global emergence, and emergence is one of the things that makes CAs so intriguing. In a world where global outcomes fuse in subtle and diverse ways with local action, CAs look like a methodological paradigm for the twenty-first century.[50] They're the source of, and inspiration for, major developments in complex adaptive systems. The promising new field of artificial life is one obvious example. What's becoming apparent is that many classes of dynamics can be simulated through CA.

Perhaps the greatest attraction of a CA-based approach to socio-economic dynamics is the equal weight given to the importance of space, time, and system attributes. When Sakoda and Schelling published their checkerboard articles, however, they didn't mention the CA concept. They seem to have been blissfully unaware of it. Yet it's clear that CA and socioeconomic dynamics have a great deal in common (as Table 5.2 shows). Checkerboard models also share some obvious features with CA, like grid structure and local neighborhoods. At the same time, Sakoda's and Schelling's checkerboard models focus primarily on "sorting and mixing," that is, agents searching for and moving to attractive locations in space. Checkerboard models don't just concentrate on cells changing their state at a given site (like CAs), but on changing their site as well. For urban simulations, this point is important. We must distinguish between models that allow individuals to move—*migration* models—and those that do not—*steady site* models.[51]

Another important feature of urban work is the definition of neighborhoods. Two kinds are often adopted in two-dimensional CA: the *von Neumann* neighborhood—with four neighboring cells north, south, east, and west of the cell in question—and the *Moore* neighborhood—with the same four cells plus those that are NW, NE, SE, and SW. Neighbors that are more distant from the central cell may have an influence on state changes, but it's assumed in strict CA that the temporal dynamics will take care of these distant effects. In other words, growth and decline imply spatial diffusion. Fortunately, a halfway house exists, embracing some CA principles but also relaxing the neighborhood definition. These are the so-called cell-space (CS) models introduced by Albin.[52]

Although many CA applications reported in the urban modeling literature relax the neighborhood effect to allow for action-at-a-distance, this is beyond the spirit of strict CA. Perhaps the most important challenge for urban simulation models is how to specify the nexus between urban changes at the physical and the human levels. The dynamic systems of interest are (1) the relatively slow developmental changes that take place across the complete networks of infrastructure constructed in cities, and (2) the relatively rapid behavioral changes that agents can implement by altering their own mental models and choices. One can argue that CA transition rules should be based on agents' local behavior. However, real urban "cells" of infrastructure—like houses, roads, and green space—are more spatial in character and are governed by a broader set of coevolutionary forces. The real challenge is to address the tangible and intangible changes interdependently.

Some recent studies have highlighted the self-organizing properties of such urban models. For example, a simple heuristic CA model, called *City*, was developed to study sociospatial segregation in a similar spirit to Schelling's work.[53] *City*'s territory is a two-dimensional square lattice of cells, each of which may be regarded as a house or a *place*. Individuals (persons, families, or households) occupy or leave various places, thereby generating the migration dynamics and sociospatial structure of the city. Residents and place-hunters base their decisions on preferences about the types of individuals in neighboring places. Model results display self-organization, local instabilities, captivity, and other interesting phenomena. Later versions—called *City-1* and *City-2*—feature two levels: a population level composed of individuals with cultural and economic properties, and a housing-stock level consisting of a two-dimensional lattice of cells.[54]

Another interesting multiagent-based model goes by the name of *SIMPOP*. Developed by a French group of social scientists, it aims to unearth a set of rules that transform systems of cities over time.[55] SIMPOP experiments with the effects of various hypotheses using a grid of hexagonal cells. Settlements are characterized by types of economic functions. The general evolutionary patterns that emerge from their work are consistent with the arguments put forward elsewhere in this book. For example, the universality of power laws and the rank-size rule is demonstrated under a variety of initial conditions. Their simulation model also suggests that transitions between different urban regimes are a necessary characteristic of urban evolution.

One of the advantages of agent-based simulation is an ability to generate simple and complex regimes of behavior. CA-based systems simplify and complexify life in its various forms. Cities are a perfect illustration of this. Their cells switch suddenly from being weakly interactive to being strongly interactive. If the pendulum swings too far too quickly, the collective outcomes can be counter-productive. For example, transport networks provide the urban arena on which an ever-increasing volume of human interactions accumulate. As the density of traffic grows, various forms of congestion arise. A traffic system suffers from unexpected phase transitions of the intimidating kind. In response to growing congestion, some innovative drivers search for novel ways to exploit these networks more efficiently. As their numbers grow, the resulting temporal and spatial innovations may increase or decrease the network's throughput. This type of coevolutionary learning is an increasingly important architect of urban and economic evolution and is discussed more fully in the next chapter.

six

Traffic Near the Edge of Chaos

As far as the laws of mathematics refer to reality, they are not certain; and as far as they are certain, they do not refer to reality.

—**Albert Einstein**

The Driver's Dilemma

What is it about driving a car that brings out the animal instinct in many of us? Road rage is on the rise in many Western countries. There seems to be no end in sight to the frantic attempts of smart-aleck drivers to "beat the system" as a whole. It's amazing just how often we're confronted with Prisoner's Dilemma-like situations, perhaps more so in traffic than in any other area of human activity. Most drivers are patient when caught in unexpected traffic jams. They choose to cooperate with other drivers. Nevertheless, there's always one or two impatient deviants who invariably choose to defect. When you're stuck in the correct lane of cars, waiting patiently to cross a busy intersection or detour past some construction work, how do you feel about those smart alecks who zoom by you on the inside lane and then butt in again at the very last moment?

Is this "me-first" attitude a feature only of congested traffic? Perhaps it happens because traffic jams are one-time Prisoner's Dilemma–like situations? You won't meet the same drivers again, so you may as well try to beat them if you can. Perhaps. But driving on a congested highway also turns out to be no simple matter.

Out on the roads we're obliged to interact with many other drivers. In plenty of learning situations, we can choose our partners, those with whom we'd like to interact.[1] But out on the roads, we have no such choice. What each driver does affects what other drivers do. How we drive depends on how others drive. We're at the mercy of those who just happen to be using that same piece of roadway at the same time. There's no way of knowing in advance who we'll meet, least of all what they're thinking. To many drivers, this can be disconcerting, even annoying. When the going gets tough, suddenly our primitive instincts can get the better of us. Some of us think to ourselves, "I can outsmart these dummies."

Traffic jams are endemic. Some even say that the best efficiency measure of a modern metropolis and its economy is the size of its traffic jams. Here are a few examples. Bangkok, once famous for its canals, is now renowned for its all-day jams on Sukhumvit Road. São Paolo's merciless delays are almost as horrifying as those in Mexico City. In the latter, the Periferico functions more like a parking lot for much of the day. On an average working day in 1996, the Netherlands had fifty motorway holdups at least two kilometers long.[2] The permanent congestion on Silicon Valley's two main freeways must be the greatest threat to its continued prosperity. Many of America's fastest growing urban areas are losing their attraction because efficient commuting has become virtually impossible. The common "attractor" is that ultimate equilibrium point—the perfect standstill!

We can't even guess our likely travel time on many urban freeways. Why? Because we're at the mercy of an unknown variable— the traffic's behavior as a whole. We simply don't know how it will behave collectively. Uncertainty breeds anxiety and too much anxiety can cause accidents. For starters, few motorists realize that driving a car is the most dangerous activity that humanity has devised. The Global Burden of Disease Study, a four-year collaboration of the World Bank and the World Health Organization, has predicted that heart disease and road accidents will soon become the world's leading causes of death and disability. All of us should feel extremely nervous about driving. But many drivers don't feel concerned at all. For them driving is simply a game, and a competitive one at that in which macho thinking prevails.

The truth is that large urban transportation networks are no different from many other phenomena discussed in this book. They're complex adaptive systems. Drivers can get trapped in a kind of El Farol world, a world that's hard to comprehend. More problematical is the fact that these systems can be devilishly difficult to manage efficiently. Due to their complexity, traffic innovations can produce counterintuitive results. Highly favored methods to alleviate congestion can have unexpected consequences, producing outcomes quite the opposite to their intention. Imagine the potential headaches for traffic planners. A perplexing culprit is the addition of a new link between two existing nodes on a congested network. Diabolically, such a simple change can lead to a reduced overall efficiency and make everyone worse off. This doesn't always happen, thank goodness. But it *can* happen.

Here's an example of *how* it can happen. It's also a quick introduction to some of the basic tools of the traffic planner's world. Take a look at Figure 6.1. Imagine that a bunch of drivers are trying to get from point A to point D within the city. There are two ways of doing this, which traffic planners call *routes*. Traffic can choose the northern route (the path ABD), using the road links labeled AB and BD, or take the southern route (the path ACD), involving the links labeled AC and CD. From our traffic studies, we know that about 360 vehicles want to traverse this network every minute during the morning peak hour.

Before anyone can estimate how many vehicles might opt for each route, they need to know how efficiently each link performs as the traffic flow changes. To solve this, traffic planners have devised what they call "link performance functions." We'll just call them LPFs. Each LPF reflects the fact that the performance level of a link is a function of its usage. Due to congestion, the travel time along roads and across intersections is an increasing function of flow. An LPF is simply an attempt to relate the travel time on each link to the flow of traffic traversing that link. Let's take a quick look at a few typical LPFs to get a feel for their characteristics.

For each of the functions shown in Figure 6.2, the travel time at zero flow is the time shown on the vertical axis labeled t. Traffic planners call it the *free-flow* travel time. If there's no traffic on a link, obviously there's no delay to you. So you can travel along that

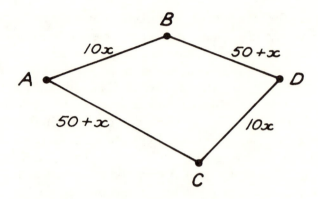

FIGURE 6.1   The initial network: Drivers choose the northern route (ABD) or the southern route (ACD).

link unaffected by other vehicles. Like a leaf floating freely down a stream, the link is said to be free-flowing. There are no obstacles impeding the flow. As the flow of vehicles increases, however, vehicles start to be affected by their closeness to other vehicles. Various degrees of congestion develop depending on the number and size of the collective population of vehicles. Intersections develop queues and travel times increase. There's an upper limit to the link flow, of course, just like there's an upper limit to the flow of water through a pipe. This is called its flow capacity. The basic idea in traffic planning is that each link's performance function is *asymptotic* to its flow capacity.

Traffic planners, engineers, and economists spend countless hours trying to devise the right combination of one-way streets, left-turn lanes, traffic light configurations, freeway interchanges, parking fees and conditions, road pricing, and the like to reduce the frequency and severity of congestion. Economists have played a major role in studies of congestion. For example, more than twenty-five years ago, a Nobel laureate in economics, William Vickrey, distinguished six types of congestion in traffic situations.[3] For traffic volumes ranging from half to almost full capacity, Vickrey suggested that link performance functions can be treated as polynomial functions in x, where x is the link flow. As we stated in the previous chapter, a polynomial function takes the following form:

$$t = t_0 + ax^k$$

where, in this case, t is the travel time (expressed in seconds) under actual driving conditions, t_0 is the free-flow travel time, and a and k are constants. The straight line shown in Figure 6.2 is a linear function, that is, k = 1. The two curved lines are quadratic functions,

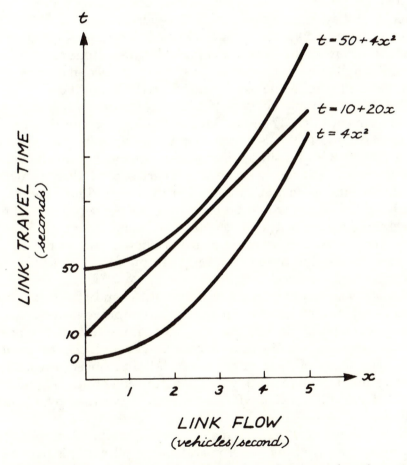

FIGURE 6.2   A sample of typical link performance functions.

that is, k = 2. In our four-link network shown in Figure 6.1, the links perform according to the linear functions written on the respective arrows forming the network.

Now we have enough data to tackle what traffic planners call the assignment problem. This means estimating the flows and travel times on the four links. The only thing we don't know is the decision rule—or mental model—that motorists use to choose between the two routes. How would you decide? Surveys have shown that most of us choose the route that we believe will minimize our own travel time between A and D. If everyone opted for this approach consistently, the traffic would redistribute itself until it converged on a stable pattern. Drivers would switch from one route to another until they found what they believed to be the best routes for their purposes. Sooner or later, a stable equilibrium assignment is reached, where no driver could improve his travel time any further by unilaterally changing routes. In traffic parlance, the name for this stable attractor is the user-equilibrium (UE) condition.

Note that our initial network (Figure 6.1) features travel symmetry in terms of LPFs. The links AB and CD have identical LPFs, as do links AC and BD. This means that we can find the user equilibrium flow pattern by simple inspection. Obviously, half the vehicles would be assigned to each route. Every second, three vehicles would take the route ABD and another three would take the route ACD. All link flows would be three vehicles per second and link travel times would be $t_{AB} = t_{CD} = 30$ seconds and $t_{AC} = t_{BD} = 53$ seconds. Irrespective of whether a driver chooses the northern or southern route, the time taken to get from A to D would be 83 seconds.

Now let's see what happens if the local transport authority decides to expand the network in an effort to improve flows, reduce peak-hour delays, and save on fuel costs and pollution. Suppose that an extra link is built from B to C. Drivers at B see the empty road to C. Many of them ought to relish the prospect of reaching their destination more quickly by taking this new route. Figure 6.3 shows the new link BC, the flow on which is governed by a linear LPF of 6x.

Drivers now have three alternative ways of getting from A to D. Clearly, the old UE flow pattern no longer applies to this new network. Once again, however, we can calculate the new equilibrium

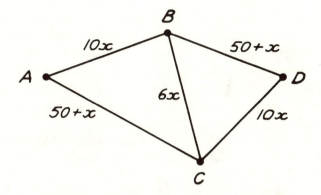

FIGURE 6.3   The expanded network: Drivers now choose among the northern, southern, and central routes.

pattern rather easily. New UE link flows turn out to be four vehicles per second on links AB and CD and two vehicles per second on links AC, BD, and BC. Associated travel times are $t_{AB} = t_{CD} = 40$ seconds, $t_{AC} = t_{BD} = 52$ seconds, and $t_{BC} = 12$ seconds. Regardless of whether route ABD, ACD, or ABCD is chosen, route travel time is now 92 seconds.

Paradoxically, the time taken by each driver has increased from 83 to 92 seconds! A link designed to ease congestion seems to have worsened the situation. What a planning disaster! Politicians have been thrown out of office for oversights far less serious than this! Traffic analysts have a name for this perplexing class of problem. It's known as Braess's Paradox.[4] How could it happen? For an explanation, we'll turn again to our old friend, the Prisoner's Dilemma.

In Whose Best Interests?

In our discussion of the Prisoner's Dilemma, remember how the safest individual strategy was to defect—provided that you weren't planning to trade repeatedly into the future. If you planned to trade on one occasion only, cooperation could you leave you upset, whereas defection risked only indifference. So you chose the Nash solution, despite the fact that your best joint strategy in payoff terms would have been to cooperate. The disappointing thing was that opting for the Nash equilibrium solution resulted in zero payoff to both of you.

As you've probably guessed already, a user equilibrium assignment of traffic turns out to be a Nash equilibrium. It's a strategy that most people pursue, because it serves individual interests best. But it's definitely not to the collective advantage of the network as a whole. Just like the conflict in the Prisoner's Dilemma, there's a conflict in congested traffic between the individual driver's optimal plans and the travel plans that yield the maximum throughput overall. This latter flow pattern is called the system optimum (SO).[5] The SO is the (imaginary) flow pattern that would result if one powerful, coordinating agent could arrange the flows in such a way that the total system cost was minimized.

A counterintuitive result like Braess's Paradox arises because these two flow patterns—the UE and the SO—rarely coincide. Oddly enough, it's not just a Prisoner's Dilemma situation. It also resembles the conflict arising between network configurations that we discussed in the previous chapter. Being the most convenient network from the perspective of individual users, the utility-maximizing network corresponds to a UE solution. It's a rational expectations equilibrium. On the other hand, the cost-minimizing Steiner solution falls at the other end of the full spectrum of ways of linking up nodes in a network. Being best for the system as a whole, the Steiner solution is a system optimum pattern.

Whenever a change is made to a road network, there's no guarantee that the traffic will reorganize itself in such a way that it renders an overall savings in travel time and travel cost. The greater the divergence between the UE and the SO, the greater the risk of a paradoxical outcome. Obviously there's no problem on an uncongested network, because drivers can happily choose their best route without any concern for other drivers. Such a traffic pattern is weakly interactive. But as the flow density of traffic increases, the two flow patterns begin to diverge more widely. Denser flows mean that cohorts of vehicles become more strongly interactive. The inevitable result is that some links reach a traffic volume that is nearer to their capacity, while others remain less congested.

To see this more clearly, consider the simple network shown in Figure 6.4. It features one origin-destination pair AD, connected by

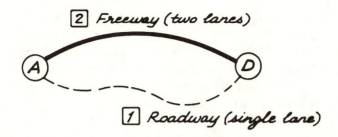

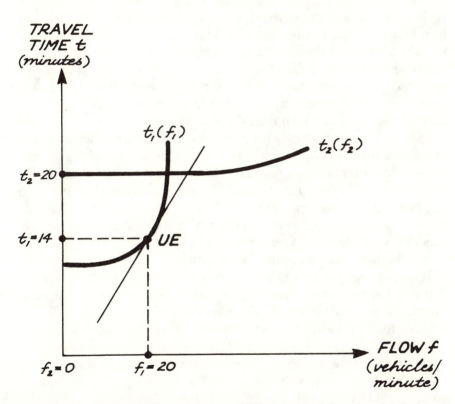

FIGURE 6.4   A two-link network equilibrium problem in which the user equilibrium is not a system optimum.

two links. The southern link (number 1) is a single-lane roadway and the northern link (number 2) is a two-lane freeway. Hypothetical LPFs for these two links are shown in the figure. If the total AD flow is F, the UE solution will be as shown in the figure ($f_1 = F$ and $f_2 = 0$). At this flow level, no driver will use the freeway. The derivative of t_1 with respect to f_1 at $f_1 = F$ is positive, and this discourages freeway use. Note, however, that if one vehicle were to shift from link 1 to link 2 every minute, the increased travel time that these freeway users would incur could be less than the total travel time saved by the remaining drivers on link 1. Thus the solution that is optimal from an individual driver's viewpoint is not likely to be a system optimum.

The SO solution may include some drivers using the freeway as well. If one driver shifts from link 1 to link 2 (at the UE flow pattern shown in the figure), his travel time would increase from $t_1(F)$ to $t_1(0)$. The travel time experienced by each of the remaining drivers on link 1 would fall, however, by the following derivative: $dt_1(F)/df_1$. From the overall perspective, one shifting driver's increase in travel time may be more than offset by the decreased travel time enjoyed by all the others using link 1.

Failure to recognize this fundamental difference between what's best for the system as a whole and what's best for each individual leads to counterintuitive scenarios like Braess's Paradox. The very existence of this paradox depends on the assumption of independent optimality underpinning a UE. Because each driver's choice is carried out without consideration of the effect of this action on other drivers, there's no reason to expect that the addition of a new link will always decrease total travel time.

Transportation scientists have derived formulae to tell us whether Braess's Paradox can occur in a given network.[6] Furthermore, economists have shown that such paradoxical outcomes can be avoided, and overall optimality retrieved, by modifying the costs incurred by some of the drivers. By levying a flow-dependent congestion fee on each driver using a particular route on the network, for example, the traffic flow pattern that results from choosing cost-minimizing routes could be made to return to a system optimum.[7]

But a fundamental question remains to be answered. Can we realistically expect a user equilibrium to be stable, even reachable, in practice? Or is Braess's Paradox symptomatic of the uncertainties associated with network connectivity, link congestability, and drivers' travel choice behavior? The current desire to implement automated route guidance systems, or management controls like congestion pricing, highlights a need to resolve some of the uncertainties about drivers' behavior. How do drivers respond in situations where their own behavior is also dependent on the behavior of others? Do variations in travel time cause them to alter their decision rules? What are the behavioral impacts of implementing route guidance systems or congestion pricing?

Sheep, Explorers, and Bounded Rationality

Granting each economic agent the ability to recognize his optimal mode of travel is a reasonable assumption in a modern city. We might call this the *know-how* of travel. But if we add to this the foresight needed to recognize his fastest route and optimal times of departure, all in such a way that his travel time cannot be improved by altering his original decisions, it's difficult to believe that each and every agent has the ability to *know-whether* his choices are optimal. Furthermore, the UE solution demands that drivers make choices in an identical and correct manner every time, having access to full information. This means that they must *know-what* the travel time is on every alternative route. To manage all this, commuters must be as clever as deductively rational economists. They must possess perfect *know-ware*.

Once again, these are unrealistic assumptions. Recognizing that perfect foresight may not hold in reality, some transport analysts have relaxed these restrictions by distinguishing between the travel time that commuters *perceive* and the *actual* travel time.[8] The perceived travel time may be looked upon as a random variable distributed across the population of drivers. The idea is that equilibrium will be reached when no traveler believes that his travel time can be improved by unilaterally changing routes. Known as a stochastic user equilibrium (or SUE), this approach takes one step in a fruitful direction: It recognizes that drivers possess incomplete information about the state of the traffic system as a whole.[9]

But the uncertainty lingers. What are the chances of actual traffic distributions ever achieving these kinds of equilibria? Rather slim if we take a look at the evidence. Recent research has shown that the collective behavior of drivers on a congested network rarely, if ever, reaches such equilibrium states.[10] This is hardly surprising once we're reminded that such equilibria are merely fixed-point attractors in a much richer space of conditional distributions that commuters and vehicles can form collectively.[11]

Not only is each individual commuter's rationality bounded by the fact that he has limited information at his disposal, but the problem itself is inherently complicated. Even if a driver turns out to be an excellent optimizer of his own actions, he has no idea how the other drivers will behave. Even if they could optimize their behavior as well, the chances of this happening simultaneously are remote. On a dense, sophisticated network, where the choice process is complicated, one is likely to find only a handful of drivers who *know* that they've done the best they can, some who *believe* that they've done the best thing, and others who have *no idea* if they've chosen well.

Because each driver's beliefs are personal and the learning process is evolving at different rates, it's also unclear how the traffic system will behave collectively. This forces all drivers into a world of subjective beliefs, and subjective beliefs about subjective beliefs. Objective, well-defined, shared expectations—the ones that are needed to reach a predictable user equilibria—simply cease to apply. On a congested city network, traffic dynamics is the collective result of thousands, even millions, of individual trip-making decisions by a heterogeneous population of drivers. Think of how expectations differ between producers, shippers, consumers, vacationers, and others. At peak-hour conditions on these networks, all drivers face route and departure time choices that are complicated and ill defined. Outcomes are unpredictable since guesswork is the order of the day!

How might drivers come to terms with such a disconcerting situation? As we learned in Chapter 2, modern psychology suggests that we're pretty good at recognizing or matching patterns.[12] For example, in traffic situations that are unpredictable, some of us look ahead for early signs of congestion or keep our other route options open for as long as possible. We develop explanatory patterns of behavior that, once recognized, help us to simplify the problem. These patterns help us to build temporary mental models of a similar kind to those we outlined when discussing the El Farol bar problem and London's Underground. Once we have such models in our minds, we carry out localized deductions based on our favored hypotheses and then act on them.[13]

As we stressed earlier, this process is coevolutionary. Feedback from our traffic experiences may strengthen or weaken our confidence in our current beliefs. Thus some of our models get discarded if they fail to live up to our expectations, being replaced with new ones as needed. In other words, whenever we can't fully understand how the traffic is likely to behave and can't be sure about the best strategy to employ, we tend to "paper over" the gaps in our understanding. In the words of Tom Sargent, we act like "economic statisticians," testing and discarding simple expectational models to fill these gaps in our knowledge.[14] As logic, such behavior is inductive. Inductive reasoning goes from a part to a whole, from the particular to the general, or from the local to the universal.

Can we find any evidence of this kind of adaptive learning among drivers on busy highways? We certainly can. In a classic paper discussing the causes of congestion, which we referred to in Chapter 3, Anthony Downs recognized two behavioral classes of driver: those with a very low propensity to change routes, called *sheep*, and those with a much higher propensity to change, called *explorers*.[15] Explorers tend to be imaginative, highly strung, aggressive drivers who constantly search for alternative options that may save them some time. They're quick to learn and may hold several beliefs in mind simultaneously. Sheep are more placid, patient, and prone to choosing the same option.[16] They tend to follow the leader and mostly cling to a particular belief because it has worked well in the past. Sheep are slow learners who must accumulate a record of failure before discarding their favored option(s).

Some recent empirical work in North America has confirmed the presence of sheep and explorer behavior in actual traffic. Using cluster analysis, scientists at the University of Washington in Seattle identified four groups among a sample of 4,000 drivers surveyed.[17] They labeled them non-changers, route changers, route-and-time changers, and pre-trip changers, based on their behavioral responses to traffic. Non-changers (or Downs's sheep) made up about one-quarter of the sample and were unwilling to modify any part of their commuting behavior (i.e., departure time, route, or mode of transportation), no matter how much traffic information they received. By way of contrast, route-and-time changers were eager to try different strategies in order to reduce their travel time.

An important element of inductive behavior is a willingness to adjust beliefs and expectations if they're found wanting. Here the role of prior experience is important. Drivers tend to form their own subjective expectations about traffic conditions based on pattern recognition and repeated learning. Expectations are conditioned by available information and updated by observed travel times, as long as there's sufficient need to revise them. Like Downs, the Japanese systems scientist Kiyoshi Kobayashi has classified drivers into two groups based on their propensity for risk: the risk-averters and the risk-neutral.[18]

Given the heterogeneity of mental models and learning rates among drivers (e.g., sheep and explorers), we might expect the collective behavior of traffic on a freeway network to fluctuate between various states. However, some fluctuations are psychological, whereas others are purely physical. Before we look into more cerebral examples of how drivers form and adjust their beliefs about traffic behavior, the next section looks into some CA-based methods that can help us to better understand those physical phase transitions that trigger such psychological reactions at the individual level.

Cellular Congestion

Like the number of music lovers heading for the El Farol bar on Thursday evenings, the flow volume on an urban freeway is totally unpredictable from day to day. In the long run, however, we do know that traffic volumes are expanding. Whenever this growing driver population pushes the flow of traffic on specific links beyond critical levels, it triggers unexpected phase transitions, heralding a qualitatively different flow pattern. Recent simulation work, using three-state CA models on a square lattice, has shown that the average speed of the traffic drops rapidly once a critical density has been reached.[19] Figure 6.5 depicts the simulated drop in mean speed. There's a dynamic jamming transition from free flow travel to start-stop waves at a critical flow density. Anyone who has been caught up in a traffic jam can vouch for the abruptness of some of these transitions.

Because this kind of phase change transforms a traffic pattern with no global communication (all cars can move independently at maximum speed) to one with a global cluster (all cars are more or less stuck in a global traffic jam), it also resembles a percolation

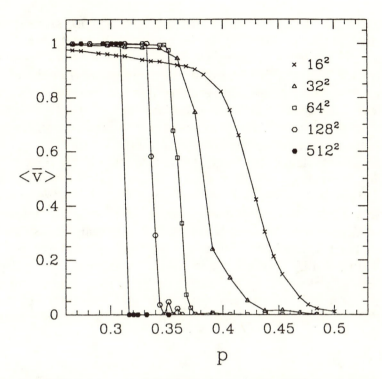

FIGURE 6.5 Average velocity (v) as a function of traffic density (p) on five cellular grids of different sizes.

transition.[20] However, work in percolation theory suggests that it's a second-order transition and has no dynamics. The jamming transition can more fruitfully be interpreted as the attainment of self-organized criticality. Note how the transition becomes much sharper as the size of the cellular grid increases. The remarkable thing is that, in some cases, this jamming transition occurs at a critical density as low as 10 percent of the system's maximum density! It's now widely agreed that this kind of transition is a general feature of traffic flow in two dimensions.

Spontaneous formation of the initial jam may be caused by nothing more than one car accidently coming too close to the one ahead of it. Although this depends only on the density of cars, it also has wider spatial implications. It means that many other cars must slow down because of the first jam. The results are back-traveling disturbances among the cars. Travel times increase significantly, even though the congestion seems relatively light at first. This is the deceptive part of jamming transitions. They tend to "creep up" on the unsuspecting driver. Local interactions can quickly add up to such an extent that they have global repercussions!

Before the onset of this jamming transition, the free-flowing travel time is approximately constant and variations from vehicle to vehicle are small. Figure 6.6 shows how the fluctuations in travel time from vehicle to vehicle go up very quickly at the onset of the jamming transition, reaching a peak near the point of critical density. This emergent phenomenon is quite striking. When passing from a weakly interactive, free-flowing state—slightly below the critical density—to a strongly interactive one featuring stop-start waves, the traffic can typically change from a regime where the travel time is highly predictable—with an error rate of no more than ±3 percent—to a regime where the error rate climbs to 65 percent or more.[21] This unpredictable state is the hallmark of traffic near "the edge of chaos." There's a critical regime near maximal ca-

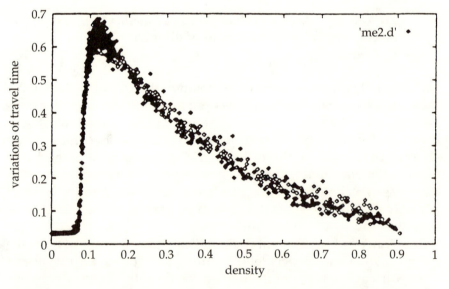

FIGURE 6.6   Travel time variations as a function of simulated traffic density.

pacity where traffic systems are sensitive to small perturbations. Travel time predictability can decrease rapidly if the system is pushed too close to this regime of maximum flow.

CA-based simulations such as these highlight a problem with traditional link performance functions like Vickrey's polynomial function. Such a function implies that the behavior of traffic under increasingly congested conditions will be smooth and reasonably predictable just short of full capacity. A growing band of CA-based simulations suggest that this picture of traffic congestion is incorrect. Even Nobel laureates get it wrong sometimes! In a manner akin to fluid dynamics, changes in traffic flow behavior can be much more abrupt and unpredictable.

In reality, revealing nonlinear phase transitions in traffic has not been the exclusive province of CA-based simulation. Fluid-dynamical approaches to traffic flow were introduced in the 1950s. In the past two decades, methods of nonlinear dynamics were successfully applied to these models, stressing the notion of a phase transition from laminar flow to stop-start waves with increasing car density. The kinetic theory of vehicular traffic, developed in the late 1960s by Ilya Progogine and Robert Herman, recognized that congested traffic can exhibit self-organizing properties.[22] They found a traffic regime in which drivers could, to some extent, act independently to achieve their microgoals and another collective regime in which the behavior of the traffic no longer depended on the desired speeds of the individual drivers. In short, their work suggested a phase transition between a simple and a complex traffic regime—predating the simulated traffic jams that CA models have generated.

As I mentioned in the previous chapter, there are two important advantages of the CA way of doing science. CA models are intrinsically dynamic and readily applicable to spatial problems. For problems involving complex geometries, such as simulations of fluid dynamics in porous media, CA approaches have proved to be superior to other methods.[23] Given the similarity of traffic flow behavior to patterns observed in fluid dynamics, one can see potential advantages for CA models in traffic studies. On the one hand, the traffic can be reduced to elemental (and cellular) forms. On the other hand, all the essential relational features of the individual elements can be incorporated in detail.

A bottom-up approach to the microsimulation of drivers and vehicles needs to start at the level where transport decisions are made. Starting with the generation of travel demands and trip decisions, followed by mode and route choices, such a silicon world would generate congestion frequencies, travel times, and levels of air quality. You might be wondering whether this kind of experimental laboratory for studying traffic behavior could be implemented for a complete city? Sounds like a mammoth task that's probably beyond our reach. Certainly it's beyond the reach of most scientific organizations. But it's not out of the question for the Los Alamos National Laboratory. In 1991, Los Alamos researcher Chris Barrett had the bright idea that the state of computer technology would make it feasible to build an electronic replica of a city like Albuquerque, complete with each and every little detail: each individual street, house, car, and driver. Fortunately for Barrett, some potential sponsors at the U.S. Department of Transportation and the Environmental Protection Agency chose to agree with him. They provided the funding to develop such a silicon city and to address issues resulting from the Intermodal Surface Transportation and Efficiency Act of 1991.

The microsimulation project underpinning the silicon city developed by Barrett and his group at Los Alamos is called TRANSIMS.[24] An early version consists of four basic modules: (1) Travel Demand and Transport System Data; (2) Trip Route Plan Generation; (3) Traffic Microsimulation; and (4) Environmental Simulation. Once all the travelers and their plans have been sprinkled onto the network, the two simulation modules generate collective outcomes for travelers and vehicle emissions, factoring in things like local congestion and accidents. It's important to note that these four modules represent processes occurring on different time scales, although they always reference individual travelers.

TRANSIMS also includes the investigation of simpler and computationally less demanding traffic simulations on individual road segments, such as the CA model that produced the travel time variations shown in Figure 6.6. Such emergent outputs are not explicitly represented at the level of the individual vehicles but are generated through the collective dynamics. They teach us that traffic systems that operate close to the point of maximum efficiency, where variations in travel time are highest, are another example of self-organized criticality.

Coevolutionary Learning in Congested Traffic

Now let's see how drivers react to the experience of driving near the edge of chaos. To explore this, we'll return to the simple network introduced in Figure 6.4. Every weekday evening, suppose that a bunch of drivers commute home from a common point downtown to a common suburb using the same single-lane roadway.[25] All drivers have a common knockoff time, and all possess identically rational expectations. They share a common view that their travel time should be not exceed a certain value—which we'll call t_{max}. Barring any unforeseen circumstances, all are able to achieve it. Although they're forced to slow down at a few points along the way, the route is mostly free-flowing. There's general agreement that the system as a whole must be close to a user equilibrium. In other words, it has stabilized near the point UE in the figure.

As long as drivers' expectations continue to be reinforced by the travel times they experience, there's no reason for any deviating expectations to arise. The rational expectations equilibrium of the literature is evolutionarily stable. Nobody has an incentive to destroy it. Thus variations in travel time between vehicles remain low.

Under these conditions, drivers are happy and the Road Traffic Authority enjoys a period of unprecedented popularity. Gradually, however, a few drivers begin to suspect that their average travel time is increasing. The slowdown is barely noticeable at first, because a number of familiar seasonal and monthly fluctuations in flow patterns have clouded the overall trend. But eventually the mist clears. It's soon evident that some of the unexpected delays are longer than before. With no viable alternative route in sight, one or two more imaginative drivers consider delaying their time of departure for home by twenty or thirty minutes. Owing to family reticence, however, they opt to postpone their decision for a week or two.

Then, on the following Monday, there's another frustrating traffic jam for no apparent reason. A few jams have occurred previously, but the frequency and duration of stop-start waves on this occasion is disturbing. Gradually, seeds of uncertainty are planted in the minds of a few more drivers. This small group begins to ponder alternative strategies for the future.

What really caused this unwelcome jam? The answer is three relatively slow processes. Population levels, mobility, and car ownership are increasing gradually in most societies. Mobility in many advanced nations has grown by an average of 3–5 percent per year throughout this century. When combined with population increases and growing levels of car ownership, a typical urban population of drivers tends to expand at 5–8 percent per year. This causes higher flow levels on most major highways, pushing travel times up. In peak periods, travel times begin to exceed the desirable level, t_{max}, more frequently.

Now let's look at how drivers' mental models of traffic behavior might be affected by repeated exposure to this kind of jamming experience. Prior to any experience of jams, each driver expects his travel time to be more or less constant; certainly not more than t_{max}. The driver population can be thought of as homogeneous, because expectations are shared and fulfilled. Order prevails on the network. This means that all the drivers can base their daily decisions on the same hypothesis:

Hypothesis S1: "I expect tomorrow's travel time to be much the same as yesterday's and certainly less than t_{max}."

This is each driver's *active* hypothesis. As long as this hypothesis proves to be correct, there's no reason for any driver to reason differently. They can all marvel at their foresightedness. Each time the predictability of travel time is shattered by a jamming transition, however, a small group of drivers loses a little confidence in the accuracy of Hypothesis S1. As more drivers realize that their "comfort zone" of travel time has been breached and that they might need to consider other options in the near future, there's an incentive to expand their own set of working hypotheses. It turns out that the most popular new hypothesis is

Hypothesis E1: "I believe that my average travel time could be reduced if I leave work twenty to thirty minutes later."[26]

This hypothesis not only focuses attention on possible improvements at the margin but also acknowledges that day-to-day variations in travel time are to be expected. It's a temporal innovation, because travel time can be improved without altering the choice of mode or route. In terms of Downs's behavioral classification, it's the strategy of an explorer. We'll refer to it as Hypothesis E1. As the frequency of traffic jams rises and the suspicion of longer average travel times increases, a growing subgroup of explorers begins to keep Hypothesis E1 in mind, in addition to Hypothesis S1.

Eventually, travel time uncertainty and the frequency of jamming transitions become sufficiently disturbing to a growing number of drivers. This group of explorers chooses to delay their departure time in an attempt to avoid the peak-period congestion. After the incidence of a few more frustrating jams, there are sufficient explorers departing later to allow a description of their evolution by a rate equation of their own. We can now describe the behavior of the peak-hour traffic system using two rate equations—one for the sheep, who do not defect, and one for those explorers who do.

To simplify matters, we'll omit the equations themselves.[27] Assuming that expectations are mutually reinforcing, the population of explorers will grow to a finite share of the driver population (restricted only by psychological or external constraints). What will happen to the population of sheep? The emergence of a stable population of (late-returning) explorers leads to an improvement in the effective use of the network. Extending the window of commuter time allows for more drivers. Nevertheless, the population of sheep will remain close to the edge of chaos.

The relief provided by the defecting explorers is temporary at best. As the driver population continues to grow, the frequency of jamming transitions starts to increase again. A different group of peak-period drivers begins to have some doubts about their choices. Gradually they start to lose faith in Hypothesis S1. Although this group is aware of Hypothesis E1, they're unable to delay their departure time after work. Instead they can make use of flexible working hours to start and finish work thirty minutes earlier. So they begin to favor another hypothesis, which is

Hypothesis E2: "I believe that my average travel time could be reduced significantly if I leave for work thirty minutes earlier and start for home thirty minutes earlier than usual."

After a few more frustrating traffic jams, there are sufficient new explorers leaving thirty minutes earlier in both the morning and the evening to create a stable population of (early-to-work, early-back-home) explorers, generating a further improvement in the effective use of the network. From this simple example, we can conclude that evolution leads to a steadily growing exploitation of time. This exploitation serves to lengthen the window of commuter time, thereby postponing the repercussions of the original peak-period congestion.

A series of temporal innovations by explorers (who favor different hypotheses) follows. Each serves to expand the flow capacity of the network by steering some more innovative drivers away from the edge of chaos, and thereby lowering their actual and expected travel times. But other drivers remain sheep forever. They may alter their active hypothesis in response to repeated jamming transitions, but their travel behavior does not vary. Some of the hypotheses that evolve in competition with Hypothesis S1 might include the following:

> Hypothesis S2: "I believe that tomorrow's travel time will be much the same as last Monday's, but it may be more than t_{max}."
> Hypothesis S3: "I believe that tomorrow's travel time will be the same as my travel time two weeks ago (two-period cycle detector)."
> Hypothesis S4: "Even allowing for the occasional traffic jam, I believe that my average travel time should still be less than t_{max}."

Although each driver keeps track of an individualized set of such hypotheses, explorers tend to monitor more at any one time. They do this because they're constantly searching for ways to improve their travel times. Among the hypotheses under consideration, each driver favors one particular hypothesis. We call this the *active* hypothesis. It's usually the one that has proven to be the most reliable within each driver's set.

Just like attendance figures at the El Farol, the complete set of active hypotheses determines how the traffic behaves and thus the travel times experienced. But the travel time history also determines the set of active hypotheses. Drivers "learn" over time which of their hypotheses work best. Occasionally, explorers discard poorly performing hypotheses and generate new ones in their place. Sheep are more conservative, only modifying their active hypotheses after a very long sequence of jamming transitions. The complete set of hunches or hypotheses forms a kind of driver ecology (or collective knowledge base). A key question of interest is how this ecology co-evolves over time. Does it ever converge to some standard equilibrium of beliefs, or does it always remain open-ended, perpetually incorporating new hunches and hypotheses?

Because the set of active hypotheses is open-ended, this is a difficult question to answer analytically. One might generate a kind of "alphabet soup" of hypotheses and then proceed by computer experiments. However, even the contours of the emergent ecology will change in our traffic problem, because the driver population is growing in number and the predicted travel times will differ for each driver. Furthermore, each driver's sensitivity to congestion will differ. Sheep and explorers also exhibit different elasticities to change. If several explorers expect peak-period congestion tomorrow, because congestion occurred two weeks ago, they're likely to alter their departure time. If several sheep face the same prospect, most will not alter their departure time.

Under certain conditions, however, the driver population can self-organize into an equilibrium of beliefs. Explorers may be innovative, but there are temporal limits to their ingenuity. Eventually traffic chaos will prevail over such a lengthy time period that the pressure for a superior alternative route becomes compelling. Because most drivers are reluctant to spend more than one hour of their daily time budget on commuting, the Road Traffic Authority can only appease such growing discontent with a major alteration to the network itself—such as the construction of a new road or the widening of an existing expressway. Suddenly, the set of hypotheses changes radically. Explorers will be quick to try out the new alternative if their average travel time has risen above t_{max}. Sheep will be slower to change, but gradually they might entertain the following hypothesis:

Hypothesis S5: "I believe that my average daily travel time could be lowered by using the new alternative."

At some stage after the new route opens, the active hypotheses of sheep and explorers may even converge to a common belief (such as Hypothesis S5). If this happens, the traditional user equilibrium might even be attained. But, as before, this equilibrium will be temporary at best. Jamming transitions among peak-period traffic on the new route will eventually occur, just as they did on the original route. Frequent congestion experience spawns a whole new family of explorers who actively pursue alternative possibilities (including the old route). There's no evidence to suggest that traffic behavior ever settles down into any stable, predictable pattern. Instead the emerging behavioral ecology becomes more complex and grows to contain an even richer population of active hypotheses. This uneven pattern of coevolutionary learning marches forever onward. Only very occasionally does it have a chance to catch its breath in the relative calm of an equilibrium state.

Edge-of-Chaos Management

An important finding from traffic simulation studies is this critical regime near maximal capacity, which for all intents and purposes looks very much like a self-organized critical state. Other analysts have dubbed it "the edge of chaos." In this region, transportation systems are very sensitive to small perturbations. The problem for those of us caught up in this kind of traffic is that small perturbations can generate large fluctuations in congestion formation and thus in travel times. It's very unnerving because we never know whether we'll be delayed or not.

Thus traffic managers face a new and perplexing problem. Their first priority is to improve the efficiency of traffic flows by every means at their disposal. Clearly, modern information technology is expected to play a key role. Sophisticated traffic controls and route guidance information are designed to improve the efficiency of the traffic as a whole. These on-line traffic management systems tend to drive the traffic closer to the above-mentioned critical regime, the "edge of chaos." By pushing for greater efficiency, they actually generate greater volatility. Travel times become more variable and further control measures can have unpredictable consequences.

This seemingly counterintuitive result is a bit like Braess's Paradox. In trying to improve the system, to your dismay you find that drivers begin to lose confidence in it. The most efficient state for a congested road network seems to be a self-organized critical state in which traffic jams of all lengths can arise to maintain the traffic flow. Small jams occur inside large jams, and a small movement of a particular car can have a large effect.[28] Such fluctuations are surely irritating to the unsuspecting driver, but they're the way to reach the most efficient flow pattern overall. Traffic management systems may try to divert traffic from overcrowded roads to undercrowded ones, thus driving both closer to the edge of chaos. Once the traffic is near this self-organized critical state, further attempts to control or reroute the traffic could have undesirable consequences.

Consider a situation where drivers have access on-line to information on traffic conditions, but the driver population is rather similar in terms of their willingness to act upon this information, that is, mostly sheep-like. Then its receipt has very little impact. It may simply reduce the number of active hypotheses currently held by the driver population. A majority of drivers continue to select the "safest bet" from their own selfish viewpoint. They might prefer shorter routes over longer ones, even if both yield about the same travel time. Since beliefs are mostly uniform, they tend to concentrate on the same routes during the same periods. The effect of helpful information in this case is to generate higher levels of congestion on the preferred routes. We'll call this result *concentration.*

What might happen when sheep and explorers coexist in a driver population? In this case, the likely impacts depend crucially on the nature of the information, when it's provided, and who receives it. Sheep seldom change their driving decisions in the short term—with or without traffic information. Explorers welcome such information, using it to modify their set of working hypotheses and, in some circumstances, to alter their active hypothesis. Particular types of information work best in various phases of the learning process. For example, the rate of defection of explorers from a congested peak period to a less-congested one can be enhanced by the provision of comparative travel times for different departure times. In the hands (i.e., minds) of a *limited* number of explorers, this comparative information could reduce levels of concentration. If given to a large number of explorers, however, this same information may lead to excessive levels of *overreaction.* Too many explorers may decide to switch to a recommended alternative.[29]

Generally, providing travel time information about different departure times and route choices will alter the ecology of active hypotheses among the driver population. This ecology, which is coevolving incessantly, has a collective "psyche" of its own. It can breed successive phases of near-chaotic behavior followed by periods of calm and order. Near-chaotic behavior corresponds to *rapidly* changing beliefs about other drivers' intentions and the best strategy to adopt. If beliefs change too quickly, however, there may be no clear behavioral pattern at all. To all intents and purposes, such a volatile state would appear to be random. Some drivers feel totally confused. It's hardly surprising to learn that their responses become unpredictable.

At the other extreme, tranquil, orderly behavior could emerge. But this can happen only if the ocean of beliefs in a driver population happens to converge on a mutually consistent set of models of one another and the traffic system as a whole. This is most unlikely in traffic suffering from even light congestion. Because sheep and explorers coexist in driver populations, there are simply too many incentives for beliefs to diverge. Thus the chances of reaching a user equilibrium are remote, and traffic assignment methods based on relaxation to an equilibrium are no longer meaningful.

For most of the time, we'd expect that drivers' mental models of each other's beliefs would be caught somewhere in between these two extremes, tending to change, poised ready to unleash avalanches of small and large changes throughout the whole belief system of the driver population. Why should we expect this? Given more information, we'd expect explorers to try to improve their set of hypotheses by constructing *more complex* mental models of traffic behavior. But these more complex models would also be more sensitive to small changes in the behavior of other drivers.

While explorers develop more complex models to improve their own decisionmaking, the coevolving system of *all* drivers' beliefs tends to be pushed further away from the orderly regime toward the chaotic one. Once an explorer's complexifying beliefs come close to the chaotic regime, however, such complexity and changeability is apt to leave him confused. He realizes that the data are inadequate. Thus he decides to simplify matters, adopting a *less complex* model of traffic behavior. Less complex models have the virtue of being less sensitive to the behavior of others and live in calmer oceans.

As we described in earlier chapters, adaptive learning produces a never-ending struggle between the need to simplify and the need to complexify. This incessant struggle underpins the coevolution of drivers' beliefs about how traffic behaves. The proverbial ocean of beliefs gets driven back and forward between the two extremes, from chaos to order and then back again. Thus, for much of the time, we might expect to find most drivers' mental states hovering nervously in between, poised somewhere near the edge of chaos.

Some key questions then arise. Is there a way out of this dilemma? Should drivers be assisted or rerouted at all? If so, which drivers should be targeted? What kind of information should be provided if the aim is to reduce the frequency or severity of congestion?

One possibility is to keep the density on each road segment just below the density of maximum throughput. This means that some drivers may have to wait to enter parts of the road network until sufficient capacity is available for them. On the other hand, if sheep and explorers coexist in a driver population, sheep could be made to pay for their intransigence. A peak-period congestion toll could be levied on those drivers who refuse repeatedly to switch to recommended alternatives. On the other hand, innovative explorers might be offered credits or bonuses for earlier or later departures, which help to keep densities below criticality. This might also help to convert some sheep into explorers. Further studies might show whether explorers should always be the beneficiaries, or if sheep might warrant inducements or compulsory education to become more adaptive. Frequent-traveler programs, designed to generate greater use of public transit, could also be introduced.

Congestion pricing seems to be the most viable approach. Two colleagues of Chris Barrett at the Los Alamos National Laboratory, Kai Nagel and Steen Rasmussen, have conducted simulation experiments, which suggest that locally operating agents could administer congestion tolls.[30] Each agent aims to keep the operation of his segment of the road network as efficient as possible, with the only means available being to adjust the toll up or down. The agent knows the performance characteristics of his segment, and from this he obtains the density that corresponds to maximum flow and thus maximum performance. Then the task is to try to keep the density on his segment at or near this particular density.

When the density gets too high, the toll is increased; otherwise it's decreased on a scale to zero. In a real network, the toll for most segments would most likely be zero for most of the time.

Driving near the edge of chaos can be a mystifying experience. Each time the predictability of travel time is shattered by a jamming transition, a few drivers lose a little faith in the validity of their beliefs. Breaching their "comfort zone" of travel time on several more occasions can transform some drivers from placid sheep, meekly following the crowd under any circumstances, into aggressive explorers, searching desperately for ways to reduce their travel time. Once a few "seeds of discontent" have been sown, explorers tend to feed on themselves. Like mutants in an ecosystem, their own growth can become self-reinforcing.

By relentlessly pursuing superior alternatives, explorers trigger fluctuations that tend to undermine the possibility of a static equilibrium in the traffic system. Self-organizing behavior is a dynamic activity. There are no simple, deterministic laws of traffic evolution. A wide diversity of decision rules can emerge and proliferate among the driver population. Each individual driver's rationality is bounded by the fact that his problem is not simple. He has little reliable information at his disposal. Because there's no single hypothesis that can be relied upon, a rich ecology of behavioral hypotheses emerges and coevolves over time.

The uneven nature of coevolutionary learning suggests that the collective behavior of drivers on a congested network will have little chance of converging to a rational expectations equilibrium. Spontaneous emergence of explorers from a seemingly homogeneous population of sheep is a nonlinear perturbation that tends to be repeated over and over again. The incentive for repetition is strong. In the true Schumpeterian spirit, each time some new explorers emerge and evolve, their innovativeness leads to an improvement in the network's throughput. Thus network exploitation becomes more efficient, despite the fact that most of the sheep are either unwilling or unable to modify their behavior, even if their chosen routes and times accumulate a convincing record of failure.

But this is not the end of the story. It's more like the beginning. One should distinguish clearly between fluctuations due to the dynamics of vehicles and fluctuations due to the learning of drivers. The real dynamics of a congested traffic system need to be explained at various levels in space and time. Three levels of evolutionary change seem to be influential: the adaptive behavior of interacting drivers (such as sheep and explorers), the dynamics of vehicular flow patterns, and the evolution of the physical network of infrastructure (see Figure 6.7). Interdependencies exist between the behavioral possibilities at each of these levels. For example, seemingly small changes in the behavioral ecology of drivers, including their attitude toward politicians, can become contagious. Ultimately, they can have profound effects on the final state of the network as a whole. Under these conditions, some emergent behavior becomes apparent only with the help of detailed microsimulations.

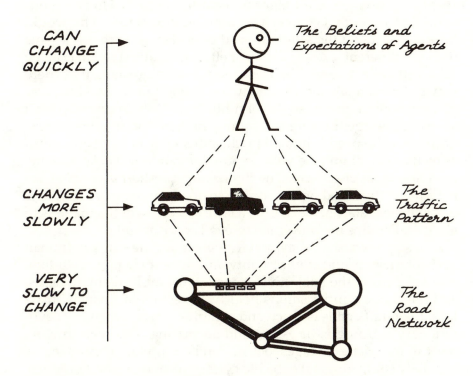

FIGURE 6.7   The multilevel nature of traffic dynamics.

There's a need to search beneath the classical aggregate view of driver behavior in order to unravel the intricate complexities. Different speeds of adjustment pose daunting problems, and paradoxes seem to abound.[31] We've seen that a predictable traffic pattern seems less and less likely the more one approaches a highly efficient traffic system. The fact that high efficiency often has the downside of high variability may not just be true of transportation systems. Chances are that it's also true of other socioeconomic systems. A higher-level simplicity is much easier to think about than some chain of complexities that caused it.[32] The true representation of a higher-level simplicity emerges only as an explicit consequence of an accurate representation of its lower-level complexities.

Traffic jams appear to have significant negative economic impacts. In 1990, for example, almost 15 percent of the U.S. GNP was spent on passenger and freight transportation costs. However, our main finding in this chapter was a little unexpected. Who would have thought that the self-organized critical state, with traffic jams of many different sizes, is the most efficient traffic state that can be achieved collectively? The message for economists is that there may be an even deeper nexus between traffic and economics. A car driver caught in the mysteries of traffic has plenty in common with an economic agent trying to improve his position in an economy. Each driver's speed is limited by the other cars on the road as well as by the speed limit. He's also exposed to random shocks from the road and from elsewhere. The interesting question is whether we may have stumbled across a new socioeconomic principle: The most efficient state achievable is a critical state with fluctuations of all sizes. Perhaps the power law prevails once again!

As a step toward a behavioral formalism for the study of human decisionmaking under uncertainty, in the next chapter we'll look more closely at the subjective expectations, multiple hypotheses, and half-hoped anticipations held by investors in financial markets. Like traffic, this is a rich and complex world, in which coevolutionary learning is incessant and surprising. Wherever traders meet to transact exchanges, beliefs can be mutually reinforcing or mutually competing. Like the life cycle of technology and products in the marketplace, beliefs are invented, establish a small niche, grow in importance, begin to dominate, mature, fall back, and finally decay. They form a turbulent ocean of interacting, competing, arising, and decaying entities. Occasionally this stormy ocean may flatten out into a simple, homogeneous equilibrium pattern. But more often than not it's heaving and deforming continuously, producing complex, ever-changing patterns in which nonequilibrium beliefs are unavoidable.

seven

Coevolving Markets

One with another, soul with soul
They kindle fire with fire.

—Arthur Pigou

Are Stock Markets Efficient?

We're ready to return to that baffling puzzle, mentioned briefly in the opening chapter. Why is it that academics, by and large, see markets quite differently from the way that actual traders see them? By now you'll have a pretty good idea of how classical economic theorists see the financial world. If you thought of equilibria and deductive rationality, you'd be right. There's simply no place for those inductive explorers we met earlier. It's sheepish risk aversion all the way. And for good reasons. If all investors possess identical, perfect foresight, then markets should behave efficiently. All the available information gets discounted into current prices. If the sole driving force behind price changes for any stock or commodity is assumed to be new information, then we can assume that traders are able to process this information so efficiently that prices will adjust instantaneously to the news. Because the news itself is assumed to appear randomly, so the argument goes, prices must move in a random fashion as well.

As mentioned earlier, the credit for this idea goes to the French mathematician Louis Bachelier. In his doctoral dissertation addressing price fluctuations on the Paris bond market, the seeds of the efficient markets hypothesis were sown.[1] He concluded that the current price of a commodity was also an unbiased estimate of its future price. Bachelier's viewpoint is a long-standing equilibrium theory. Price changes are considered to be unpredictable, and technical trading using price charts is regarded as a waste of time. Today economists make use of *martingales*, a sort of random process that Bachelier introduced in passing. In fact, his notion of efficiency has proved to be extremely influential. The vast majority of academic economists accept that this is the way real markets work.

That's the explanation in theory. But what about in practice? What's meant by an *efficient* market in practical terms? The stock exchange provides one answer. Common stocks are traded on well-organized exchanges like the New York Stock Exchange or in dealer markets called over-the-counter markets. This allows a rapid execution of buy and sell orders. The price response to any change in demand caused by new information can be almost instantaneous. Such stock markets are also competitive due to the large number of participating individuals, institutions, corporations, and others. Competitive forces also tend to cause prices to reflect available information quickly. A market that quickly and accurately reflects available information is thought of as an efficient market. Those that adjust more rapidly and accurately are considered more efficient.

Are markets efficient? Yes, according to many economists. Like rationality, however, this efficiency is simply *assumed*. There's no actual proof. It's virtually impossible to test for market efficiency since the "correct" prices can't be observed. To get over this hurdle, most tests examine the ability of information-based trading strategies to make above-normal returns.[2] But the results of such tests don't really prove whether markets are efficient. Therein lies the basic dilemma. Given that stock markets have certain characteristics that are thought to make them more efficient than other markets, they seem like a reasonable place to start our investigation in earnest. Let's take a brief look at what the efficient market hypothesis posits in this setting.

Eugene Fama coined the term "efficient market" and suggested three levels of efficiency.[3] Studies of *weak-form* market efficiency began with Bachelier and concluded that stock prices follow a random walk. The *random walk* hypothesis means that at a given point in time, the size and direction of the next price change is random with respect to the knowledge available at that point in time. This implies that charting and all other forms of technical analysis practiced by various investors, amateur and professional alike, are doomed to fail. Market efficiency can also take a *semistrong form* or a *strong form,* but these two classes needn't concern us here.[4] It'll be enough to take a critical look at weak-form efficiency. If this form's credibility tends to unravel, then so will the others.

Market efficiency also seems to have its roots in the idea of *intrinsic value.* Although the value of most goods is acknowledged to be a function of consumer beliefs, preferences, and endowments, securities have often been treated as having a value independent of these consumer characteristics. Their value is based on the characteristics of the firm behind the security. This is a supply-side approach. The price of any security, however, depends not only on the characteristics of the firm or commodity involved but also on the demand for the security. In other words, it depends on the characteristics of the *investor.*

To date, the most commonly used model to relate investors' current price expectations with future price distributions is one that we've met earlier: the *rational expectations* equilibrium model. A fully revealing, rational expectations equilibrium occurs when prices reveal all the information held by individual investors. In other words, when price expectations are realized in a future period. But *whose* expectations? If investors possess *homogeneous* beliefs, the choice of whose expectations to use is greatly simplified. As Rubinstein states, "In a perfect and competitive economy composed of rational individuals with homogeneous beliefs about future prices, by any meaningful definition present security prices must fully reflect all available information about future prices."[5]

Now the real problem of defining market efficiency becomes clear. Overlooking the fact that investors might not have access to the same information, what happens if these investors happen to be different psychologically? From earlier chapters, we know that individuals possess different expectations in everyday situations. We know, for instance, that sheep and explorers coexist in traffic. When it comes to choosing alternative strategies, some drivers are risk-averse, whereas others are willing to experiment. Similar variability exists among the strategies of fishermen or technological imitators and innovators. Some search in familiar zones, and others are willing to risk uncharted waters. The truth of the matter is that any population possesses a rich spectrum of different beliefs, hypotheses, and expectations. We need look no further than the electoral boxes for proof of that! Why should it be any different in stock markets?

The basic problem with the efficient market hypothesis and the theory of random walks is that they concentrate exclusively on the security itself and the information relating to it. The demand side of the market is trivialized. All the idiosyncrasies of human nature are ignored. Furthermore, all these homogeneous investors are locked up in a static world. Expectations aren't allowed to vary. Yet real marketplaces are incredibly *dynamic* and *interactive.* Just ask any trader on the floor or in the pits. Different investors attempt to maximize their returns over different time horizons. Each has a different personality. What each investor does individually affects what the market does collectively, and in turn, what the market does collectively affects each investor individually. There are plenty of positive feedback loops at work. In other words, markets are coevolutionary in character, and learning is the engine of change.

Perhaps this explains why the newspapers and financial tabloids are full of graphs and advertisements by self-professed "chartists" claiming insights into future price movements. Could it be that these traders "see" something in those market gyrations that the academics have missed? Perhaps they feel that the geometry of price histories is important. Maybe it's just seasonal variations? Or does the position of the stars matter most? In any event, traders and academics view markets differently. Many traders believe that technical trading can be consistently profitable. They also believe that factors such as market "psychology" and "herd" effects do affect price changes.

Which group should hold sway? Markets do appear to be reasonably efficient in a limited sense of the word. Stock prices seem to reflect available information, despite traders' different information sets, beliefs, attitudes toward risk, and trading horizons. As stressed in Chapter 1, however, statistical tests have shown that technical trading can produce consistent profits over time.[6] The widespread use of technical trading rules continues to be a puzzle in academic finance. Yet other studies have also shown that trading volume and price movements are more volatile in real markets than the standard theory predicts.[7] Temporary bubbles and crashes, like the major crash in 1987, are well beyond the scope of rational adjustments to market news. Although some economists have looked for signs that prices are being generated by chaotic mechanisms, we'll not dwell on these tests here. It suffices to say that the evidence implicating chaos as a factor influencing price fluctuations in financial markets is mixed.[8] To learn more about how the market evolves over time, let's take a closer look at a favorite tool of the technical traders: the patterns formed by price gyrations.

Pattern Recognizers

Many technical traders believe that patterns of price movements in the marketplace tend to repeat themselves as human nature weaves its collective spell. There's plenty of evidence to support their view. Records of historical price changes show countless configurations that seem too striking to be attributable to mere chance. One of the earliest observers to find repetition in the market's price gyrations was Charles Dow. Dow started the Dow Jones Chemical Company and was the founding editor of the *Wall Street Journal*. During the last few years of his life, he wrote a few editorials dealing with stock price movements, which are the only personal record we have of his recognition of recurring patterns in price histories.[9] His theory is arguably the oldest and most famous technical trading approach in existence, and there are many versions of it still alive today.

Dow realized that the market did not resemble a balloon bobbing about aimlessly in the wind. Rather than bouncing along in a random fashion, he surmised that it moved through discernable sequences. As Dow stated: "The market is always considered as having three movements, all going at the same time. The first is the narrow movement from day to day. The second is the short swing, running from two weeks to a month or more; the third is the main movement, covering at least four years in duration."[10] Dow theory practitioners refer to these three components as daily fluctuations, secondary movements, and primary trends. They're really *time horizons*, extending over the short, medium, and long term. The

longer horizons, or primary trends, are commonly called *bull* or
bear markets. To search for patterns in these trends over time, technical analysts use various charts—such as line, bar, and point-and-
figure charts. Some of the price patterns formed by market action,
and recognized by technical traders, are shown in Figure 7.1.

Two of Dow's less discussed principles are of special interest. He
argued that in its primary uptrend, the market was characterized
by three upward swings. The first swing he attributed to a rebound
from the "over-pessimism" of the preceding primary downswing;

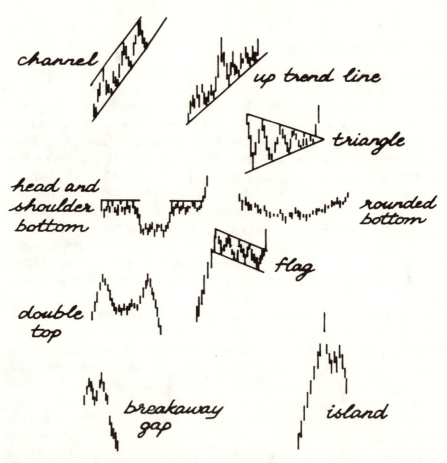

**FIGURE 7.1   Pattern formation in financial markets: typical bar charts
of price histories.**

the second upward swing geared into the improving business and earnings picture; the third and last swing was an overdiscounting of value. Dow's second principle was geometrical. This asserted that at some point in every market swing, whether up or down, there would be a reverse movement (or reaction) canceling 40 percent to 60 percent of that swing. It's hard to know if he thought of such geometrical regularities as being shaped by the human factor, but such repetition could hardly be judged as purely accidental.

More than eighty years after Dow's death, the Options Division of an annual tournament conducted by the Financial Traders Association in the United States was won by a former drummer in a rock band, one Robert Prechter. Prechter, who also holds a psychology degree from Yale University, managed to increase the value of his portfolio by a whopping 444.4 percent in the allotted four months![11] By 1989, the Financial News Network had named him "Guru of the Decade." One could be forgiven for thinking that Prechter's approach was novel. But the truth is that it was based on a more sophisticated form of Dow's geometrical principles. Let's take a quick look at this intriguing pattern recognizer, known as the *Elliott wave principle*.[12]

Prechter's mentor, Ralph N. Elliott, was a Los Angeles accountant and an expert on cafeteria management. He was also a keen student of all the gyrations in the Dow Jones averages. Having lost his job and part of his savings on Wall Street in 1929, he had plenty of time on his hands to search for a better way to play the markets. Like Dow, Elliott discerned repetitive patterns, but his discoveries went beyond Dow theory in comprehensiveness and exactitude. What Dow outlined with broad strokes of his brush, Elliott painted in careful detail. The wave principle is Elliott's discovery that investor behavior trends and reverses collectively in recognizable patterns. The basic pattern is shown in Figure 7.2.

Market action unfolds according to a basic rhythm of five waves up and three waves down to form a complete cycle of eight waves. Note that in its primary uptrend, there are three rising waves or upswings—just as Dow observed. What Dow called primary trend upswings or downswings, Elliott called *impulse* waves. In Elliott's jargon, waves numbered 2 and 4 are *corrective* waves. A complete Elliott cycle consists of eight waves: a primary uptrend of five

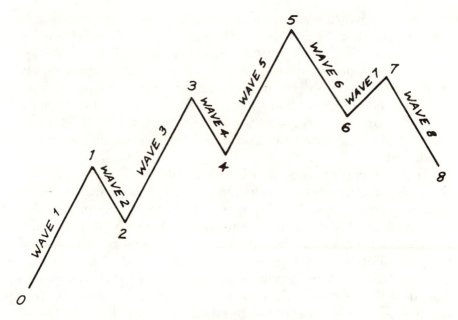

FIGURE 7.2   The basic Elliott wave pattern.

waves (1–2–3–4–5) being corrected by a secondary downtrend of three waves (6–7–8).

Following completion of this cycle, a second cycle of similar form begins. Once again, there are five upward waves and three downward waves. A third then follows, but this time there are only five waves up. This completes a major five-wave-up movement over a longer time horizon. Then follows a major three-wave-down movement, correcting the preceding major five-wave-up movement. Each of these "phases" is actually a wave in its own right but is one degree larger (or longer) than the waves of which it is composed.[13] The complete thirty-four-wave pattern is shown in the lower part of Figure 7.3.

Note how closely the geometrical form of this *major* wave pattern resembles that of its component *minor* wave pattern. According to Elliott, two waves of a particular degree can be broken into eight waves of the next lower degree; then those eight waves can be subdivided in exactly the same manner to reveal thirty-four waves of the next lower degree. The wave principle recognizes that

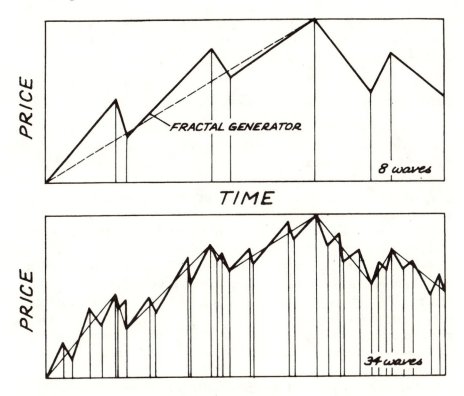

FIGURE 7.3   A nested Elliott wave pattern.

waves of any degree fulfill a dual role. They can be subdivided into waves of lesser degree, but they're also components of waves of higher degree. For example, the corrective pattern shown in the major wave illustrated in Figure 7.3 subdivides into a 5–3–5 pattern. If we could place this corrective pattern under a "microscope," it would also reveal a 5–3–5 pattern. Waves (1) and (2) in the thirty-four-wave movement shown in Figure 7.3 take on the same form as waves [1] and [2], confirming the phenomenon of constant form within ever-changing scale. This suggests that Elliott waves at different levels may be self-similar.

Self-similarity, or invariance against changes in scale or size, is a familiar attribute of many natural phenomena in the world around us. But who would have thought it might apply to financial markets? Because more than one scale factor is involved, strictly speaking these markets don't exhibit self-similarity. Instead they're said to be *self-affine,* which turns out to be a close relative of self-similarity. Both these concepts are explained in the next section.

Scaling the Market's Peaks

What does self-similarity of form really mean? Underlying the wave principle is the idea that financial markets exhibit a very special kind of symmetry: nature's symmetry. In effect, price gyrations display fractal geometry. The science of fractals is a relatively new one, which is gradually commanding the recognition that it deserves. Much of nature conforms to specific patterns and relationships, some of which are identical to those that Elliott recognized and described in the stock market. But there's a practical difficulty with Elliott's wave principle. It's virtually impossible to apply the technique successfully in an objective and repetitive manner.[14] In other words, it fails to provide a "descriptive phenomenology" that is organized tightly enough to ensure a degree of understanding and consistent application. Fortunately, the science of fractals features the statistical notion of "scaling," which helps to restore this objectivity.

Scaling is a morphological term. Starting from the rules that govern the variability of price on one particular timescale, higher-frequency and lower-frequency variation is found to be governed by the same rules, but acting faster or more slowly.[15] The founder of the fractal concept, Benoit Mandelbrot, suggests that a wealth of features beloved by chartists (and Elliott wave theorists) need not be judged subjectively, but may follow inevitably from suitable forms of random variability. In other words, we shouldn't be surprised by the fact that the market seems to trace out characteristic patterns at all levels—such as charts of similar general shape on different timescales. Even major market corrections, like the "October crashes" of 1929 and 1987, may simply be larger versions of what's happening all the time on smaller timescales.

Mandelbrot's scaling principle is more objective than Elliott's wave principle. His key idea is that much in economics is *self-affine.* This almost visual notion allows us to test the idea that "all charts look similar." Consider what happens if you inspect a financial chart from up close, then far away. Often you can "see" a pattern, like the basic Elliott wave pattern of five waves up then three waves down. Many smaller and larger patterns often look similar. Look what happens if we take a complete pattern, then diverse pieces of it, and resize each to the same horizontal format. Two such renormalized charts are never perfectly identical, of course, but they're often remarkably similar. Resizing in this way is known technically as "renormalizing by performing an affinity." This motivated Mandelbrot to coin the term "self-affinity."[16]

Self-affinity designates a property that's closely related to self-similarity, since it also involves a transformation from a whole to its parts. But it's not a similarity that reduces both coordinates in the same ratio. Instead it's an affinity that reduces time in one ratio and the other coordinate in a different but related ratio. Thus if two price charts, or two parts of one chart, happen to look very much alike, technically speaking they could be *self-affine*—statistically invariant by dilation or reduction. Two sequences of price gyrations that appear to be self-affine are shown in Figure 7.4. Far from being a rarity, such resemblances are rife throughout all financial markets. These fascinating discoveries have important implications for much of economics and finance. To date, they remain unexplained.

Mandelbrot posed a key question: Is the mathematical notion of chance powerful enough to bring about the strong degree of irregularity and variability in financial charts as well as in coastlines? The answer to that question came as a surprise. Not only is it powerful enough, but there's a tendency to underestimate the ability of chance to generate ordered structures that have not been anticipated in advance.[17] Chance remains important over a wide range of levels, including the macroscopic one. Several decades after Elliott, Mandelbrot's pioneering studies of fractals have confirmed that nature and markets abound with this special kind of symmetry.

In Chapter 1, we mentioned that Mandelbrot collected daily and monthly price data for various commodities. Logarithmic plots of the resulting size classes of price variations revealed that the distribution of price variations did not change over fifty-year periods or longer, except for scale. All of his curves could be superposed on each other by horizontal translation, confirming a strong quantitative symptom of scaling. Once again, a set of economic outcomes seems to be under the spell of a power law distribution.

220

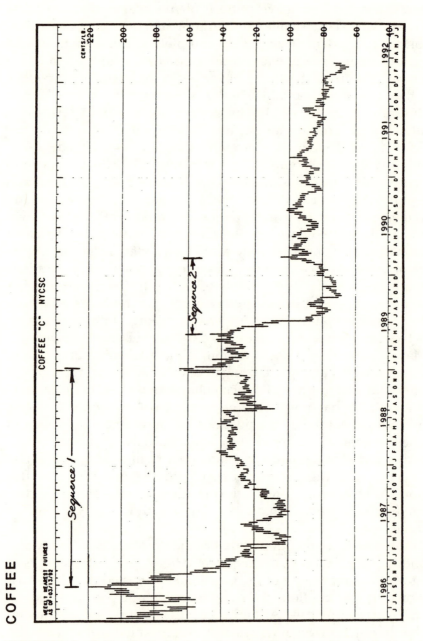

FIGURE 7.4   Self-affinity in the price gyrations of coffee futures.

But Mandelbrot went much further than this. To achieve a workable description of price changes, of firm sizes, or of income distribution, he argued that we must use random variables that have an infinite population variance. Thus he expected a revival of interest in the family of statistical distributions that adhere to a power law. These are exemplified by Pareto's law for the distribution of personal income, Zipf's law, and the work of the probability theorist Paul Lévy. Mandelbrot's work recognized a kinship between these closely related empirical laws and the theoretical power laws that occur in probability theory. More importantly, he managed to interpret various power laws in terms of scaling. Sadly, the revival of interest he had hoped for has not yet materialized.

More recently, studies of multifractals have revealed that the price variations recorded by Mandelbrot and others exhibit self-affinity.[18] Such price changes have no typical or preferred size of variation. They're "scale-free," just like the sandpile avalanches that we discussed earlier. It would seem that prices and sandpiles do have something in common after all. They're both capable of evolving to a self-organized critical state.

To create a multifractal from a unifractal, you must lengthen or shorten the horizontal time axis so that the pieces of the generator are stretched or squeezed. Meanwhile, the vertical price axis can remain untouched. Market activity may speed up in the interval of time represented by the first piece of the generator and slow down in the interval that corresponds to the second piece. Such simple alterations can produce a full replication of price fluctuations over a given period, including the periods of very high or very low volatility. On a more practical level, these findings suggest that fractal generators could be developed based on historical market data. Such generators would help to introduce some much-needed order to the seemingly chaotic gyrations of financial markets.

What's most disturbing is that much of Mandelbrot's important work has largely been ignored. It's hard to understand why. Is it because his ideas don't fit into the traditional picture or because he's a physicist rather than an economist? Perhaps his notions are too esoteric for economists to fully comprehend. Most classical economists attribute large events—like the stock market crashes of 1929 and 1987—to one-time, abnormal circumstances, such as depressions or the automated responses of computer trading programs. They look to econometric models for the explanation, paying scant attention to the statistical distributions underlying the actual geometry of price histories. Mandelbrot's results suggest otherwise. Eventually they will change the statistical underpinnings of economics in a fundamental way.

Fibonacci Magic

The emerging pattern of price gyrations and market evolution involves many interrelated dynamic principles—Elliott waves, fractals, self-affinity, and power laws, to name just a few. We're tempted to ask if these dynamic perspectives have anything more in common. By the time you reach the end of this chapter, you may want to decide for yourself. For some readers, the material in this section will appear to be nothing more than an amusing mathematical diversion from our mainstream discussion of financial markets. Others, however, may feel it deserves to be taken more seriously!

The ancient world was full of outstanding mathematicians. When Elliott wrote *Nature's Law,* he referred specifically to a sequence of numbers discovered in the thirteenth century by the mathematician Leonardo da Pisa. Better known by his nickname, Fibonacci, this remarkable mathematician was taught the Arabic system of numbers by the Mohammedans of Barbary.[19] In 1202, he published a voluminous book titled *Liber Abaci,* in which he introduced Europeans to the Arabic system and to nearly all the arithmetic and algebraic knowledge of those times. Among the many mathematical examples to be found in this "Book of the Abacus," Fibonacci discussed a breeding problem of the following kind: How many pairs of rabbits can be produced in a single year from one pair of baby rabbits, if a pair of baby rabbits requires one month to grow to adulthood and each pair of adult rabbits gives birth to a new pair of baby rabbits after one month?

For the first two months, obviously there will only be one pair of rabbits. The sequence of numbers defining the population of rabbit pairs thus begins with the digits 1, 1. This population doubles by the end of the second month, so that there are two pairs at the start of the third month. Of these two, only the older pair begets a third pair the following month, so that at the beginning of the fourth month, the sequence is 1, 1, 2, 3. Of these three, the two older pairs reproduce, so the number of rabbit pairs expands to five. Of these five, the three older pairs reproduce, so that the next entry in the sequence is eight.

In the comparatively short period of twelve months, Mr. and Mrs. Rabbit would have a family of 144 rabbit pairs. Their monthly breeding program gives rise to the following sequence of rabbit pairs:

1, 1, 2, 3, 5, 8, 13, 21, 34, 55, 89, 144.

This justly famous sequence of numbers is known today as the Fibonacci sequence. Should they opt to continue their breeding habits for several years, the number of rabbit pairs would grow to astronomical proportions. After one hundred months, for example, we would be facing a rabbit population of 354,224,848,179,261,915,075 pairs!

No doubt you're wondering what this rabbit breeding problem can possibly have to do with price histories in financial markets. One thing to note is that the Fibonacci sequence has many interesting properties in itself. For example, the sum of any two numbers in the sequence equals the next number in the sequence. 1 plus 1 equals 2, 1 plus 2 equals 3, 2 plus 3 equals 5, 3 plus 5 equals 8, and so on to infinity. Secondly, and more importantly, the ratio of any two numbers in the sequence approaches 1.618, or its inverse, 0.618, after the first few pairs of numbers. The ratio of any number to the next higher number, called *phi,* is about 0.618 to 1 and to the next lower number is about 1.618. The higher the numbers in the sequence, the closer to 0.618 and 1.618 are the ratios between the numbers.

For some unknown reason, the ratio 1.618 (or 0.618) to 1 seems to be pleasing to the senses. The Greeks based much of their art and architecture upon this proportion, calling it the *Golden Mean.* Among mathematicians, it's commonly known as the *Golden Ratio,* an irrational number defined to be $(1 + \sqrt{5})/2$.[20] It's the mathematical basis for the shape of Greek vases and the Parthenon, sunflowers and snail shells, the logarithmic spiral and the spiral galaxies of outer space. It seems to imply a natural harmony that feels good, looks good, and even sounds good. Music, for instance, is based on the eight-note octave. On a piano, this is represented by five black keys and eight white ones—thirteen in all. Perhaps it's no accident that the musical harmony that seems to give us the greatest satisfaction is the major sixth. The note E vibrates at a ratio of 0.625 to the note C, just slightly above the Golden Ratio. Note that the ear is also an organ that happens to be shaped in the form of a logarithmic spiral.

Nature seems to have adopted the Golden Ratio as a geometrical rule in its magical handiwork, from miniscule forms, like atomic structure and DNA molecules, to systems as large as planetary orbits and galaxies.[21] It's also involved in many diverse phenomena such as quasi crystal arrangements, reflections of light beams on glass surfaces, the brain and nervous system, and the structure of many plants and animals. Some have even suggested that the Golden Ratio is a basic proportional principle of nature. Could it be an *emergent* property of certain classes of natural systems?

Some of the greatest surprises of nonlinear dynamics and chaos theory have been the discovery of emergent simplicities, deep universal patterns concealed within the erratic behavior of dynamical systems. One of the first of these unexpected simplicities was found by Mitchell Feigenbaum and is known as the Feigenbaum number. Virtually any mathematical equation with a period-doubling bifurcation produces the same universal ratio: 4.669 and a bit! This was a totally unexpected new number in mathematics, emerging from some of the most complex behaviors known to mathematicians.[22] The period-doubling cascade (depicted in Figure 7.5) is important because it's one of the most common routes from order to chaos. Despite the fact that the Feigenbaum number is an emergent feature of period-doubling dynamical systems, we've only known about it for the past twenty years. Such emergent simplicities may be viewed as peaks in the landscapes of the possible.

Different kinds of simplicities can emerge from underlying chaos—numbers, shapes, patterns of repetitive behavior. Some of these features have their own internal structure. Another fascinating example is Mandelbrot's fractal set. It's one of the most intricate geometric objects ever to have decorated a child's bedroom wall (see Figure 7.6). On viewing it, we might believe that it's extremely complex. Yet the computer program that generates it is just a few

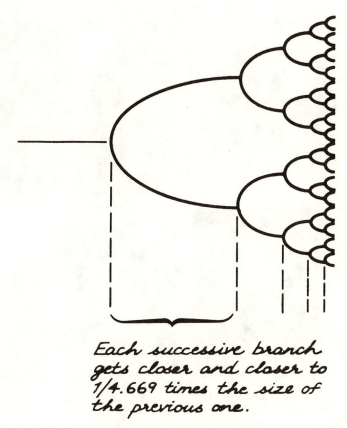

Each successive branch gets closer and closer to 1/4.669 times the size of the previous one.

FIGURE 7.5 The Feigenbaum number lurks within every period-doubling cascade.

instructions long. As Murray Gell-Mann suggests, it has logical depth rather than effective complexity.[23] Putting it more bluntly, Mandelbrot's set is as simple as the rule that generates it. It only looks complicated because you don't know what the rule is. It's another case of simple rules producing seemingly complex results.

Perhaps the Golden Ratio is like the Feigenbaum number or Mandelbrot's set. After all, iteration is one of the richest sources of self-similarity. Given a proper start, any repeated application of some self-same operation, be it geometric, arithmetic, or symbolic, leads almost invariably to self-similarity. Take the Fibonacci

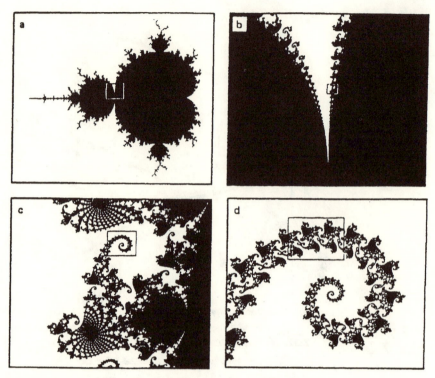

FIGURE 7.6   The Mandelbrot set.

sequence of numbers. If we multiply each number by the Golden Ratio and round to the nearest integer, we get

0, 2, 2, 3, 5, 8, 13, 21, 34, 55, 89, 144, . . .

which is the Fibonacci sequence again, except for a few initial terms (and perhaps some later ones). The Golden Ratio reveals its own self-similarity if it's written down as a *continued fraction*. Like so many self-similar objects, the Fibonacci sequence of numbers contains within it the seeds of chaos.

If natural law permeates the universe, might it not permeate the world of people as well? How different from nature's laws are the laws of human nature? Nothing in nature suggests that life is disorderly or formless. We mustn't reject the possibility that human progress, which is a by-product of human nature, also possesses order and form. If we examine the plentiful data on price gyrations in the stock market, the unmistakable self-affinity of these gyrations over different timescales suggests that they're sustained by the Golden Ratio. This was the basis for Elliott's wave principle. Two waves of a particular size can be broken into eight waves of a smaller size; then those eight waves can be subdivided in exactly the same manner to reveal thirty-four waves of an even smaller size (as depicted in Figure 7.3).[24] Both fractals and market action discern constant form within ever-changing scale.

We can generate the complete Fibonacci sequence by using Elliott's concept of the progression of the market.[25] The same basic pattern of movement that shows up in minor waves, using hourly plots, also shows up in what Elliott calls supercycles and grand supercycles, using yearly plots. Take a look at the two graphs in Figure 7.7. They trace out extraordinarily similar patterns of movement despite a difference in the time horizon of more than 1000 to 1. No preference is shown for any particular timescale. Instead the evolving pattern reflects the properties of the Fibonacci sequence. Waves may sometimes appear to be stretched or compressed, but underlying patterns never change. This is consistent with Mandelbrot's notion of self-affinity. The spiral-like form of market action conforms repeatedly to the Golden Ratio.

From the working of the Golden Ratio as a "five up, three down" movement of the stock market cycle, the astute reader might anticipate that the ensuing correction after the completion of any bull phase would be three-fifths of the previous rise in time or amplitude. Unfortunately, such simplicity is rarely seen within individual waves. However, time and amplitude ratios do play their part over longer timescales. For example, one of the great Dow theorists, Robert Rhea, found that over a thirty-six-year time period (1896 to 1932), bear markets ran 61.1 percent of the time assigned to bull markets. He later corrected this figure to 62.1 percent. Thus Rhea discovered, without knowing it, that the Golden Ratio relates bull phases to bear phases in both time and amplitude.

Robert Prechter, that "Guru of the Decade" we met earlier in this chapter, sees the wave principle as a major breakthrough in sociology. He believes that the personality of each wave in the Elliott

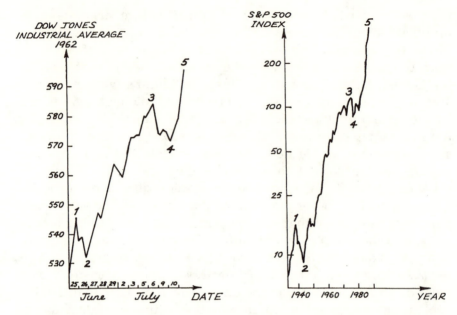

FIGURE 7.7 Hourly and yearly fluctuations in the U.S. stock market.

sequence is an integral part of the mass psychology it embodies. Some waves are powerful and may subdivide or feature extensions. Others are short and abrupt. Nevertheless, the progression of mass emotions from optimism to pessimism and back again tends to trace out a roughly similar wave sequence each time around. These emotions lead to cycles of overvaluation and undervaluation, producing similar circumstances at each corresponding stage in its wave-like structure. The Golden Ratio helps to shape progress overall. But each wave reflects a collective mood or personality of its own.

Because the stock market is one of the finest reflectors of mass psychology available to us, perhaps it's not surprising that it illustrates the scaling principle so vividly. Is such a principle everywhere present? Perhaps it shapes the minds of investors and hence movements of the market in a coevolutionary dance to the tune of the Golden Ratio! The answer to this intriguing question is left to the reader's imagination.

Market Moods

Elliott and Prechter were not the first to focus on the moods and attitudes of investors en masse. In a remarkable book attempting to explain the peaks and troughs in the business cycle in the 1920s, the English economist Arthur Pigou placed special emphasis on the human element.[26] He surmised that *changes in expectations* were the proximate causes of variations in the economic marketplace. Although his interest was in the changing demand for labor, his theory helps to explain excessive volatility and other vagaries observed in financial markets.

What was Pigou's theory? He began by classifying the causes of expectations into three groups: (a) *real* causes, namely changes in actual conditions, (b) *psychological* causes, namely changes in men's attitude of mind, and (c) *autonomous monetary* causes, namely events like gold discoveries that affect the money supply. Also he claimed that in our day-to-day world, real causes and psychological causes exist simultaneously, and they react to one another. Once started, these reactions may become reciprocating and continuous. A real cause prompts a psychological reaction, this in turn adds further to the real cause, this in turn adds something further to the psychological cause, and so on.

If you're thinking that there's something familiar about this, you'd be right. Pigou was describing a positive feedback loop. We can illustrate his ideas in the familiar financial arena of commodity markets. Imagine that news of major strike action by members of the transport workers' union reaches the marketplace, triggering concern among farmers about livestock and fruit deliveries. Soon they express this concern publicly in the media, prompting further concern by the transport workers that a prolonged dispute may put their jobs at risk. Gradually the mood of the market as a whole begins to sour, exacerbating the importance of the news even further. As the strike lingers on, progressively angrier responses by the farmers serve only to trigger an even more defiant stance by the union. The *real* cause—industrial action—has triggered a *psychological* response, which adds further fuel to the gravity of the real cause, which adds further to the worries of all the individuals and collectives involved.[27] Thus undue pessimism develops.

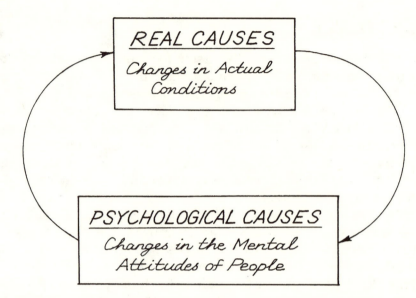

FIGURE 7.8   Positive feedback in Pigou's industrial economy.

This is a highly self-reinforcing feedback loop (see Figure 7.8). Swings in optimism or pessimism arise as a psychological reflex from the original real cause(s). Pigou emphasized that these swings occur simultaneously over a large number of people because of "psychological interdependence, sympathetic or epidemic excitement, or mutual suggestion."[28] He did not believe in the theory of rational expectations, pointing to an "instability in the facts being assumed." Psychological causes arise because *expected* facts are substituted for accomplished facts as the impulse to action. This leads to errors of undue optimism or undue pessimism.

In summary, Pigou felt that the upward and downward swings seen in markets are partly caused by excesses of human optimism followed by excesses of pessimism. It's as if the pendulum swings too far one way and there is glut, then it swings too far the other way and there's scarcity. An excess in one direction breeds an excess in the other, diastole and systole in never-ending succession.[29] There's plenty of evidence of such cycles of overreaction. Psychologists acknowledge the moody, contagious nature of crowds. There's a degree of psychological interdependence that can magnify the initial response. An error of optimism by one person can pump up the optimism of others. It's almost like an epidemic. When prices rise in the stock market, for example, because a few more businessmen become more prosperous, they're apt to look on the brighter side. This serves as a spur to optimistic error among others. Thus the error is magnified.

There's another interesting twist to Pigou's theory. Once they're discovered, errors of optimism can quickly change to errors of pessimism, and vice versa. This keeps the pendulum swinging too far in both directions. The result is a relentless ebb and flow in the tide of emotions affecting investors' stock market decisions. If Pigou happens to be right, then the implication is that human nature doesn't change. Despite the errors in optimism and pessimism, certain patterns will tend to repeat themselves as human nature weaves its spell. Suddenly, those patterns of self-affinity that we've observed in market gyrations take on a new meaning. Could self-affine price histories—those same patterns displaying fractal geometry and conforming to power laws—simply be reflecting the collective moods and vagaries of human nature? Perhaps the marketplace experiences mental phase transitions, transforming it from a simpler to a more complex regime, and later back again.

Pigou was one of the earliest scholars to question the validity of the efficient markets hypothesis from a psychological viewpoint. Others have followed recently in his footsteps. Robert Shiller, professor of economics at Yale University's Cowles Foundation, typifies a group of modern scholars exploring the idea that price movements in speculative markets may be due to changes in opinion or psychology. He poses the following basic question:

> Can we trace the source of movements back in a logical manner to fundamental shocks affecting the economy, the shocks to technology, to consumer preferences, to demographics, to natural resources, to monetary policy or to other instruments of government control? Or are price movements due to changes in opinion or psychology, that is, changes in confidence, speculative enthusiasm, or other aspects of the worldview of investors, shocks that are best thought of as coming ultimately from people's minds?[30]

Shiller finds that investor attitudes are of great importance in determining the course of prices of speculative assets. Prices change in substantial measure because the investing public en masse capriciously changes its mind. He found clear evidence of price volatility, relative to the predictions of efficient markets theories, particularly in the stock market.[31] This means that the variability of price movements is too large to be justified in terms of efficient markets models, given the relatively low variability of fundamentals and given the correlation of price with fundamentals.

Shiller studies various kinds of popular models—simple, qualitative hypotheses of what may happen to prices. Many popular models focus on behavioral patterns observed in the marketplace. They bear a striking resemblance to Brian Arthur's temporary mental models associated with the processes of pattern recognition and inductive reasoning (see Chapter 2). They're also reminiscent of the temporary hypotheses that drivers adopt in their attempts to combat traffic jams (see Chapter 6).

A well-known example of a popular model in the stock market is the sequence of price movements surrounding the crash of October 1929. People who adopt this model think that this particular pattern of price movements may happen again at a later date. Because they're easy for the general public to understand, models like these usually get plenty of attention in the press. For example, there was an article advancing the "1929 hypothesis" in the *Wall Street Journal* on October 19, 1987—the very morning of the day the stock market crashed again!

Singling out patterns like the one in 1929 for so much attention is rather arbitrary. History provides many more episodes that might be used for comparison than ever enter the public's mind. Other dramatic stock market rises, as well as many less dramatic stock market episodes, are largely forgotten—because investors mostly fear the major crash. Yet the self-similarity of these gyrations over different timescales may be the potent, pattern-making feature of markets in general. Why concentrate on a very infrequent part of this overall picture? Shiller argues that such popular models may create a vicious circle, or feedback loop in our terminology, whereby people's reaction to price changes causes further price changes, yet more reaction, and so on. We've argued in earlier chapters that economists should examine these mental models directly. The approximation of allowing economic theorists to model human behavior, without collecting information on the popular models of the world, has serious drawbacks. Nowhere are these limitations more apparent than in the study of speculative markets.

Reading the Market's Mind

Now let's turn to the ideas of two of the most successful investors to have put their pens to paper for our benefit. One has become a household name by virtue of his aggressive currency plays, which have challenged the stability of nations. The other is largely unknown outside his close-knit circle of enthusiastic disciples. Both can justifiably claim to understand the "mind" of the market. More importantly, their highly profitable records are living proof of the potential fallibility of the efficient markets hypothesis.

Until recently, George Soros managed his own international fund management group. Its flagship vehicle, the Quantum Fund, is a Curaçao-based investment firm headquartered in Manhattan. Despite the recent corrections among various hedge funds (including Quantum), typical annual gains in earlier periods exceeded 50 percent.[32] But much of Soros's fame (and notoriety) stems from the fact that he made a billion dollars going up against the British pound. Some say he rescued England from recession. Others are less complimentary. Dubbed by *Business Week* as "The Man Who Moves Markets," Soros is arguably one of the most powerful and profitable investors in the world today.[33] He has all the trappings of an intelligent thinker and sponsors major philanthropic efforts. For our purpose, it's enough to concentrate on his philosophical train of thought.

Soros is highly critical of the way in which economists use the concept of equilibrium. As he views it, the deception lies with their emphasis on the final outcome instead of the process that leads up to it. This endows the equilibrium concept with an aura of empirical certainty. Yet that's not the case in reality. Equilibria have rarely been observed in real life. Market prices have a habit of fluctuating incessantly. We've seen historical examples of price fluctuations in earlier sections. More will appear later in this chapter. If market participants are actually adapting to a constantly moving target, calling their behavior an adjustment process may be a misnomer, and equilibrium theory becomes irrelevant to the real world.

The assumption that Soros found so unacceptable as a student of economics was that of *perfect knowledge*. How could one's own understanding of a situation, in which one participates and interacts with others, possibly qualify as full knowledge of that situation? Because we're more aware today of the limits to knowledge, modern theories of perfect competition and efficient markets merely postulate perfect *information*. But this merely shirks the real issue. By assigning themselves the task of studying the relationship between supply and demand, and not either by itself, economists disguise a sweeping assumption behind the facade of a methodological device. The sweeping assumption is that each participant knows all that needs to be known to make a correct decision.

As I've argued in earlier chapters, this kind of assumption is untenable. Even the shapes of supply and demand curves cannot be taken as independently given, because both are built on the participants' expectations (or hypotheses) about events that are, in turn, shaped collectively by their own expectations. Anyone who trades in markets where prices are changing incessantly knows that participants are strongly influenced by market developments. As Soros suggests, "Buy and sell decisions are based on expectations about future prices, and future prices, in turn, are contingent on present buy and sell decisions."[34] Rising prices, fueled by buyer interest exceeding that of sellers, tend to attract even more buyers. Likewise falling prices tend to attract more sellers.

There's plenty of evidence of positive feedback loops in financial markets of all varieties. How could such self-reinforcing trends persist if supply and demand curves were independent of market prices? In the normal course of events, a speculative price rise provokes counteracting forces: Supply is increased and demand reduced. Thus temporary excesses are corrected with the passage of time. But Soros disputes that this always happens. In the stock market, for example, the performance of a stock may affect the performance of the company in question in a variety of ways. He contends that such paradoxical behavior is typical of all financial markets that serve as a discounting mechanism for future developments, notably stock markets, foreign exchange markets, banking, and all forms of credit.

Soros points to the need to understand the process of change that we can observe all around us. We're both instigators of, and reactors to, change. In his own words, "The presence of thinking participants complicates the structure of events enormously: the participants' thinking affects the course of events and the course of events affects the participants' thinking." From this we can identify the core of Soros's thesis about the dynamics of financial markets. It's a process of coevolutionary learning. Just as we've discussed at length, economic agents must base their decisions on an inherently imperfect understanding of the situation in which they participate. We saw that it baffles music lovers at the El Farol, that it provokes defection in the Trader's Dilemma, and that it frustrates drivers on a congested highway. Thinking always plays a dual role. First, participants seek to understand the situation in which they participate. Second, their imperfect understanding serves as the basis of decisions that influence the actual course of events.

What makes the participants' understanding imperfect is that their thinking affects the very situation to which it applies. They're caught up as participants in the process that they're trying to understand. Because there's a discrepancy between the expectations (or favored hypothesis) held by each participant and the outcome itself, invariably some participants "change their mind" next time around. This also changes future outcomes. Soros gives this discrepancy a special name. He calls it the participants' *bias*. The actual course of events is very likely to differ from the participants' expectations, and this divergence gives an indication of the participants' bias.

It's this bias that forms the centerpiece of what he calls his *theory of reflexivity*. Soros splits the divergence into two components: (1) the *cognitive function* is the participants' effort to understand the situation, and (2) the *participating function* is the impact of their thinking on the real world.[35] We've used slightly different terms, namely *inductive reasoning* and the *collective outcomes*. When both functions operate simultaneously, they interfere with each other. Instead of a determinate result, we have an interplay in which both the situation and the participants' views are dependent variables, so that an initial change precipitates further changes both in the situation and the participants' views. He calls this particular kind of positive feedback process "reflexivity."[36] Reflexivity doesn't produce an equilibrium. Because the two recursive functions belong to the world of morphogenesis, they produce a never-ending process of change. People are groping to anticipate the future with whatever guideposts they can establish. Outcomes tend to diverge from expectations, leading to constantly changing expectations and constantly changing outcomes.

The idea of a distinction between near-equilibrium and far-from-equilibrium conditions has been emphasized before. Clearly Soros believes that such distinctions are also important in financial markets. But he's quick to add the following rider: "Since far-from-equilibrium conditions arise only intermittently, economic theory is only intermittently false."[37] In other words, his notion of reflexivity operates intermittently. Thus it has strikingly similar properties to the theory of punctuated equilibria and self-organized criticality (introduced in Chapter 1).

Soros claims that it's possible to treat the evolution of prices in all financial markets as a reflexive, historical process. There are long fallow periods when the movements in these markets do not seem to follow a reflexive tune but resemble the random walks mandated by the efficient markets hypothesis. Because the whole process is open-ended, however, discontinuities arise unexpectedly. These sudden changes are shaped by the misconceptions of the participants. In this respect, Soros's thesis closely resembles that of Pigou. Real causes and psychological causes are reacting upon each other. In both cases, price histories are built on fertile fallacies. In both cases, the efficient markets hypothesis is found wanting.

Despite his earlier success as a global investor, in this perplexing era where old and new economies vie for future superiority Soros is vague about how to play today's markets and win. Also, he shrouds his past methods in a cloak of mystery. In contrast, Charles Lindsay's recipe for trading success is remarkably simple and clear. Having probed extensively into the self-affinity issue in real markets, Lindsay's strategy embodies many unconventional concepts discussed in this chapter. He maintains that all events, real or imagined, cause prices to fluctuate as traders and speculators react to these events and rumors. Because rumors abound, he believes that a successful trading system must ignore the rumors themselves, taking only the market's net reaction to them into account. This is the basis of his trading approach.[38]

Lindsay believes that prices are as unstable as waves pounding onto a beach. They reflect the incessant struggle between buyers and sellers. Whenever buying pressure exceeds selling pressure, prices move upward. Whenever selling pressure exceeds buying pressure, prices move downward. If buying and selling pressure are equal, the price moves sideways. Lindsay likens such price swings to those associated with the pressure in a hose as water is forced through its nozzle. He defines a *Trident price* as the price at which buying (or selling) pressure is overcome by its opposite. In other words, it's the price at a turning point. Price fluctuation in the same trend direction is called a price swing, joining the lowest price in the trend to the highest price in the trend, or vice versa depending on trend direction. Figure 7.9 illustrates various price swings from one Trident price to the next. Trident prices are nothing more than local maxima or minima in the recent price history. For example, all the depicted swings from P_1 to P_2, and from P_2 to P_3, are swings from a local maximum (or minimum) to a local minimum (or maximum). Such turning points define those occasions when buying or selling pressure is overcome by its opposite.

The chart depicting price variations in the market for live hogs highlights a typical trading opportunity using Trident analysis. Note that the drop in price from P_1 to P_2 is about 20 cents per pound. Then the price rises again—from P_2 to P_3—by about 12 cents per pound. According to Trident theory, the next downward swing—namely P_3 to P_4—should reach a target price of about 39.5 cents per pound. As the historical chart shows, the realized price, P_4, dipped slightly below 39 cents per pound. In Trident terms, this trade was fully successful since it exceeded its target price.[39]

Like Elliott wave theory, Trident analysis is a trading strategy that's based on an investor's ability to recognize various patterns formed by sequential price gyrations in the marketplace. The model itself consists of a collection of formulae deduced from analyses of price swings and price action. It is path dependent in the sense that a future price depends sensitively on the cumulative sequence of historical price movements. In practical terms, the strategy allows the investor to calculate an "ideal" target price and potential profit for each "tradable" price swing. The price swing P_3 to P_4—shown in Figure 7.9—depicts only one best trade: Buy at P_3

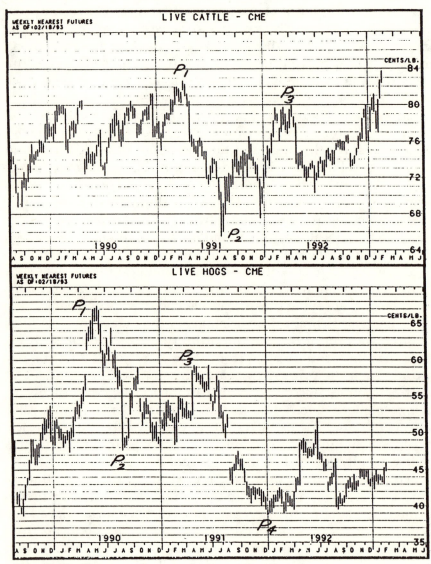

Price Fluctuations

FIGURE 7.9   Typical price fluctuations in commodity markets.

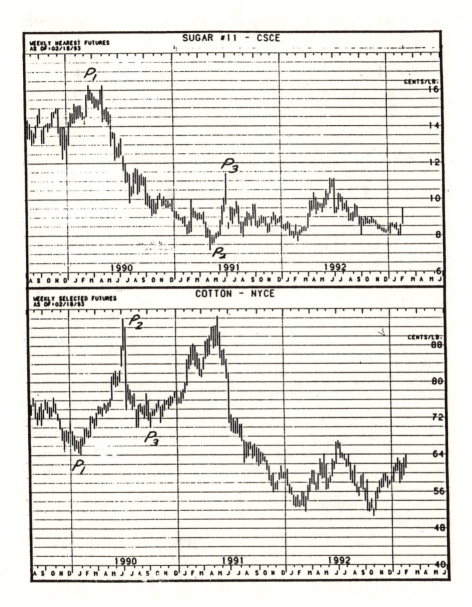

and sell at P_4. Thus, the Trident model assumes that the next price swing will resemble the previous swing in the same direction. In other words, it assumes the same kind of symmetry that underlies the principles of fractal geometry: self-similarity.

The target price is ideal in the sense that it serves as an optimistic forecast rather than a hard-and-fast prediction. Targets aren't always reached, but the one algorithm holds true for calculating swing targets at all levels. Lindsay's simple algorithm is built on the notion that price action is not random but sequential, path dependent, and often close to symmetrical. A host of different markets contain numerous examples of Trident price formation and target completion. In practice, ideal targets are reached about 40 percent of the time. Potentially profitable trades occur far more frequently, because trades can be terminated early if their ideal targets turn out to be unattainable. The proof of Trident is in the bank. Many of Lindsay's devout students have accumulated impressive fortunes.

Like Elliott, the key to Lindsay's success lies in the recognition that prices fluctuating over several levels of time increment continuously and simultaneously. He distinguishes between five levels, claiming that his Trident analysis is effective at each level: (1) microswings, which occur during a daily trading session (e.g., at fifteen-minute intervals); (2) minor swings, which are measured from the highest daily high to the lowest daily low in sequence, then from the lowest daily low to the highest daily high in sequence; (3) intermediate swings, which are measured from the highest minor high to the lowest minor low in sequence and from the lowest minor low to the highest minor high in sequence; (4) major swings, which are measured from the highest intermediate high to the lowest intermediate low in sequence and from the lowest intermediate low to the highest intermediate high in sequence; and (5) master swings, which take several years to form and are defined by sequential life of contract highs and lows.

Full details of Lindsay's trading method will not be discussed here.[40] That would breach an oath of commercial confidentiality. My modest aim is to show that relatively simple but effective trading strategies can be founded on multifractal scaling principles. Such methods are easier to apply than Elliott's wave principle, yet the underlying forces shaping price fluctuations are similar. Importantly, each method recognizes that the market is always right. The market coevolves, and you, as a trader, must coevolve with it. One fascinating feature of the Trident algorithm is that success hinges upon the investor's ability to recognize a tradable situation. Two key criteria defining "tradability" are what Lindsay calls "determinate" and "trend reversal" prices. Both of these are defined in terms of a single fraction of earlier price swings. That fraction just happens to be 0.625, remarkably close to the Golden Ratio!

How Markets Learn

We've seen how price histories trace out remarkably symmetrical geometrical patterns over different timescales. It's as if markets possess a collective mind of their own, a *fractal* mind. We've also learned that some of the most successful players in the investment game—people like Robert Prechter, George Soros, and Charles Lindsay—believe that individual decisions can "move" markets and, in turn, that the market's collective mind affects individual investors. Once again, the self-reinforcing engine behind all of these observations is the unfolding process of coevolutionary learning.

Is there a way of relating these two sets of observations? Can we test whether fractal geometry is consistent with Soros's theory of reflexivity or Pigou's thesis on the excesses of human optimism and pessimism? This would appear to be impossible if we choose to resort to traditional modeling techniques. Closed-form models cannot handle a diverse population of investors harboring literally hundreds of different hypotheses about market behavior. But a possible way out of this dilemma has been mentioned in earlier chapters. Agent-based simulations may be able to accommodate the vastly heterogeneous beliefs held by market participants, thereby uncovering some of their emergent features.

Instead of confining ourselves to the vehicles themselves, in Chapter 6 we looked at traffic behavior in terms of drivers' *psychology*. We saw that the beliefs and expectations of drivers are constantly being tested in a world that forms from their and others' actions and subjective beliefs. Perhaps the same may be true of the stock market. After all, the typical investor is not so different from the typical driver! For both, prediction usually means a short-term, beat-the-crowd anticipation of tomorrow's situation (i.e., prices or travel times). Why not view the stock market as a diverse collection of beliefs, expectations, and mental models?

Brian Arthur is one Santa Fe Institute economist who opted to test this approach to financial markets. Together with John Holland, Blake Le Baron, Richard Palmer, and Paul Tayler, Arthur created an artificial stock market on the computer, inhabited by "investors" who are individual, artificially intelligent programs that can reason inductively.[41] In this market-within-a-machine, artificial investors act like those economic statisticians we described in Chapter 6. They're constantly testing and discarding expectational hypotheses of how the market works and which way prices will move. These subjective, expectational models are a bit like the ones used by Arthur's "silicon patrons" at the El Farol bar. Just as there's no way of telling how many devotees of Irish music plan to come to the El Farol next Thursday evening, or how many drivers plan to take the same expressway home after work tonight, there's no way that investors can tell what tomorrow's prices will be in the stock market.

There are plenty of clues around, of course. For example, a popular guide to the state of prices the next day is the value of tomorrow's stock index in the futures market. If that value is above today's closing value, it means that the bulk of investors expect tomorrow's prices to rise. But there are literally hundreds of different hypotheses about tomorrow's state of play. Here are a couple of other possibilities:

IF today's price is higher than its average in the last one hundred days,
THEN predict that tomorrow's price will be 3 percent higher than today's.

or

IF today's price breaks below the latest trendline upward,
THEN predict that next week's price will be 5 percent lower than this week's.

Some investors may keep many such models in mind, others may retain only one at a time. In the Prediction Company's artificial stock market, each agent adopts his "most reliable" model—the one that performs best in the market's current state. Naturally enough, different expectational models may perform better than others at different times. Thus investors must retain and adopt a suite of models for their buy and sell decisions. Eventually, the poorer performing models are discarded. Agents use a generic algorithm to produce new forecasting models from time to time.

The learning process in this silicon world comes from two sources: discovering "new" expectational models and identifying the ones that perform best from among the current set.[42] Prices form endogenously from the bids and offers of the silicon agents, and thus ultimately from their beliefs. Such expectational models are akin to Pigou's "changes in men's attitudes of mind," and they display some feedback effects inherent in his theory. For example, if enough traders in the market happen to adopt similar expectational models, positive feedback can turn such models into self-fulfilling prophecies.[43] The agent-based experiments conducted by the Prediction Company have typically involved about one hundred artificial investors each armed with sixty expectational models. As this pool of six thousand expectational models coevolves over time, expectations turn out to be mutually reinforcing or mutually negating. Temporary price bubbles and crashes arise, of the very kind that Pigou attributed to excesses of human optimism or pessimism. These more volatile states may be attributed to the spontaneous emergence of self-fulfilling prophecies.

A key aspect of agent-based simulations are their internal dynamics. Expectations come and go in an ocean of beliefs that form a coevolving ecology. How do the beliefs of fundamentalists fare in this silicon world? Do technical trading beliefs ever gain a firm footing? The results so far suggest that both views are upheld, but under different conditions.[44] If a majority of investors believe the fundamentalist model, the resulting prices will validate it, and deviant predictions that arise by mutation in the population of expectational models will be rendered inaccurate. Thus they can never get a solid foothold in the market. Necessity prevails. But if the initial expectations happen to be randomly distributed uniformly about the fundamentalist ones, trend-following beliefs that appear by chance have enough density to become self-reinforcing in the ecology of beliefs. Chance shatters the conventional wisdom. Then the use of past prices to forecast future ones becomes an emergent property.

In this mutated regime, no stationary equilibrium seems to be reached. The market keeps evolving continuously. If initially successful agents are "frozen" for a while, then injected back into the market much later, they do no better than average. The market seems to be impatient, moving on and discovering new strategies that replace earlier ones. There's no evidence yet of market "moods," but there is evidence of GARCH.[45] The presence of GARCH means that there are periods of persistent high volatility in the price series, followed randomly by periods of persistent low volatility. Such phenomena make no sense under an efficient market hypothesis. But in an evolutionary marketplace, prices might continue in a stable pattern for quite some time, until new expectations are discovered that exploit that pattern. Then there'll be very rapid expectational changes. These transform the market itself, causing avalanches of further change. Once again, there's evidence of punctuated equilibria and self-organized criticality. Perhaps that see-sawing action we observe in markets is symptomatic of a system driving itself toward then away from the edge of chaos![46]

If it does, this would be further evidence that markets undergo phase transitions. Observable states look like they're poised between necessity and chance, between the deterministic and the seemingly chaotic, between the simple and the complex. In summing up, Arthur states:

> We can conclude that given sufficient homogeneity of beliefs, the standard equilibrium of the literature is upheld. The market in a sense in this regime is essentially "dead." As the dial of heterogeneity of initial beliefs is turned up, the market undergoes a phase transition and "comes to life." It develops a rich psychology and displays phenomena regarded as anomalies in the standard theory but observed in real markets. The inductive, ecology-of-expectations model we have outlined is by definition an *adaptive linear network*.[47] In its heterogeneous mode it displays complex, pattern-forming, nonstationary behavior. We could therefore rename the two regimes or phases *simple* and *complex*. There's growing evidence suggesting that actual financial markets live within the complex regime.[48]

It seems that market participants are involved in an incessant game of coevolutionary learning. Agent-based simulation experiments like the Santa Fe Artificial Stock Market offer a keyhole through which we can gain useful insights into adaptive behavior. Similar studies by others have also shown that heterogeneous behavior on the part of participants can provide opportunities for making consistent profits, that participants with stable bankrolls appear to have an advantage over those who don't, and that small perturbations can sometimes drastically alter the behavior of the participants.[49] As empirical evidence mounts against the view that markets are efficient, new explanatory approaches like that of the adaptive, boundedly rational investor will gain more credibility. Scaling principles and simulation experiments will play an increasingly important part in this new behavioral revolution. Behavioral experiments in such silicon worlds may even herald a new kind of economics, an experimental economics that relies heavily on agent-based simulation. This new approach to social science is the subject of the final chapter.

eight

Artificial Economics

Truth is much too complicated to allow anything but approximations.

—John von Neumann

Limits to Knowledge

It's hard to let old beliefs go. They're so familiar and comforting that we depend heavily on them for peace of mind. Most of us forget Kant's message that the way the world looks is nothing more than the way we happen to see it through our own particular set of lenses. So it has been in economics. That old set of lenses, still the most popular pair on the block, remains stubbornly homogeneous, static, and linear. But a new set have arrived on the scene. These new lenses are dauntingly heterogeneous, dynamic, and nonlinear.

A pressing need for new lenses has prompted a focus in this book on the less predictable elements underpinning economic change, those chance events that punctuate the calm, deterministic landscape of the classical economic system, propelling it into an uncertain future. I hope I've convinced you that real economies evolve in fits and starts. Calm is merely the precursor of the next storm. These fits and starts contain structure and recurrent pattern. In an evolving economy, morphogenesis and disequilibrium are more often the norm than stasis and equilibrium.

But this is only symptomatic of a more complicated problem. As we've stressed throughout, the real difficulty is that each of us is part of the very economy that we're desperately trying to understand. This has the hallmark of a systems problem. But it's not a classical systems problem, like how a clock "tells the time" or how a car "moves."[1] Clocks and cars are structurally complex, but they're behaviorally simple. Their behavioral simplicity transcends the structural complexity of their intricate parts. An economy, however, is behaviorally complex. Because the "parts" are human agents, they're observers as well as participants, learning from their experiences while contributing to the collective outcome. Playing these dual roles really puts the cat among the pigeons! What people believe affects what happens to the economy, and what happens to the economy affects what people believe. Because each agent's beliefs are affected differently, nobody knows exactly what will happen!

Whenever agents learn from, and react to, the moves of other agents, building a simple predictive model to forecast the collective future is fraught with danger unless the economy is linear. A linear economy obeys the principle of superposition. It's easy to analyze because we can extrapolate our understanding of the agents in isolation. Learning is only weakly interactive, so the economy's behavior is just the sum of the behavior of its constituent parts.

But weakly interactive learning, like that which is associated with repetition of much the same problem, is subject to diminishing returns. We're trapped in the frozen world of stasis. For learning to be truly adaptive, the stimulus situations must themselves be steadily evolving rather than merely repeating conditions. The existence of a recursive, nonlinear feedback loop is the familiar signature of coevolutionary learning. People learn and adapt in response to their *interactive* experiences. In turn, the whole economy reacts and adapts collectively based on the choices that people make. In other words, the behavior of the whole is more than the sum of its parts.

Under strongly interactive conditions, we've seen that collective outcomes can differ from what each agent expected or intended. Unexpected outcomes trigger avalanches of uncertainty, causing each agent to modify his view of the world. As Kant has suggested, nobody can have certain knowledge of things "in themselves." Each of us knows only how things seem to us. If we're privy to only part of the information about the economy, then there are clear limits to what we can know. Each agent's mind sets these limits. When we ask questions about the economy, we're asking about a totality of which we're but a small part. We can never know an economy completely, nor can we see into the minds of all its agents and their idiosyncracies.

From the above, it's pretty clear that knowledge becomes a much fuzzier concept in a coevolutionary economy. If there are definite limits to what we can know, then our ability to reach identical conclusions under similar conditions should not be taken for granted. We're unique products of our uniquely individual experiences. Our personal knowledge is honed by the constructs, models, and predictors that we choose to use to represent it. All of this has to be created, put together over time by us as well as by others in society as a whole. Despite the fact that learning can be strongly interactive, it can also be frustratingly slow, partly because some knowledge stocks are surprisingly resilient to change. They're also surprisingly complex.

In Chapter 2, we mentioned that deductive rationality fails us when we're forced to deal with complicated decision problems. Beyond a certain degree of complicatedness, our rationality is bounded. Even more ominous was the fact that in strongly interactive decision situations, each agent may be forced to guess the behavior of other agents. Suddenly we're all plunged into a world of subjective beliefs, and subjective beliefs about subjective beliefs. Complete, consistent, well-defined premises are impossible under these trying conditions. Deductive reasoning breaks down because the problem has become ill defined.

Whenever deductive reasoning breaks down, human agents tend to resort to inductive reasoning. In other words, we search for patterns.[2] The right-hand side of the brain handles pattern recognition, intuition, sensitivity, and creative insights. By putting a combination of these processes to work, we use perceived patterns to fashion temporary constructs in our mind. These simple constructs fill the gaps in our understanding. They "localize" our decision-making, in the sense that we can do no better than act on the best construct at our disposal. When feedback changes our perceptions, thereby strengthening or weakening our confidence in our current set of constructs, we may decide to discard some and retain others.

We looked at the importance of inductive reasoning in three economic contexts: (1) estimating the periodic demand for a public facility; (2) estimating travel times and costs on a congested highway;

and (3) estimating price movements in financial markets. Each of these examples typifies a broader class of problems that arise in economics.[3] Yet all three possess common features. If there was an obvious model that all agents could use to forecast the outcome, then a deductive solution would be possible. But no such model has been found to date. Irrespective of recent history, a wide range of plausible hypotheses could be adopted to predict future behavior. This multiplicity of possibilities means that nobody can choose their own strategy in a well-defined manner. Each problem is ill defined, and the agents involved are catapulted into an uncertain world. Thus they're forced to resort to intuition and other inductive modes of reasoning.

There's an even more diabolical dimension to each of these problems: Any shared expectations will tend to be broken up. For example, if all of our bar lovers believe that most will go to the El Farol next Thursday night, then nobody will go. But by all staying home, that common belief will be destroyed immediately. If all of our peak-hour commuters believe that most drivers will choose to commute at peak hour, then most explorers will search for ways to avoid peak-hour congestion. On the other hand, if all believe few will do this, then all will commute at peak hour, thereby undermining that belief. Not only do expectations differ, but they're also changing incessantly. Adaptive agents, who persistently alter their mental models of other agents' behavior, will decide and behave differently.[4] They're forever changing their mental images of each other's likely behavior. Beliefs about beliefs are mostly volatile. There's no evidence to suggest that adaptive behavior ever settles down into a steady, predictable pattern.

Adaptive Agents and the Science of Surprise

The key to understanding adaptive behavior lies with explanation rather than prediction. When economic agents interact, when they must think about what other agents may or may not be thinking, their coevolving behavior can take a variety of forms. Sometimes it may look chaotic, sometimes it may appear to be ordered, but more often than not it will lie somewhere in between. At one end of the spectrum, chaotic behavior would correspond to rapidly changing models of other agents' beliefs. If beliefs change too quickly, however, there may be no clear pattern at all. Such a volatile state could simply appear to be random. At the other end of the spectrum, ordered behavior could emerge, but only if the ocean of beliefs happens to converge onto a mutually consistent set of models of one another. One familiar example is that stalwart of the economic theorist's world—a state of equilibrium among a set of deductively rational agents.

For most of the time, however, we'd expect that mental models of each other's beliefs would lie somewhere in between these two extremes, poised and ready to unleash avalanches of many small and a few large changes throughout the whole population of inter-acting agents. Why should we expect this? The plentiful evidence supporting the ubiquitous applicability of power laws is one reason. Given more data, we would expect each agent to improve his ability to generalize about the other agents' behavior by construct-ing *more complex* models of their behavior. These more complex models would also be more sensitive to small alterations in the other agents' behavior. Thus as agents develop more complex models to better predict outcomes, the coevolving system of agents tends to be driven away from the ordered regime toward the chaotic regime. Near the chaotic regime, however, such complexity and changeability would leave each agent with very little reliable data about the other agents' behavior. Thus they would be forced to simplify, to build less complex models of the other agents' be-havior. Such simplified models can succeed in calmer times.

Economic enigmas—like the periodic demand for public facili-ties, for road space, or for financial instruments—have several key features in common. Each contains the essential elements of a com-plex adaptive system (CAS). A CAS possesses three important at-tributes. First, it involves a large (but not infinite) number of agents. Second, these agents are adaptive and intelligent, making decisions on the basis of mental models (like travel time predictors or financial models), which they modify in the light of their experi-ences and replace with new ones if necessary. Finally, no single agent knows what all the other agents are (thinking of) doing, be-cause each has access to only a limited amount of information.

The upshot of all this is that there's no optimal predictor in a CAS. The best each agent can do is apply the predictor that has worked best so far, be willing to reevaluate the effectiveness of his favorite predictor, and adopt more convincing ones as new information becomes available. An agent's active predictor may be the most plausible or most profitable one at the time. But the total population of active predictors coevolves incessantly. As we've stressed repeatedly, coevolutionary learning means that the total population of active predictors determines the outcome, but the outcome history also shapes the total population of active predictors.

One of the difficulties with a CAS is that nobody really knows the total population of active predictors at any point in time. Because it's impossible to formulate a closed-form model to deduce future outcomes, traditional economic models fail in this environment. In John Holland's terminology, the population of predictors forms an ecology. If we want to understand how this ecology might evolve over time, we're forced to resort to simulation experiments. Simulation doesn't simplify the economy, but incorporates as much detail as necessary to produce emergent behavior. There's simply no other way of accommodating such a large, ever-changing population of active predictors.

The defining characteristic of a CAS is that some of its global behaviors cannot be predicted simply from knowledge of the underlying interactions.[5] In previous chapters we explored emergence. An emergent phenomenon was defined as collective behavior that doesn't seem to have any clear explanation in terms of its microscopic parts. What does this kind of emergent simplicity tell us? It tells us that an economic system of interacting agents (like urban residents, bar attendees, traffic commuters, or traders in a financial market) can spontaneously develop collective properties that are not at all obvious from our knowledge of the agents themselves. These statistical regularities are large-scale features that emerge purely from the microdynamics. They signify order despite change. Sometimes, they display self-similarity at different scales.

Furthermore, the laws governing economic change can't be understood by limiting our study to a single human lifetime or a few generations. A deeper understanding of how the economy coevolves can be gained only by adopting a long-term perspective. Only then can we see that the best thing to do—to move or not to move, to go or not to go, to commute or not to commute, to buy or to sell—really depends on what everyone else is doing. But since no individual agent knows what everyone else will do, all he can do is apply the set of predictors that has worked best for him so far.

Since the study of CAS, with changing patterns of interactions between adaptive agents, often gets too difficult for a mathematical solution, finding a new way of doing social science has become imperative. We might call the new kid on the block the science of "surprise." This kind of science is gradually gaining ground, as various social scientists enlist their computers as laboratories for social science experiments. The primary research tool in this new field is simulation.

The simulation of agents and their interactions goes by different names: agent-based modeling, bottom-up modeling, and artificial social systems, to name a few. What's crystal clear, however, is its purpose. Agent-based simulation attempts to gain a deeper understanding of CAS through the analysis of simulations. As Robert Axelrod suggests, this new method of doing social science can be contrasted with the two standard methods discussed throughout this book: deduction and induction. Like deduction, it starts with a set of explicit assumptions. But unlike deduction, it does not prove theorems. Instead, an agent-based model generates simulated data that can be analyzed inductively. The simulated data come from a rigorously specified set of rules rather than from direct measurement of the real world.[6] Whereas the aim of induction is to discern patterns in data, and that of deduction is to discover consequences of assumptions, the aim of agent-based modeling is to enhance our intuition.

Numerous examples and experiments presented throughout this book have shown how locally interacting agents can produce surprising, large-scale effects. Agent-based simulation is a rigorous way of conducting such "thought experiments." The assumptions are often simple, but the full consequences are rarely obvious. We have referred to the large-scale effects of locally interacting agents as emergent properties. Emergent properties seem surprising because it can be difficult to anticipate the consequences of even very simple forms of interaction. In an economy, for example, emergent properties arise from seemingly simple interactions between agents engaged in the business of exchange. Congestion and market volatility are two unwelcome emergent properties of such socioeconomic interactions.

A Harvard systems scientist, Vince Darley, has argued that emergence is purely the result of a phase change in the amount of computation necessary for the optimal prediction of certain phenomena.[7] Imagine that $s(n)$ denotes the amount of computation required to simulate a system of size n and arrive at a prediction of the given phenomenon. Further imagine that $u(n)$ is the amount of computation needed to arrive at the same result by way of a creative analysis—founded, for example, on a deeper understanding of the system. Darley suggests that if $u(n) < s(n)$, the system is nonemergent, but if $u(n) > s(n)$, the system is emergent.

We can visualize Darley's phase change in the context of traffic congestion. In Chapter 6, we discussed dynamic jamming transitions. Remember how they transform the traffic from a free-flowing state to stop-start waves at a critical traffic density. As long as the density of vehicles remains below this critical threshold, it's rather easy to estimate individual travel times. They're roughly the same for each driver, and variations between vehicles are small. Experience engenders reliable predictions. We can deduce the outcome readily from our understanding of the system's performance as a whole. We can do this because the behavior of this simple system is easily understandable. There's no need to carry out a detailed simulation of it to arrive at a travel time prediction. In light traffic, obviously $u(n) < s(n)$, and the traffic system is nonemergent.

Once the critical density is exceeded, however, travel time predictability quickly starts to fade. As discussed earlier, the traffic can change from a regime where the travel time is predictable with an error rate of 3 percent to a regime where the error rate climbs to 65 percent or higher. There's a critical region around maximal capacity where the traffic as a whole is very sensitive to small perturbations. This emergent phase transition in the traffic's collective behavior results in a much greater spread of individual travel times. The business of predicting your own travel time suddenly becomes much more challenging. Under heavily congested conditions, perfect understanding of the system is replaced by a bemuddled picture of what's happening. In this emergent situation, $u(n) > s(n)$. Under these conditions, we must resort to simulation if we wish to improve our understanding of the way the traffic behaves collectively.

The surprising thing about self-organization is that it can transform a seemingly simple, incoherent system (e.g., light traffic) into an ordered, coherent whole (a strongly interactive traffic jam). Adding a few more vehicles at a crucial stage transforms the system from a state in which the individual vehicles follow their own local dynamics to a critical state where the emergent dynamics are global. This involves a phase transition of an unusual kind: a nonequilibrium phase transition. Space scales change suddenly from microscopic to macroscopic. A new organizing mechanism, not restricted to local interactions, has taken over. Occasional jamming transitions will even span the whole vehicle population, because the traffic has become a complex system with its own emergent dynamics. What's most important is that the emergence of stop-start waves and jams, with widely varying populations of affected vehicles, could not have been anticipated from the properties of the individual drivers or their vehicles.

As the size and rule complexity of many classes of socioeconomic system changes, various phase changes can occur when the curves u(n) and s(n) cross (see Figure 8.1). Darley argues that there's no discontinuity separating nonemergent and emergent systems, just a phase change in the optimal means of prediction. Beyond this, perfect understanding of the system does no better than a simulation. Our astonishment at the fact that we seem unable to predict emergent properties does not stem from any inability to understand but from the inherent properties of the system attributable to the accumulation of interactions. As systems become more emergent, the propagation of information through accumulated interaction will blur the boundaries of any analysis that we try to perform. All useful predictive knowledge is contained in the accumulation of interactions.

The advantage of an agent-based approach to any CAS is that the system's dynamics are generated by way of the simulation. Interactions can accumulate, multiple pathways can be recognized, and emergent properties can be revealed, all without making any ad hoc assumptions or aggregated models for these properties. The major disadvantages of simulation are the extremely high computational demands and the fact that it may not always lead to a better understanding of the basic mechanisms that caused the

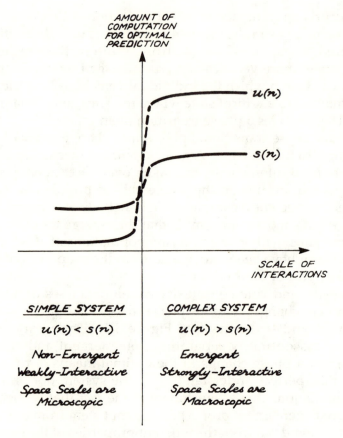

FIGURE 8.1   A phase change between nonemergent and emergent systems.

dynamics. Although the inherent dynamics are revealed, they're not always explained.

The fact that a given system lies far beyond the realms of deductive reasoning does not necessarily mean that we should lose all faith in our traditional means of comprehension, explanation, and prediction. Consider the game of chess, first discussed in Chapter 2. Modern computer chess programs use extremely sophisticated, brute force approaches to simulate the game and decide on moves. By way of contrast, human grand masters use a subtle combination of pattern recognition, generalization, and analogy making to "understand" the game and make their decisions. In this instance, the phase change where the curves u(n) and s(n) cross is at such a value that humans can still boast superiority at determining such elusive concepts as positional advantage.[8] But the computer is rapidly bridging such gaps.

Many scientists now believe that chess lies on the emergent side of the phase boundary, so much so that solution by simulation is ultimately the best approach. However, human experience and understanding can often do surprisingly well, despite all the limits of knowledge and reasoning. Perhaps a sophisticated combination of both approaches may be the best bet for predicting the behavior of a CAS. The brain itself is an extremely complex system, one whose functioning would appear to lie far beyond the phase change. Our state of mind seems to be an emergent property of our brains, more mysterious than the motion of a car because we can't see the mental wheels going around. A human mind is a process, not a thing, emerging from the collective interactions of appropriately organized bits of ordinary matter. This has very important ramifications for the youthful field of artificial life.[9] We look at some of the economic ramifications of these exciting new developments in the next section.

The New Age of Artificial Economics

There's no universally agreed upon definition of economic activity. Classical economics texts place most of their emphasis on exchange processes, such as trade between producers and consumers. In other words, they emphasize transactions between agents. In this book, our emphasis has not been on the transactional character of economic interactions but on the dynamic, learning aspects. Why? Because the adaptive behavior of human agents makes a dynamic approach obligatory. Human learning means that economies are not just transactional systems to be analyzed as if they're simply part of a giant accounting system. Instead, economies should be treated as something very much "alive."

Traditionally, the scientific study of life has been restricted to biology. But some economists have recognized the nexus between biology and economics. It was Alfred Marshall who contended that biology, not mechanics, is the true Mecca of economics.[10] Economics should be a branch of biology concerned with the study of socioeconomic life. That makes it cultural and dynamic, not purely financial and transactional. Economics must embrace a cluster of properties associated with life in general: self-organization, emergence, growth, development, reproduction, evolution, coevolution, adaptation, and morphogenesis.[11]

Above all, economic development depends crucially on path-dependent principles of self-organization and coevolution, unfamiliar processes that have remained largely untouched by traditional analytical tools. The challenge is to create a bottom-up approach, a *synthetic* methodology in which the behavior of agents is examined in each other's presence. Its pursuit lies at the heart of agent-based simulation. The collective behavior that results from such an approach can be radically different to that posited from studies of agents in isolation.

The time seems ripe for a radically new approach to economics. We might call it *artificial economics!* Like its mentor and predecessor, artificial life, this new field of artificial economics (AE) would adopt a synthetic approach. Instead of taking economies apart, piece by piece, AE would attempt to put economies together in a coevolutionary environment. Its primary aim would be to link economic macrostructure to agents' microeconomic behavior in a consistent, path-dependent manner. We might even find that such a synthetic approach could lead us beyond known economic phenomena: beyond *economic-life-as-we-know-it* and into the less familiar world of *economic-life-as-it-could-be.*[12]

Instead of those stubbornly homogeneous agents who dominate the classical economist's world, AE would concern itself with a rich diversity of agents generating *lifelike* economic behavior. To produce lifelike economic outcomes, AE would create diverse *behavior generators*. This problem is partly psychological and partly computational. We've discussed behavior generators in earlier chapters, under the guise of constructs, predictors, and mental models. Many of the mechanisms by which economic reasoning and behavior arises are known. There are still some gaps in our knowledge, but the general picture is falling into place. Like nature, an economy is fundamentally parallel. Thus AE can start by recapturing economic life as if it's *fundamentally and massively paral-*

lel.[13] If our models are to be true to economic life, they must also be highly distributed and massively parallel.

AE would be concerned with the synthetic application of computers to the study of complex, economic phenomena. This doesn't mean that the computational paradigm would be the underlying methodology of behavior generation.[14] Nor would AE seek to explain economic life as a kind of computer program. Instead, for example, it might use insights from evolutionary biology and human psychology to explore the dynamics of interacting agents and the resulting collective economic outcomes. This was the synthetic approach in the El Farol problem. Artificial music lovers were assigned different sets of predictors to aid in their decisionmaking. If the ecology of active predictors is suitably diverse, it's likely that it would mimic the diverse approaches of an assortment of real music lovers. The same may be said of artificial commuters and artificial investors.

In the days before computers, economists worked primarily with systems whose defining equations could be solved analytically. For obvious reasons, they politely ignored those whose defining equations could *not* be solved. This has led to gross approximations, sometimes even to gross misrepresentations! With the advent of computers, however, mundane calculations can be handled routinely. Agent-based simulation allows one to explore an economic system's behavior under a wide range of parameter settings and conditions. The heuristic value of this kind of experimentation cannot be overestimated. One gains much richer insights into the potential dynamics of an economy by observing the behavior of its agents under many different conditions. Let's look briefly at a product of this new age of artificial economics: the evolution of an artificial society of agents, initially engaged in some relatively primitive economic activity.

Growing a Silicon Society

It has been said that the ultimate goal of the social sciences is to discover laws of cultural dynamics. Economic development in the very long run must play a part in this scientific exercise. The problem is that most economic analyses focus on the short to medium run. Furthermore, what economists typically regard as the long run is only a relatively short-run movement from the perspective of archaeologists. For the latter, a generation or even a century is a relatively short period. Archaeologists tend to think in terms of millennia when considering changes in human culture.

Archaeology can help economics because the field has gleaned a reasonably clear picture of socioeconomic development in the very long run. In terms of broad epochs, that development has taken us from the epoch of hunting and gathering to horticultural settlements and complex, nonliterate societies, then to the historical epoch of urban civilization, household agriculture, and trading empires, and more recently to the industrialized economy.[15] There's plenty of evidence suggesting that we're currently in the midst of another major transition to a new epoch of postindustrialization, largely associated with the advent of a knowledge-based economy and increasingly sophisticated information-processing devices.

Sometimes the transition between epochs seems to have been smooth, but on other occasions there's evidence of crises and abrupt upheavals prior to the successful adoption of a new regime. Much of the archaeological evidence supports the notion of a series of punctuated equilibria, as discussed in earlier chapters. Examples even exist where a rapid collapse and reversion to a previous regime has occurred. In some well-known cases of relatively isolated cultures, the socioeconomic process seems to have stuck in a more or less stationary or fluctuating state for a very long time. All these documented examples provide convincing evidence in support of the multiplicity of outcomes that are possible as the economic agents in a society coevolve.

One of the more baffling cultures to have challenged the minds of archaeologists is that of the Anasazi Indians. The earliest settlement built by this Native American culture dates from A.D. 100, but nobody seems to know where they lived before they set up house in northeastern Arizona. What is known is that over a period of 1,200 years, the Anasazi established a flourishing culture of villages, shrines, and farms. They enjoyed a golden age of more than a hundred years toward the end of the thirteenth century. Then, quite suddenly, they abandoned their elaborate dwellings and fertile farmland and traveled southeast to the Rio Grande and to Arizona's White Mountains. No one seems to know why the Indians abandoned the place that had been their fertile home for more than a thousand years. But after the exodus, the number of Anasazi dwindled to a third of what it was in its heyday. Today only a few remnants of their culture have survived, such as their pottery and agriculture. Most of their ancient history has been lost.

But now the Indians have been brought back to "life." This ancient tribe has been resurrected, and their native landscape is once again dotted with Anasazi settlements. The big difference on this occasion is that each Anasazi community is actually a colored zone on a grid that sits inside the memory of a Macintosh computer. In a broader sense, this artificial society consists of two main elements: a population of "agents" (like the Anasazi), and an environment in which these agents "live." This two-level, silicon world is the joint brainchild of Joshua Epstein and Robert Axtell, two researchers at the Brookings Institution in Washington, D.C.

Epstein and Axtell set out to "grow" a social order from scratch, by creating an ever-changing environment and a set of agents who interact with each other and their environment according to a set of behavioral rules. History is said to be an experience that's run only once. Clearly Epstein and Axtell don't hold with that view. Their idea is that an entire society like the Anasazi—complete with its own production, trade, and culture—could be "recreated" or evolved from the interactions among the agents. As Epstein suggests, "You don't solve it, you evolve it." They call the laboratory in which they conduct their simulation experiments a Compu-Terrarium, and the landscape that the interacting agents inhabit a Sugarscape.16 Let's take a closer look at how socioeconomic life develops in this artificial world.

The action takes place on a small grid of fifty-by-fifty cells. But Sugarscape is not a pure CA. The landscape denoted by this grid is not blank, as it is on a typical CA. On it is scattered this silicon world's only resource: sugar. In order to survive, the entities that inhabit this sweetened landscape must find and eat the sugar. The entities themselves are not just cells that can be turned on or off, mimicking life or death. Each is an agent that is imbued with a variety of attributes and abilities. Epstein and Axtell call these internal states and behavioral rules. Some states are fixed for the agent's life, whereas others change through interaction with other agents or with the environment. For example, an agent's sex, metabolic rate, and vision are hard-wired for life. But individual preferences, wealth, cultural identity, and health can all change as agents move around and interact.

Although every interacting agent appears on the grid as a colored dot, each may be quite different. Some are farsighted, spotting sugar from afar. Others are thrifty, burning the sugar they eat so slowly that each meal lasts an eternity. Still others are shortsighted or wasteful. Rapacious consumers eat their sugar too quickly. The obvious advantage of this heterogeneity is that it's capable of mimicking (albeit simplistically) the rich diversity of human populations in terms of their preferences and physiological needs. Any agent that can't find enough sugar to sustain its search must face that ultimate equilibrium state. It simply dies!

Sugarscape resembles a traditional CA in its retention of rules. There are rules of behavior for the agents and for the environmental sites (i.e., the cells) that they occupy. Rules are kept simple and are no more than the commonsense ones for survival and reproduction. For example, a simple movement rule might be: *Look around as far as you can, find the nearest location containing sugar, go there, eat as much as you need to maintain your metabolism, save the rest.* Epstein and Axtell speak of this as an agent-environment rule. A rule for reproduction might be: *Breed only if you've accumulated sufficient energy and sugar.* Also, there are rules governing socioeconomic behavior, such as: *Retain your current cultural identity (e.g., consumer preferences) unless you see that you're surrounded by many agents of a different kind; if you are, change your identity to fit in with your neighbors or try to find a culture like your own.* This rule smacks of Schelling's segregation model, because it highlights coevolutionary possibilities among nearby neighbors.

The CompuTerrarium leaps into action when hundreds of agents are unleashed randomly onto the grid. Colored dots distinguish agents who can spy sugar easily from more myopic agents. Naturally, all the agents rush toward the sugar. The latter may be piled into two or more huge heaps or scattered more evenly throughout the landscape. Strikingly, many agents tend to "stick" to their own terrace, adjacent to their "birthplace." Because natural selection tends to favor those agents with good eyesight and a low metabolic rate, they survive and prosper at the expense of the shortsighted, rapacious consumers. In short, the ecological principle of carrying capacity quickly becomes evident. Soon the landscape is covered entirely with red dots (high-vision agents).

Even with relatively simple rules, fascinating things start to happen as soon as the agents begin to interact on the Sugarscape. For example, when seasons are introduced and sugar concentrations change periodically over time, high-vision agents migrate. But low vision, low metabolism agents prefer to hibernate. Agents with low vision and high metabolism usually die, because they're selected against.

All of the time, the surviving artificial agents are accumulating wealth (i.e., sugar). Thus there's an emergent wealth distribution on the Sugarscape. Herein lies the first topic of particular interest to economists. Will the overall wealth be distributed equally, or will agents self-organize into a Pareto distribution? In other words, will equity prevail or will the ubiquity of power laws prevail again? No doubt you've guessed already. Although quite symmetrical at the start, the wealth histogram on the Sugarscape ends up highly skewed. Because such skewed distributions turn up under a wide range of agent and environment conditions, they resemble an emergent structure—a stable macroscopic pattern induced by the local interaction of agents. Self-organization is on the job as usual, and the power law wins out again!

Although these few examples are a useful way of illustrating the variety of artificial life evolvable inside the CompuTerrarium, they hardly herald an impending revolution in our understanding of how an economy evolves. For that we must expand the behavioral repertoire of our agents, allowing us to study more complex socioeconomic phenomena. Epstein and Axtell have made a start on this expansion. When a second commodity, spice, is added to the landscape, a primitive trading economy emerges. By portraying trade as welfare-improving barter between agents, reminiscent of those Merchants of Venice that we met in Chapter 4, they implement a trading rule of the form: *Look around for a neighbor with a commodity you desire, bargain with that neighbor until you agree on a mutually acceptable price, then make an exchange if both of you will be better off.*

Surprisingly, this primitive exchange economy allows us to test the credentials of that classical theory of market behavior: the efficient market hypothesis. The first stage of the test involves imbuing agents with attributes consistent with neoclassical economic wisdom—homogeneous preferences and infinite lifespans for processing information. Under these conditions, an equilibrium price is approached. But this equilibrium is not the general equilibrium price of neoclassical theory. It's *statistical* in nature. Furthermore, the resulting resource allocations, though locally optimal, don't deliver the expected global optimum. There remain additional gains from trade that the agents can't extract. What we find is that two competing processes—exchange and production—yield an economy that's perpetually out of equilibrium.

Once we imbue agents with human qualities—like finite lives, the ability to reproduce sexually, and the ability to change preferences—the trading price never settles down to a single level. It keeps swinging between highs and lows, very much like price oscillations in real markets (as discussed in the previous chapter). Basically, it appears to be a random distribution. But it turns out that there's structure after all! Although the seemingly random price fluctuations continue indefinitely, the fluctuations appear to be variations from an identifiable price level. This particular price just happens to be the same equilibrium level as the one attained under those all-too-unrealistic assumptions underpinning the efficient market hypothesis. Thus we gain the distinct impression that any equilibrium state associated with the efficient market hypothesis is nothing more than a limiting case among a rich panorama of possible states that may arise in the marketplace. As Epstein suggests, "If the agents aren't textbook agents—if they look a little bit human—there is no reason to assume markets will perform the way economic textbooks tell us they should."

How is the distribution of wealth affected by trade? It turns out that the overall effect of trade is to further skew the Sugarscape's distribution of wealth. By increasing the carrying capacity and allowing more agents to survive, trade magnifies differences in wealth. Trade increases the interactions between agents, thereby strengthening the power law fit even further. Experiments with a wider set of choice possibilities endorsed the view that it's devilishly difficult to find conditions under which a society's wealth ends up being evenly distributed. We may conclude that there's a definite trade-off between economic equality and economic performance. This bears a striking qualitative similarity to findings in various economies around the world.

There's so much more to say about the socioeconomic laboratory constructed by Epstein and Axtell. When agents can enter into credit relationships, for example, some turn out to be borrowers and lenders simultaneously. This is of fundamental importance for economic evolution. Many other issues—such as the emergence of cultural groups, webs of economic intercourse, social clusters, institutional structures, and disease—can all be scrutinized under the Sugarscape microscope. The pair of researchers are now working to extend the Sugarscape in order to capture the way of human life in the late twentieth century. Thus far, the agents have sex but there are no families, no cities, no firms, and no government. Over the next few years, they hope to produce conditions under which all of these things emerge spontaneously. As life on the Sugarscape is in its infancy at present, who's to say what might happen in time?

Sugarscape is an important example of agent-based simulation for several reasons. First, although economists and other social scientists study society, they do so in isolation. Economists, geographers, psychologists, and archaeologists rarely interact meaningfully or pool the knowledge they've accumulated. The organization of university departments further endorses this regrettable divide. Yet life on the Sugarscape brings all these narrow views together, broadening our understanding in a meaningful way. Second, Sugarscape activities are interactive and dynamic. Thus it's far more process-dependent than classical models. Third, Sugarscape recognizes and preserves differences in culture and skills that human populations exhibit. Finally, for the first time in history, the social sciences have the opportunity to conduct and repeat experiments and test hypotheses concerning socioeconomic behavior. Sugarscape typifies this new way of doing social science as we enter the unprecedented era of artificial economics. So if your business is modeling economic behavior, it's an excellent starting point for rule-based simulation experiments.

Some Final Words

Like it or not, computers have handed scientists a new paradigm for understanding the ways of the world. With the incredible drop in the cost of computing power, computers are now capable of simulating many physical systems from first principles. For example, it's now possible to model turbulent flow in a fluid by simulating the motions of its constituent particles—not just approximating changes in concentrations of particles at particular points, but actually computing their motions exactly. But such advances may not be unique to the physical world. It may not be so long before we can model the turbulence observed in financial markets in much the same way.

Agent-based simulation models like Sugarscape, TRANSIMS, and the Santa Fe Artificial Stock Market have shown us that complex behavior need not have complex origins. Some of the complex behavior exhibited collectively by economic agents, for example, may come from relatively simple predictors. Other emergent behavior may be attributable to predictors that differ in terms of the time horizons over which they're applied. Since it's hard to work backward from a complex outcome to its generator(s), but far simpler to create and test many different generators and thus synthesize complex behavior, a promising approach to the study of complex economic systems is to undertake a general study of the kinds of collective outcomes that can emerge from different sets of predictors as behavior generators.[17] As we've stressed already, most work of this kind must be done by simulation experiments.

There are many exciting new efforts underway that attempt to replicate inside the computer the rich diversity of socioeconomic life. We've discussed a few of these in this book. Sadly, space has precluded discussion of them all. The common feature of these experiments is that the main behaviors of interest are properties of the *interactions between agents*, rather than the agents themselves. Accumulations of interactions constitute the fundamental parts of nonlinear economic systems. They're the *virtual parts* of an economy, which depend on nonlinear interactions between human agents for their very existence. If we choose to isolate the agents, then the virtual parts disappear. If we choose to aggregate the agents, then the virtual parts disappear. Artificial economics is seeking the virtual parts of an economy. The goal is *synthesis* rather than *analysis.* In this quest, synthesis by simulation is the primary methodological tool, and the computer is the scientific laboratory.

Like nature, economies coevolve incessantly. They add and subtract mechanisms, components, and interactions over time. They're just as alive as any biological organism. Their unique quality is an evolutionary drive that selects for human agents with an ability to learn and adapt rather than for those choosing optimal behavior. Because economic diversity springs from the heterogeneity of human learning and creativity, economic evolution may be subject to the "Baldwin effect."[18] The importance of adaptive learning shows up more clearly when the economy is viewed in a long-run perspective. Learning and adaptation should not be addenda to the central theory of economics. They should be right at its core in strongly interactive environments of high complexity.

As interactions grow, the natural trend of human progress is toward the more complex. In fact, it is the very complexity of economic reality that makes the analysis of interactions so helpful as an aid to better understanding. But the path of progress is not a smooth curve, and never will be, unless human nature is somehow repealed. It's a very haphazard path, straight enough for much of the time, but boasting tortuous twists and turns at unexpected times. Economic progress looks like a series of punctuated equilibria. So does the path of environmental quality. Because the interactions between agents in an economy can produce robust, self-organized dynamic equilibria, the frequency of disturbances from this critical state may obey a power law distribution with respect to size. Power law distributions seem to be ubiquitous in nature and human societies. Thus we shouldn't be surprised by occasional large fluctuations. Archaeologists never are. Very big changes are part of a frequency distribution that reflects many more small changes alongside fewer large changes.

In the preceding chapters, we've looked at how positive feedback economies (and their parts) can self-organize. Self-organization in a complex economy results from a set of agents, driven by their own behavioral biases, interacting to produce and reinforce unexpected collective outcomes. The goals, strategies, ethics, and understanding of these agents fashion the collective behavior that emerges, which in turn forces each agent to react and adapt differently. Sometimes something new emerges and a different regime takes over. Future expectations and decision strategies change accordingly. So do future collective outcomes.

If nothing else, an appreciation of power laws, adaptive learning, and self-organization teaches us humility. Perhaps science is revealing our own limitations. Understanding that we can't know everything is a crucial step in the quest for wisdom. Our inability to predict can be soothed by a growing ability to adapt and co-evolve harmoniously—just like we find in nature. We live in a world full of remarkable emergence and diversity. History matters. We can't be sure where we're going next, but fortunately we're getting to know some of the rules by which the game is being played. What's most reassuring is that sometimes we seem to get something for nothing—emergent order on this never-ending road to know-ware.

Notes

Chapter One

1. Krugman presents some enjoyable anecdotes about economic sense and nonsense in the political economy of the last few decades in the United States. For a closer look at why our expectations have diminished, see Krugman (1994b, 1994c).

2. A typical example of policy entrepreneurship was the spurious "supply-side economics," which proliferated during Ronald Reagan's term of presidency.

3. See Krugman (1994c), page xi.

4. Krugman is certainly not alone in this belief. Another of like mind is Herbert Simon, who has argued that the seemingly "soft" social sciences are really "hard" (i.e., difficult); see Simon (1987).

5. See Samuelson (1976), page 10.

6. For an entertaining summary of the arguments both for and against the contention that no objective reality exists independent of an observer, see Casti (1989, Chapter 7).

7. The term "stasis" is an abbreviated form of the word "morphostasis," a group of negative feedback processes studied in cybernetics. Since its inception, cybernetics has been more or less regarded as the science of self-regulating and equilibrating systems. But its scope turns out to be broader, as we'll learn in Chapters 2 and 3.

8. This simple analogy was suggested by the physicist Per Bak. For an unconventional look at the boundary between the natural world and the social sciences, see Bak (1996, especially Chapter 11).

9. Tank A can be thought of as "selling" thirty liters of water to Tank B. In this abstract case, the "selling" price would need to cover the price of the pipe.

10. In 1972, Hugo Sonnenschein surprised many mathematical economists by showing that the rule of price adjustment arising from a given set of agent preferences and endowments can literally be *any* rule you like. More importantly, it need not be the kind of rule that leads to one of Adam Smith's invisible-hand equilibria. In view of this result, a static equilibrium becomes a very unlikely state of economic affairs. For a discussion of Sonnenschein's result, as well as some other paradoxical aspects of economic processes, see Saari (1995).

11. For the technically-minded, a *fixed-point* attractor contains only one state; a *periodic* attractor set is a sequence of states periodically occupied by the system at each iteration; a *chaotic* attractor doesn't show any simple geometrical structure, but is often fractal, and is such that the sequence of states depends sensitively on the initial state.

12. See Nicolis and Prigogine (1989), page 3.

13. Archaeologists think in terms of millennia instead of merely generations or centuries. Thus they know that economies can collapse rapidly and revert to a more primitive regime. In relatively isolated cultures, the socioeconomic process can also become trapped in a more or less stationary or fluctuating state for a very long time. A simulated example of this kind of socioeconomic dynamics is discussed in Chapter 8. Another unusual model describing socioeconomic evolution in the very long run can be found in Day and Walter (1995).

14. See Monod (1971), page 118.

15. See Bak (1996).

16. The effects of friction in economics have been at the core of distribution and welfare issues for more than a century. For a review of such frictional effects, see Griffin (1998). Other chapters in the same book also highlight the importance of friction; see Åkerman (1998).

17. See Kauffman (1995), page 209.

18. Schelling's ideas on complexity and self-organization can be found in a book titled *Micromotives and Macrobehavior.* Krugman suggests that the first chapter of this book is "surely the best essay on what economic analysis is about, on the nature of economic reasoning, that has ever been written" (Krugman 1996, page 16). The two chapters on "sorting and mixing" provide an excellent, nonmathematical introduction to the idea of self-organization in economics. See Schelling (1978) for the original material and Krugman's book for a modern interpretation.

19. An equivalent way of stating this rule is that each individual is satisfied as long as at least 37 percent of his or her neighbors are of his or her type.

20. This layout is one of a number of possibilities, since the order in which individuals move remains unspecified. The final outcome will also be sensitive to the initial conditions (as depicted in Figure 1.4b). As Schelling noted, repeating the experiment several times will produce slightly different configurations, but an emergent pattern of segregation will be obvious each time.

21. The notion of phase transitions has its roots in the physical sciences, but its relevance to economic evolution has been recognized recently. In the social sciences, phase transitions are difficult to grasp because the *qualitative* changes are hard to see. Far more transparent is the effect of temperature changes on water. As a liquid, water is a state of matter in which the molecules move in all possible directions, mostly without recognizing each other. When we lower its temperature below freezing point, however, it changes to a crystal lattice—a new solid phase of matter. Suddenly, its properties are no longer identical in all directions. The translational symmetry characterizing the liquid has been broken. This type of change is known as an equilibrium phase transition. Recent advances in systems theory, especially studies led by Ilya Prigogine and the Brussels school of thermodynamicists, have discovered a new class of phase transitions—one in which the lowering of temperature is replaced by the progressively intensifying application of nonequilibrium constraints. These nonequilibrium phase transitions are the ones associated with the process of self-organization. See, for example, Nicolis and Prigogine (1977, 1989).

22. See von Neumann (1966).

23. In later chapters, I discuss various examples of cellular automata that have been used to sharpen our intuition about socioeconomic behavior through computer simulation. Schelling's model is not strictly a cellular automaton, since it allows agents to migrate from one cell to another. The interested reader can find a cellular automaton defined and applied to urban dynamics in Chapter 5.

24. In a delightful book about fractals, chaos, and power laws, Manfred Schroeder reviews the abundance and significance of power laws in nature and human life; see Schroeder (1991).

25. See Pareto (1896).

26. See Eldredge and Gould (1972).

27. In Ray's experimental world, which he calls *Tierra* (the Spanish word for Earth), self-reproducing programs compete for CPU time and memory. These programs show all of the evolutionary splendor that we have come to admire in the natural world. For further details of this digital life, which takes place inside a computer, see Ray (1992).

28. See Kuhn (1962).

29. See Schumpeter (1942), page 83, footnote 2.

30. This hypothesis was not widely appreciated at the time, since it appeared in his doctoral dissertation on price fluctuations in the Paris bond market; see Bachelier (1900).

31. See, for example, Brock, Hsieh, and LeBaron (1991).

32. See, for example, Shiller (1981, 1989).

33. Two admirable summaries of recent findings in the ongoing search for chaos in financial markets can be found in Brock, Hsieh, and LeBaron (1991) and Benhabib (1992).

34. For an overview of Elliott's wave principle, see Frost and Prechter (1985).

35. Mandelbrot suggests that most scientists did not expect to encounter power-law distributions and thus were unwilling to acknowledge their existence. An account of his work on cotton prices appears in Mandelbrot (1963). For a fuller account of his work on fractals and scaling in finance, see Mandelbrot (1997).

36. Mandelbrot refers to the power-law distribution as the scaling distribution.

37. Critics of economic theory see this "stable, closed-world" model as a vast abstraction from reality. For example, Daniel Bell regards it as a convenient utopia dreamt up by John Locke and Adam Smith. He points to the need for studies of human behavior, the codification of theoretical knowledge, and the influence of time and history. Clearly, many economists have begun to realize that they cannot afford to ignore the nature and relentless pace of social and technological change. For a blunt view of what's been wrong with economics for some time, see Bell (1981).

38. See Maruyama (1963).

39. See Arthur (1994b).

40. See Allen and Sanglier (1981) and Arthur (1994b).

41. See Arrow (1962).

42. See Arthur (1994b), page 50.

43. This conjecture seems to be turning into a serious hypothesis. To gain an accurate picture of urban development, for example, Peter Allen and Michele

Sanglier have demonstrated that a dynamic model of a central place system must consider the self-organizing aspects of urban evolution; see Allen and Sanglier (1979, 1981). Although the monopolistically competitive general equilibrium model formulated by Paul Krugman demonstrated that the process of city formation is one of cumulative causation (i.e., positive feedback), he found that the eventual locations of cities tend to have a roughly central-place pattern; see Krugman (1993). The Kyoto scholar Kiyoshi Kobayashi has shown that Japanese industrial R&D laboratories tend to cluster in one dominant location, which depends on geographical attractiveness as well as the historical choices of others; see Kobayashi, Kunihasa, and Fukuyama (2000). These modeling and simulation experiments confirm the importance of chance and determinism in the evolution of urban systems. In other words, pluralism prevails.

44. See Forrester (1987).

45. See Arthur (1994b).

46. Some of this simulation work is discussed in later chapters.

47. See Kauffman (1995), page 202.

48. If we think of the market as being segmented over time, then the learning curve can also be regarded as embodying economies of scope. For a discussion of this idea, see Spence (1981).

49. In a simplified network of producers and consumers, like those represented in the classical input-output model, intermediate producers play the dual role of purchasers and vendors. It's possible to demonstrate that small initial shocks to parts of such an economy can sometimes trigger large avalanches of orders and back orders. The collaborative work between Per Bak and two economists at the University of Chicago—Jose Scheinkman and Michael Woodford—goes even further. It suggests that some large fluctuations observed in economics are indicative of an economy operating at the self-organized critical state, in which minor shocks can lead to avalanches of all sizes. For further details on economic avalanches of this kind, see Bak et al. (1993) and Scheinkman and Woodford (1994).

Chapter Two

1. For a fuller account of the distribution of knowledge handlers in the American economy, see Machlup (1962).

2. The Swedish study and its results are discussed in Andersson (1986).

3. One way of monitoring research collaboration is to measure the number of internationally coauthored scientific articles. Work of this kind has been reported recently by Swedish researchers. For example, Andersson and Persson claim that in recent decades, such collaboration has been growing at an average of 14 percent per year; see Andersson and Persson (1993).

4. For an interesting analysis of the effect of distance on collaboration between the United Kingdom, Canada, and Australia, see Katz (1993). He normalized the distance variable as a fraction of the largest distance between pairs of universities in each country and found that the frictional impedance effect was exponential. A

similar result can be found in Beckmann (1994), whose theoretical analysis weighed the advantages of collaboration against its cost. His results suggest that we should expect an exponential distance effect.

5. This highly contentious issue can be relied upon to raise a storm of debate among researchers claiming expertise in the field. But independent research has shown that the strongest proponents supporting each argument tend to have vested interests in their particular point of view. For a hierarchical treatment of the knowledge exchange issue, see Batten, Kobayashi, and Andersson (1989).

6. See Schrödinger (1956), page 93.

7. This suggestion came from Kenneth Boulding.

8. Both animal and human behavior can be thoughtful, and learning depends on some kind of thinking. It's easy to regard thinking as something we *do* and knowledge as something we *have*. But this may be an oversimplification. We don't just store our knowledge; we also use and improve it. Ryle (1949) points out that we can also use it without necessarily being able to explain what it is that we know. He introduced a distinction between "knowing that" and "knowing how," partly to reinforce his idea that intelligence is a characteristic of performance. For a summary of Ryle's thesis, and an interesting analysis of thinking as an activity that "unfolds" in time, see Eiser (1994).

9. Reasoning from the general to the particular is a top-down approach. It leads to the concept of a representative agent like the "average citizen." General rules of behavior are determined at the macrolevel and then assigned unilaterally to all individual agents. Thus the population of agents is regarded as being homogeneous.

10. For a summary of some of these experiments in deductive reasoning, see Johnson-Laird and Byrne (1991).

11. See Arthur (1994a), page 406.

12. These two outcomes assume that all remaining moves are the best possible ones.

13. Quads is a game between two players, each of whom attempt to place 18 different pieces on a game board of 36 squares. Players take turns, choosing and placing one of their pieces on the board in such a way that it borders at least one other piece. The sides facing each other must be identical. The game ends as soon as one of the players cannot place another piece on the board. The other player is the winner.

14. For an extensive discussion of inductive reasoning and its prominent role in the learning process, see Holland, Holyoak, Nisbett, and Thagard (1986).

15. A revealing finding was that grand masters' mistakes involved placing whole *groups* of pieces in the wrong place, which left the game almost the same to the master but bewildering to the novice. Even more revealing was the fact that when pieces were assigned randomly to the squares on the board instead of being copied from actual games, grand masters were found to be no better than novices in reconstructing such random boards.

16. For a wide range of chess openings, see Horowitz (1964).

17. For an introduction to synergetics, see Haken (1977).

18. The growing importance of computer simulation can be gauged from the improved performance of silicon "agents" in high-level chess games. Since 1997,

when IBM's Deep Blue defeated Garry Kasparov in their second round of games, this third way of reasoning in open-ended situations has been recognized as full of promise.

19. For a full description of his computer experiments, see Arthur (1994a).

20. See Cohen and Stewart (1994), page 232.

21. The Prisoner's Dilemma first appeared in 1952, in an unpublished memorandum from the Rand Corporation discussing some experimental games. It remained unnamed in those early days, until A. W. Tucker called it the Prisoner's Dilemma. Tucker saw in it a perverse analog of the American criminal justice system, where prosecutors extract confessions on the promise of reduced sentences (plea bargaining).

22. For a comprehensive discussion of the Prisoner's Dilemma and the insights it can provide for various problems of collective action in social and economic contexts, see Axelrod (1984) and Hardin (1982). These two authors have recently updated their original work; see Axelrod (1997) and Hardin (1995).

23. See Olson (1965).

24. If your perilous journey to reach Thebes was taken into account, however, you may feel that zero is far too generous.

25. See Kauffman (1995), page 218.

26. See Axelrod (1984, 1997).

27. For an overview of the Prisoner's Dilemma game, along with some of the background to TIT FOR TAT, see Rapoport and Chammah (1965).

28. Boyd and Lorberbaum's (1987) claim that no pure strategy is evolutionarily stable was disputed recently by Bendor and Swistak (1998), who found that strategies that are nice and retaliatory (like TIT FOR TAT) are the most stable against possible invasions.

29. TIT FOR TAT is sensitive to the occurrence of mistakes or misunderstandings, commonly called noise. Noise played a part in the simulation study reported in *Nature* by Nowak and Sigmund (1993). Unlike TIT FOR TAT, their WIN-STAY, LOSE-SHIFT strategy defects after the other player is exploited and cooperates after a mutual defection. Axelrod's reaction to their study was to feel a little protective of TIT FOR TAT. With the help of a postdoctoral fellow, he found that adding either generosity or contrition to TIT FOR TAT was an effective way of coping with noise. Furthermore, the WIN-STAY, LOSE-SHIFT strategy did not perform as well in this variegated environment. For further details, see Axelrod (1997).

30. See Axelrod (1984), page 69.

31. See Hardin (1995), page 45.

32. A good example is the case where two industrial nations have erected trade barriers to each other's exports. Because of the mutual advantages of free trade, both countries would be better off if these barriers were eliminated. But if only one eliminated its barriers, it would face terms of trade that hurt its own economy. In fact, whatever one country does, the other country is better off retaining its own barriers.

33. For further details, see Lindgren (1992).

34. For a comprehensive discussion of fitness landscapes, see Kauffman (1993; 1995, especially Chapter 8).

35. See Lindgren (1992).

Chapter Three

1. By the end of this chapter, however, I'll argue that *both* are systems problems, because a single human brain is just as much a complex adaptive system as a group of human brains.

2. See Samuelson (1976), page 14.

3. See Bossomaier and Green (1998).

4. For an interesting information contagion model, designed to isolate the effects of informational feedback on the market-share allocation process, see Lane (1997).

5. The tale of these twins can be found in a book addressing the possible creation of a "science of surprise." For the part on Twain's tale, see Casti (1994), pages 171–172.

6. Time is rather special in other ways as well. Whether we think of it as flowing like sand, or turning on wheels within wheels, time escapes irretrievably. It simply keeps on keeping on. All that a clock really does is mark that progress for us. Timepieces don't really keep time, they just keep up with it!

7. Here we should distinguish conventional modeling from simulation. Many complex economic systems can be "modeled" with the aid of *agent-based simulation,* a new way of doing science and a topic that is discussed in later chapters.

8. See Schumpeter (1942), page 61.

9. According to Magoroh Maruyama, the field of cybernetics has been more or less identified as a science of self-regulating and equilibrating systems. By focusing mostly on the deviation-counteracting aspects of mutual causal relationships, cyberneticians have paid less attention to systems in which the mutual causal relationships are deviation-amplifying. Yet such systems are ubiquitous in nature and in human society. For a more complete discussion of these distinctions, see Maruyama (1963).

10. For a penetrating insight into misleading trade statistics in the global economy, including an assertion that the United States has no "foreign" trade as long as it's buying in dollars, see Ohmae (1991, especially Chapter 9).

11. See Krugman (1994b), Chapter 11.

12. For a fuller discussion of the connectivity properties of random graphs, see Erdos and Renyi (1960) and Kauffman (1993, 1995).

13. Erdos and Renyi (1960) were the first to demonstrate this rapid transition, in which a single gigantic connected component emerges—linking most of the nodes!

14. For a comprehensive discussion of the mathematical aspects of percolation theory, see Stauffer (1985) and Grimmett (1998).

15. The terms "sheep" and "explorers" were suggested by the traffic planner Anthony Downs (1962) to explain how peak-hour traffic congestion causes some drivers to search actively for faster alternatives, whereas others stubbornly tolerate the long delays caused by congestion. We'll explore this issue more deeply in Chapter 7.

16. Richard Nelson, Sidney Winter, Stuart Metcalfe, Giovanni Dosi, Gerry Silverberg, and others have developed an important class of evolutionary models in which technology and the structure of industry are said to *coevolve;* see, for

example, Nelson and Winter (1982). This process leads to productivity growth that is a statistical property of the system as a whole. The *technological* notion of coevolution described in their work complements the *behavioral* one discussed in this book.

17. See Schumpeter (1934), page 68.

18. Perhaps one should not rule out this idea too quickly. Signed digraphs may be a natural way of attempting to simplify a complex set of relationships into manageable components. Such links and arrows may play a basic part in the "mental modeling" of human beings. For a discussion of the role of links, arrows, and networks in human thought, see Johnson (1995).

19. I am grateful to Jeff Johnson, a systems scientist at the Open University in Milton Keynes, for pointing this fact out to me; see Johnson (1995), pages 26–28.

20. Rule-based mental models are central to the dynamic analysis of problem solving and induction described by Holland, Holyoak, Nisbett, and Thagard (1986). The reader is directed to this source for a comprehensive discussion of the kind of inductive behavior described in this book. This is not to imply that a rule-based approach to artificial intelligence is likely to succeed. To build a device that even approaches real intelligence would require a rule-based program far larger than anything that could be managed in a human's lifetime.

Chapter Four

1. Pirenne's hypothesis is laid out in Pirenne (1925, 1936). Its controversial nature has prompted discussion in many forums. Refreshingly unbiased critiques can be found in Bloch (1962), and North and Thomas (1973).

2. A full description of this analysis can be found in Mees (1975).

3. The notion of attractiveness invoked here is purely one of potential income, thus avoiding more abstract notions like standard of living or perceived opportunities.

4. Three pioneers of nonequilibrium systems—all of whom have emphasized the importance of self-organizing processes—are Hermann Haken, Gregoire Nicolis, and Ilya Prigogine. For glimpses into their early work, see Haken (1977) and Nicolis and Prigogine (1977).

5. Some economic historians have argued that the development and expansion of Europe's market economy in this period was fueled by population growth and its redistribution over space; see, for example, North and Thomas (1973). Putting the emphasis on migration instead of trade merely reinforces Mees's argument, since both are external sources of increased interaction.

6. See Schumpeter (1934).

7. Pirenne (1936) suggests that a "clerk" formed part of the equipment of every merchant ship sailing abroad, and from this we can infer that ship owners and seafaring merchants of that era had learned to keep accounts and to dispatch letters to their correspondents.

8. The above rules could also be used to specify a general trading network equilibrium for any pair of regions and any commodity. A discussion of this kind of equilibrium model can be found in Andersson (1995).

9. In the literature on induction, the above rules have been called *diachronic* because they specify the manner in which the environment may be expected to change over time. Diachronic rules may be divided into two classes: *predictor* rules, which tell the agent what to expect in the future, and *effector* rules, which cause the agent to act on the environment. In our chosen economic environment, the set of conditions relating to route security are predictor rules, whereas those pertaining to profitability are effector rules. For a comprehensive discussion of mental models as rule systems, see Holland, Holyoak, Nisbett, and Thagard (1986).

10. See Pirenne (1936), page 94.

11. In the valley of the Seine, it was the Paris Hanse of water merchants. In Flanders, an association of city gilds engaged in trade with England came to be known as the London Hanse. In Italy, the attraction of the Champagne fairs led to the formation of the *Universitas mercatorum Italiae nundinas Campaniae ac regni Franciae frequentantium*. For further details, see Pirenne (1936), pages 95–96.

12. See Pirenne (1936), page 124.

13. See Pirenne (1936), page 94.

14. See Pirenne (1936), page 22.

15. In England it was at Stourbridge; Germany at Aix-la-Chapelle, Frankfurt, and Constance; the Low Countries at Bruges, Lille, Messines, Thourout, and Ypres; Castile at Seville and Medina del Campo; Italy at Bari, Lucca, and Venice.

16. At the peak of their life cycle in the middle of the thirteenth century, each fair lasted from sixteen to fifty days and was succeeded soon thereafter by a new fair in another town within the district of Champagne. The four towns that shared between them the Champagne and Brie fairs in the Middle Ages, namely Troyes, Bar-sur-Aube, Provins, and Lagny, were constantly "passing the parcel." The net result was an annual agenda of six fairs that rotated between the four towns from January to October each year.

17. North and Thomas (1973, page 55) state that "ratios were quoted on the basis of one sou or twelve derniers, equal to some amount of a foreign currency."

18. See Braudel (1982), page 92.

19. North and Thomas argue that Champagne's destiny as a permanent international marketplace might have been realized had not royal taxation penalized the fairs at the same crucial period when a new direct sea route between Italy and the Low Countries had just been opened; see North and Thomas (1973), page 56.

20. Logistical networks are those networks in space and time that are responsible for the movement of goods, people, money, and information. For a fascinating analysis of the development of the world economy in terms of four "logistical revolutions," see Andersson (1986).

Chapter Five

1. The Shortest Network Problem was originally known in the literature as Steiner's Problem, because it was tackled first by Jacob Steiner, a geometrician at the University of Bonn. For an update on progress with this class of problem, see the January 1989 issue of *Scientific American*.

2. A group of Australian mathematicians showed recently that in the special case when the original points lie on a smooth curve, the problem of finding the Steiner network can be solved in polynomial time.

3. The Steiner solution has a tendency to form a series of Steiner trees (three links connected to each Steiner point at an angle of 120 degrees), resulting in roughly hexagonal patterns. This may be compared with the classical location problem in economics. In order to achieve the optimal location pattern for both producers and consumers, Walter Christaller and August Lösch showed that producers should locate at the centers of space-filling, hexagonal market areas—if their market areas interact.

4. See Bunge (1966).

5. Dudley Dillard was among the main protagonists; see Dillard (1967).

6. Although it's also true that urban growth in the five preceding decades (1790–1840) was rapid, the railroad age ushered in two decades of unprecedented city expansion. By 1860, close to 20 percent of the population were living in cities of 2,500 or more, compared with only 7 percent in 1820. For further details, see Chandler (1965).

7. See Rostow (1960).

8. Freight costs for users of the National Road were typically from 25 to 50 cents per ton-mile, whereas the comparable costs on the Erie Canal were 0.5 cents per ton-mile for raw goods and 3 cents per ton-mile for dry goods. These cost figures came from Dillard (1967) and Pred (1966).

9. See Fogel (1964).

10. In his groundbreaking book, William Cronon (1991) explores the ecological and economic changes that reshaped the American landscape and transformed American culture during the second half of the nineteenth century. Although principally a story about Chicago, it gives an excellent overview of the way in which competition between various western cities shaped the evolving landscape at that time.

11. Cronon suggests that the most important work on the boosters is that of Charles N. Glaab, to which his discussion is indebted. My discussion of boosters is indebted to Cronon.

12. See Cronon (1991), page 34.

13. The boosters' interest in Newton's law of gravity can be seen as a forerunner of the more formal theories of the gravitational kind, which emerged in economic geography and regional science during the course of the twentieth century.

14. See Goodin (1851), page 306.

15. Krugman (1996, page 9) points out that the popular, 900-page economics principles textbook by William Baumol and Alan Blinder contains not a single reference to the spatial dimension. Its major rival, an 1,100-page text by Joseph Stiglitz, contains just one reference to cities—in the context of rural-urban migration in less-developed countries! To assist in rectifying this imbalance, Krugman has recently attempted a synthesis of the field of spatial economics, together with two "distant" colleagues (see Fujita, Krugman, and Venables, 1999).

16. Complete details of the land rent/transport cost trade-off can be found in von Thünen (1826). For an interesting extension of von Thünen's theory, see Puu (1997).

17. The conventional theory in many fields—economics, history, anthropology—assumes that cities are built on a rural economic base. Jane Jacobs, for one, believes that the reverse is true: that is, rural economies and their work are directly built upon city economies and their work; see Jacobs (1969).

18. See Christaller (1933) and Lösch (1944).

19. See Goodin (1851), page 312.

20. Perhaps because of this, Chicago's early boosters rarely stressed natural transportation advantages as much as boosters in other cities.

21. See Cronon (1991), page 52.

22. The Chicago River lay close to the divide between the Great Lakes and the Mississippi watersheds. By digging a canal across the glacial moraine at this point, the dream of an inland ship passage between New York and New Orleans became a reality.

23. See Scott (1876).

24. This abrupt explosion of unbalanced growth not only confounded proponents of the central place model but also destroyed the credibility of the famous frontier thesis put forward by the historian Frederick Jackson Turner. Turner (1920) viewed the different Wests as sequential growth phases of the American frontier, repeating the social evolution of human civilization in Europe "like a huge page in the history of society." Only at the end of this sequence, according to Turner, would come an industrial city like Chicago. Whatever the merits of this thesis may be, it fits poorly with the explosive world of Chicago in the 1830s. For a fuller account of the weaknesses in Turner's thesis, see Cronon (1991), pages 31–32 and 46–54. For a similar criticism of the theory of rural or frontier primacy, see Jacobs (1969).

25. See Cronon (1991), page 34.

26. Chicago seems to have grown to metropolitan status less from being what the boosters called *central* than from being *peripheral.* For a fuller discussion of this point, see Cronon (1991), pages 90–91.

27. See Marx (1973), page 524.

28. For a vivid description of the federal government's four-year investigation of the Chicago futures markets, see Greising and Morse (1991).

29. See Cronon (1991), page 112.

30. According to figures quoted in the Chicago Board of Trade's annual reports.

31. See Cronon (1991), pages 120–132.

32. See Rothstein (1982), page 58.

33. *Chicago Tribune,* April 17, 1875.

34. The rank-size rule is sometimes called Zipf's law, in recognition of his observation of regularities in systems of human origin; see Zipf (1941, 1949). But Zipf's discovery was predated by Felix Auerbach (1913), whose German publication hasn't been recognized by the English-speaking world. Others to have beaten Zipf to the rule include Lotka in 1925, Gibrat in 1931, and Singer in 1936. Singer (1936) stressed that Gibrat's "law of proportional effect" is more general and that the rank-size rule is perfectly analogous to Pareto's law of income distribution.

35. In a comparative study of thirty-eight countries at varying levels of economic development, Berry (1961) found that thirteen of them had city-size

distributions that conformed to the rank-size rule. Later studies have confirmed that many more rank-size distributions can be found in Asian and European nations; for example, see Sendut (1966) and de Vries (1984).

36. Portugal has several overseas colonies.

37. See Sendut (1966), page 166.

38. The Kansai or Keihanshin region of Japan includes the cities of Osaka, Kyoto, and Kobe, as well as a number of smaller cities. Because of the desire of these cities to foster exchange and cooperate more closely, they appear to be coevolving into a "network city." For a portrayal of the Kansai conurbation's development as a network city, see Batten (1995).

39. See Zipf (1949), pages 427–431.

40. Perhaps the earliest model linking centers to complementary areas, and thus generating systems of cities consistent with the rank-size rule, was devised by Martin Beckmann; see Beckmann (1958).

41. See Berry (1961), page 587.

42. For a technical account of the evidence supporting the rank-size distribution as a stable attractor, see Haag and Max (1993).

43. See Sendut (1966).

44. Zipf's law proved interesting to Benoit Mandelbrot when he was a postdoctoral student at MIT. It propelled Mandelbrot on a path that led to finance and economics, and later to fractals; see Mandelbrot (1997), especially Chapter E7.

45. See Zipf (1949), especially Chapter 9.

46. Krugman asserts that when Marshallian dynamics are added to the traditional constant-returns, competitive model of international trade, they result in a rather simple landscape—one where the whole space of possible resource allocations drains to a single point; see Krugman (1994a), page 412.

47. See Haag (1994) and Mandelbrot (1997).

48. See Sakoda (1971), page 121.

49. John von Neumann and Stanislaw Ulam were the first to introduce the CA concept about fifty years ago; see von Neumann (1966). But it's pretty safe to say that John Conway popularized the concept through his invention of the game of Life. In Life, cells come alive (i.e., "turn on"), stay alive (i.e., "stay on"), or die (i.e., "turn off"), depending on the states of neighboring cells. Although Life is the best known CA, it's perhaps the least applicable to real configurations.

50. In their introduction to a special issue of the journal *Environment and Planning B*, devoted to urban systems as CA, Batty, Couclelis, and Eichen (1997) make this suggestion. The reader is directed to this issue for an overview of ways in which urban dynamics can be simulated through CA.

51. A distinction between migration models and steady site models was made by Hegselmann (1996). He also points out that allowing for migration doesn't imply an extension to the CA concept. The moving of an agent to an empty cell in his neighborhood can be treated as an application of a rule by which an occupied cell and a neighboring empty one exchange their states.

52. See Albin (1975).

53. See Portugali, Benenson, and Omer (1994).

54. In the later versions, immigrants and inhabitants interact with each other and with the system of cells (houses), and this interaction results in (1) intracity

and intercity migration dynamics, (2) changes in the properties of individuals, and (3) changes in the properties of the cells. For further details, see Portugali, Benenson, and Omer (1997).

55. See Sanders et al. (1997).

Chapter Six

1. Science is a good example of this freedom-of-choice situation.

2. For a lively summary of the state of the world's major urban expressways, the interested reader's attention is directed to a survey on commuting that appeared in the *Economist* on 5 September 1998.

3. Vickrey proposed the following six traffic states: (1) single interaction, (2) multiple interaction, (3) bottleneck, (4) triggerneck, (5) network and control, and (6) general density. For further details, see Vickrey (1969).

4. Braess constructed an intriguing network example that showed that introducing a new link in a congested network can actually increase network-wide congestion or the travel costs of each driver. For full details, see Braess (1968).

5. For a discussion of the economic ramifications of this conflict, see Arnott, de Palma, and Lindsay (1993).

6. Revealing discussions of Braess and other traffic network paradoxes can be found in Dafermos and Nagurney (1984) and in Yang and Bell (1998).

7. One pair of transport economists harboring this view are Johansson and Mattsson (1995).

8. See, for example, Daganzo and Sheffi (1977).

9. For an introduction to some of the analytical aspects of deterministic and stochastic user equilibria, see Sheffi (1985).

10. For a representative study which points in this direction, see Harker (1988).

11. As shown by Kobayashi (1993).

12. An introduction to the role of pattern recognition in learning theories can be found in Bower and Hilgard (1981), Chapter 12.

13. For a discussion of the role of pattern recognition and inductive modes of decisionmaking in economics, see Arthur (1994a).

14. See Sargent (1993).

15. See Downs (1962).

16. These attributes have also been noted by Ben-Akiva, de Palma, and Kaysi (1991).

17. See Conquest et al. (1993).

18. Kobayashi's two classes of behavior correspond closely to Downs's sheep and explorers; see Kobayashi (1993).

19. CA-based traffic simulation studies that have demonstrated these jamming transitions include Biham, Middleton, and Levine (1992); Nagel and Schreckenberg (1992); and Nagel and Rasmussen (1995). Other approaches to the analysis of traffic flows as nonlinear dynamic phenomena include spin glass systems; see, e.g., Kulkarni, Stough, and Haynes (1996).

20. For a comprehensive discussion of percolation theory, see Stauffer (1985) or Grimmett (1998).

21. The Golden Ratio has also been called the Golden Section, the Golden Cut, the Divine Proportion, the Fibonacci number, and the Mean of Phidias. For a focused discussion of this ratio and the Fibonacci sequence of numbers, see Frost and Prechter (1990, Chapter 3), Schroeder (1991), and Dunlap (1997).

22. For a deeper discussion of period-doubling cascades and the Feigenbaum number, see Cohen and Stewart (1994), pages 228–230.

23. Murray Gell-Mann contends that something entirely random, with practically no regularities, has effective complexity near zero. So does something completely regular, such as a bit string consisting only of zeros. Effective complexity can be high only in a region intermediate between total order and complete disorder. Logical depth is a crude measure of the difficulty of making predictions from theories. It's often hard to tell whether something possesses a great deal of effective complexity or reflects instead underlying simplicity and some logical depth. For further elaboration, see Gell-Mann (1995).

24. The cycles shown in Figures 7.2 and 7.3 are idealized in the sense that perfect wave symmetry is rarely observed in real markets. Although most five-wave formations have definite wave-like characteristics, many contain what Elliott called "extensions." Extensions are exaggerated or elongated movements that generally appear in one of the three impulse waves. Because these extensions can be of a similar amplitude and duration to the other four main waves, they give the impression that the total count is nine waves instead of the normal five. This makes the application of Elliott's wave principle more difficult in practice. For a comprehensive discussion of extensions, and other irregularities like "truncated fifths" and "diagonal triangles," see Frost and Prechter (1990).

25. A discussion of the market's progression, and the many links between the Fibonacci sequence and Elliott's wave principle, can be found in Frost and Prechter (1990).

26. See Pigou (1927).

27. Pigou's definition of real causes included crop variations, inventions and technological improvements, industrial disputes, changes of taste or fashion, and changes in foreign demand.

28. See Pigou (1927), page 86.

29. See Frost and Prechter (1990), page 11.

30. See Shiller (1989), page 1.

31. Shiller's research concentrates on the ultimate causes of price volatility in speculative markets, including the influence of fashions, fads, and other social movements. Impressive evidence is amassed in stock, bond, and real estate markets; see Shiller (1989).

32. For example, the Quantum Fund gained 68.6 percent in 1992 and 61.5 percent in 1993.

33. The introductory material in this paragraph has been drawn from a cover of his book *The Alchemy of Finance: Reading the Mind of the Market*. For further details and an exciting read, see Soros (1994).

34. See Soros (1994), page 29.

35. Soros cites "learning from experience" as an obvious example of the cognitive function.

36. The word "reflexivity" is used in the sense that the French do when they describe a verb whose object and subject are the same.

37. See Soros (1994), page 9.

38. A full account of his trading strategy can be found in Lindsay (1991).

39. Trident analysis functions just as well in falling (i.e., bear) markets as it does in rising (i.e., bull) markets.

40. To get hold of Lindsay's Trident strategy and start playing the markets, I suggest that the interested reader write directly to Lindsay's publisher: Windsor Books, Brightwaters, N.Y.

41. The Santa Fe Artificial Stock Market has existed in various forms since 1989. Like most artificial markets, it can be modified, tested, and studied in a variety of ways. For glimpses into this new silicon world and its methods of mimicking the marketplace and its gyrations, see Arthur (1995), and Arthur, Holland, Le Baron, Palmer and Tayler (1997).

42. "New" expectational models are mostly recombinations of existing hypotheses that work better.

43. In a series of interesting studies—typified by Delong, Shleifer, Summers, and Waldmann (1990) and Farmer (1993)—it has been shown analytically that expectations can be self-fulfilling. Thus we may conclude that positive feedback loops, or Pigovian herd effects, do have a significant role in shaping the market's coevolutionary patterns.

44. This is reminiscent of our earlier discussion on punctuated equilibria. In proposing his general theory of reflexivity, George Soros suggested that "since far-from-equilibrium conditions arise only intermittently, economic theory is only intermittently false. . . . There are long fallow periods when the movements in financial markets do not seem to follow a reflexive tune but rather resemble the random walks mandated by the efficient market theory"; see Soros (1994), page 9.

45. GARCH = Generalized AutoRegressive Conditional Hederoscedastic behavior.

46. Peter Allen has pointed out that an *adaptive* trading strategy is one that can give good results despite the fact that we cannot know the future, because there are different possible futures. When discernable trends become apparent, the strategy must be able to react to this. By taking such actions, however, the strategy will change what subsequently occurs in reality. This coevolutionary behavior implies that markets will always drive themselves to the "edge of predictability," in other words, to the *edge of chaos*.

47. For a precise definition of an adaptive linear network, see Holland (1988).

48. See Arthur (1995), page 25.

49. Such a set of simulation experiments can be found in de la Maza and Yuret (1995).

Chapter Eight

1. As Cohen and Stewart have noted, "You can dissect axles and gears out of a car but you will never dissect out a tiny piece of motion"; see Cohen and Stewart (1994), page 169.

2. Induction as a search for patterns should be distinguished from mathematical induction, the latter being a technique for proving theorems.

3. For example, the need to estimate the periodic demand for a facility applies to crowding problems at annual meetings, at monthly luncheons, at weekly sporting events, at weekend markets, or at daily shopping centers.

4. There is a lengthy literature on mental models, although the term has been used in many different ways. For a good review, see Rouse and Morris (1986). For an interesting discussion about their use in the scientific field, see Gorman (1992).

5. See Darley (1995), page 411.

6. However, the rules themselves are usually based on direct observations of the real world. For a more comprehensive discussion of agent-based simulation, see Axelrod (1997).

7. See Darley (1995), page 413.

8. Especially if the usual time constraints on moves are removed.

9. Traditional knowledge-based approaches to artificial intelligence, based on conceptual ideas and understanding, are less likely to succeed than approaches relying on agent-based, interactive phenomena. The latter belong to the growing field of artificial life.

10. "But economics has no clear kinship with any physical science. It is a branch of biology broadly interpreted" (Marshall 1920, page 772).

11. Some early attempts to make progress in these directions can be found in Allen and Sanglier (1979, 1981) and Batten (1982). Interest in coevolution and self-organization has grown in the 1990s, especially within the field of economic geography; see Fujita (1996) and Krugman (1996).

12. Some recent work by David Lane, in which he describes a class of models called artificial worlds, designed to provide insights into a process called emergent hierarchical organization, could be said to typify the kinds of experiments that fall under the heading of artificial economics. For details of these artificial worlds, see Lane (1993).

13. Massively parallel "architecture" means that living systems consist of many millions of parts, each one of which has its own behavioral repertoire.

14. This has been the approach taken in artificial intelligence. Methodologies to be explored in artificial economics have much more in common with the embryonic field of artificial life. For an introduction to artificial life, see Langton (1996).

15. For an interesting discussion of economic change in the very long run, see Day and Walter (1995).

16. For a full account of life on the Sugarscape, see Epstein and Axtell (1996). Readable summaries of this metaphoric world of artificial life can be found in Casti (1997, Chapter 4) and Ward (1999, Chapter 2).

17. For a deeper discussion of behavior generators and the theory of simulation, see Rasmussen and Barrett (1995) and Barrett, Thord, and Reidys (1998).

18. First proposed in the late nineteenth century, the Baldwin effect suggests that the course of evolutionary change can be influenced by individually learned behavior. The existence of this effect is still a hotly debated topic in biology and related fields. For evidence of how the Baldwin effect may alter the course of evolution, see Hinton and Nowlan (1987) and French and Messinger (1995).

References

Åkerman, N. (1998) *The Necessity of Friction*. Boulder: Westview Press.

Albin, P. (1975) *The Analysis of Complex Socio-Economic Systems*. Lexington, MA: Lexington Books.

Allen, P., and M. Sanglier. (1979) "A Dynamic Model of Growth in a Central Place System." *Geographical Analysis*, vol. 11, pp. 256–272.

_____. (1981) "Urban Evolution, Self-Organization, and Decisionmaking." *Environment and Planning A*, vol. 13, pp. 167–183.

Andersson, Å. E. (1986) "Presidential Address: The Four Logistical Revolutions." *Papers of the Regional Science Association*, vol. 59, pp. 1–12.

_____. (1995) "Economic Network Synergetics." In *Networks in Action*, ed. D. F. Batten, J. L. Casti, and R. Thord, pp. 309–318. Berlin: Springer Verlag.

Andersson, Å. E., and O. Persson. (1993) "Networking Scientists." *Annals of Regional Science*, vol. 27, pp. 11–21.

Arnott, R., A. de Palma, and R. Lindsay. (1993) "A Structural Model of Peak-Period Congestion: A Traffic Bottleneck with Elastic Demand." *American Economic Review*, vol. 83, pp. 161–179.

Arrow, K. (1962) "The Economic Implications of Learning by Doing." *Review of Economic Studies*, vol. 29, pp. 155–173.

Arthur, W. B. (1994a) "Inductive Behavior and Bounded Rationality." *American Economic Review*, vol. 84, pp. 406–411.

_____. (1994b) *Increasing Returns and Path Dependence in the Economy*. Ann Arbor: University of Michigan Press.

_____. (1995) "Complexity in Economic and Financial Markets." *Complexity*, vol. 1, pp. 20–25.

Arthur, W. B., J. H. Holland, B. Le Baron, R. Palmer, and P. Tayler. (1997) "Asset Pricing Under Endogenous Expectations in an Artificial Stock Market." In *The Economy as an Evolving Complex System II*, ed. W. B. Arthur, S. N. Durlauf, and D. A. Lane, pp. 15–44. Reading, MA: Addison-Wesley.

Auerbach, F. (1913) "Das Gesetz der Bevölkerungskonzentration." *Petermanns Geographische Mitteilungen*, no. 59, pp. 74–76.

Axelrod, R. (1984) *The Evolution of Cooperation*. New York: Basic Books.

_____. (1997) *The Complexity of Cooperation: Agent-Based Models of Competition and Collaboration*. Princeton: Princeton University Press.

Bachelier, L. (1900) "Théorie de la Spéculation." Doctoral Dissertation in Mathematical Sciences, Faculté des Sciences de Paris, defended 29 March.

Bairoch, P. (1988) *Cities and Economic Development: From the Dawn of History to the Present*. Translated by Christopher Braider. Chicago: University of Chicago Press.

Bak, P. (1996) *How Nature Works: The Science of Self-Organized Criticality.* New York: Springer-Verlag.

Bak, P., K. Chen, J. A. Scheinkman, and M. Woodford. (1993) "Aggregate Fluctuations from Independent Shocks: Self-Organized Criticality in a Model of Production and Inventory Dynamics." *Ricerche Economiche,* vol. 47, pp. 3–24.

Barrett, C. L., R. Thord, and C. Reidys. (1998) "Simulations in Decision Making for Socio-Technical Systems." In *Knowledge and Networks in a Dynamic Economy,* ed. M. J. Beckmann, B. Johansson, F. Snickars, and R. Thord, pp. 59–82. Berlin: Springer-Verlag.

Batten, D. F. (1982) "On the Dynamics of Industrial Evolution." *Regional Science and Urban Economics,* vol. 12, pp. 449–462.

_____. (1995) "Network Cities: Creative Urban Agglomerations for the Twenty-First Century." *Urban Studies,* vol. 32, pp. 313–327.

_____. (1998) "Coevolutionary Learning on Networks." In *Knowledge and Networks in a Dynamical Economy,* ed. M. Beckmann, B. Johansson, F. Snickars, and R. Thord, pp. 311–332. Berlin: Springer-Verlag.

Batten, D. F., and B. Johansson. (1989) "The Dynamics of Metropolitan Change." *Geographical Analysis,* vol. 19, pp. 189–199.

Batten, D. F., K. Kobayashi, and Å. E. Andersson. (1989) "Knowledge, Nodes, and Networks: An Analytical Perspective." In *Knowledge and Industrial Organization,* ed. Å. E. Andersson, D. F. Batten, and C. Karlsson, pp. 31–46. Berlin: Springer-Verlag.

Batty, M., H. Couclelis, and M. Eichen. (1997) "Urban Systems as Cellular Automata." *Environment and Planning B,* vol. 24, pp. 159–164.

Beckmann, M. J. (1958) "City Hierarchies and the Distribution of City Size." *Economic Development and Cultural Change,* vol. 6, pp. 243–248.

_____. (1994) "On Knowledge Networks in Science: Collaboration among Equals." *Annals of Regional Science,* vol. 28, pp. 233–242.

Bell, D. (1981) "Models and Reality in Economic Discourse." In *The Crisis in Economic Theory,* ed. D. Bell and I. Kristol. New York: Basic Books.

Ben-Akiva, M., A. de Palma, and I. Kaysi. (1991) "Dynamic Network Models and Driver Information Systems." *Transportation Research A,* vol. 25, pp. 251–266.

Bendor, J., and P. Swistak. (1998) "The Evolutionary Advantage of Conditional Cooperation." *Complexity,* vol. 4, pp. 15–18.

Benhabib, J., ed. (1992) *Cycles and Chaos in Economic Equilibrium.* Princeton: Princeton University Press.

Berry, B.J.L. (1961) "City-Size Distributions and Economic Development." *Economic Development and Cultural Change,* vol. 9, pp. 573–588.

Biham, O., A. Middleton, and D. Levine. (1992) "Self-Organization and a Dynamical Transition in Traffic-Flow Models." *Physical Review A,* vol. 46, pp. R6124–6127.

Bloch, M. (1962). *Feudal Society.* Translated by L. A. Manyon. London: Routledge & Kegan Paul.

Bossomaier, T., and D. Green. (1998) *Patterns in the Sand: Computers, Complexity, and Life.* Sydney: Allen and Unwin.

Bower, G. H., and E. R. Hilgard. (1981) *Theories of Learning.* Englewood Cliffs, NJ: Prentice-Hall.

Boyd, R., and J. P. Lorberbaum. (1987) "No Pure Strategy Is Evolutionarily Stable in the Iterated Prisoner's Dilemma Game." *Nature,* vol. 327, pp. 58–59.

Braess, D. (1968) "Über ein Paradoxon aus der Verkehrsplanung." *Unternehmensforschung,* vol. 12, pp. 258–268.

Braudel, F. (1982) *The Wheels of Commerce.* London: William Collins.

Brock, W., D. Hsieh, and B. Le Baron. (1991) *Nonlinear Dynamics, Chaos, and Instability: Statistical Theory and Economic Evidence.* Cambridge: MIT Press.

Bunge, W. (1966) *Theoretical Geography.* Lund Studies in Geography. Royal University of Lund, Series C, no. 1.

Casti, J. L. (1989) *Paradigms Lost.* New York: Avon.

———. (1994) *Complexification.* London: Abacus.

———. (1997) *Would-Be Worlds.* New York: Wiley.

Chandler Jr, A. D. (1965) *The Railroads: The Nation's First Big Business.* New York: Harcourt Brace Jovanovich.

Christaller, W. ([1933] 1966) *Central Places in Southern Germany.* Translated by Carlisle W. Baskin. Englewood Cliffs, NJ: Prentice Hall.

Cohen, J., and I. Stewart. (1994) *The Collapse of Chaos.* New York: Penguin.

Conquest, L., J. Spyridakis, M. Haselkorn, and W. Barfield. (1993) "The Effect of Motorist Information on Commuter Behaviour: Classification of Drivers into Commuter Groups." *Transportation Research C,* vol. 1, pp. 183–201.

Cronon, W. (1991) *Nature's Metropolis: Chicago and the Great West.* New York: W. W. Norton.

Dafermos, S., and A. Nagurney. (1984) "On Some Traffic Equilibrium Theory Paradoxes." *Transportation Research B,* vol. 18, pp. 101–110.

Daganzo, C., and Y. Sheffi. (1977) "On Stochastic Models of Traffic Assignment." *Transportation Science,* vol. 11, pp. 253–274.

Darley, V. (1995) "Emergent Phenomena and Complexity." In *Artificial Life IV: Proceedings of the Fourth International Workshop on the Synthesis and Simulation of Living Systems,* ed. R. A. Brooks and P. Maes, pp. 411–416. Cambridge: MIT Press.

Day, R. H., and J. L. Walter. (1995) "Economic Growth in the Very Long Run: On the Multiple-Phase Interaction of Population, Technology, and Social Infrastructure." In *Economic Complexity: Chaos, Sunspots, Bubbles, and Nonlinearity,* ed. W. A. Barnett, J. Geweke, and K. Shell, pp. 253–288. Cambridge: Cambridge University Press.

De Bondt, W., and R. Thaler. (1985) "Does the Stock Market Overreact?" *Journal of Finance,* vol. 60, pp. 793–805.

Delong, J. B., A. Schleifer, L. H. Summers, and J. Waldmann. (1990) "Positive Feedback and Destabilizing Rational Speculation." *Journal of Finance,* vol. 45, pp. 379–395.

Dillard, D. (1967) *Economic Development of the North Atlantic Community.* Englewood Cliffs, NJ: Prentice-Hall.

Downs, A. (1962) "The Law of Peak-Hour Expressway Congestion." *Traffic Quarterly,* vol. 16, pp. 393–409.

Dunlap, R. A. (1997) *The Golden Ratio and Fibonacci Numbers.* Singapore: World Scientific.

Dyckman, T. R., and D. Morse. (1986) *Efficient Capital Markets and Accounting: A Critical Analysis.* Englewood Cliffs, NJ: Prentice-Hall.

Eiser, J. R. (1994) *Attitudes, Chaos, and the Connectionist Mind.* Oxford: Blackwell.

Eldredge, N., and S. Gould. (1972) "Punctuated Equilibria: An Alternative to Phyletic Gradualism." In *Models in Paleobiology,* ed. T. J. M. Schopf, pp. 82–115. San Francisco: Freeman Cooper.

Elliott, R. N. (1946) *Nature's Law: The Secret of the Universe.* Reprinted in R. N. Elliott, *R. N. Elliott's Masterworks: The Definitive Collection.* Gainesville, GA: New Classics Library, 1994.

Epstein, J., and R. Axtell. (1996) *Growing Artificial Societies.* Cambridge: MIT Press.

Erdos, P., and A. Renyi. (1960) "On the Evolution of Random Graphs." Institute of Mathematics, Hungarian Academy of Sciences, Publication no. 5.

Fama, E. (1970) "Efficient Capital Markets: A Review of Theory and Empirical Work." *Journal of Finance,* vol. 25, pp. 383–417.

Farmer, R. A. (1993) *The Macroeconomics of Self-Fulfilling Prophecies.* Cambridge: MIT Press.

Fogel, R. W. (1964) *Railroads and American Economic Growth.* Baltimore: Johns Hopkins Press.

Forrester, J. W. (1987) "Nonlinearity in High-Order Models of Social Systems." *European Journal of Operational Research,* vol. 30, pp. 104–109.

French, R. M., and A. Messinger. (1995) "Genes, Phenes, and the Baldwin Effect: Learning and Evolution in a Simulated Population." In *Artificial Life IV: Proceedings of the Fourth International Workshop on the Synthesis and Simulation of Living Systems,* ed. R. A. Brooks and P. Maes, pp. 277–282. Cambridge: MIT Press..

Frost, A. J., and R. P. Prechter. (1990) *Elliott Wave Principle: Key to Stock Market Profits.* Gainesville, GA: New Classics Library.

Fujita, M. (1996) "On the Self-Organization and Evolution of Economic Geography." *Japanese Economic Review,* vol. 47, pp. 34–61.

Fujita, M., P. Krugman, and A. J. Venables. (1999) *The Spatial Economy: Cities, Regions, and International Trade.* Cambridge: MIT Press.

Gell-Mann, M. (1995) "What Is Complexity?" *Complexity,* vol. 1, pp. 16–19.

Goodin, S. H. (1851) "Cincinnati: Its Destiny." In *Sketches and Statistics of Cincinnati in 1851,* ed. C. Cist. Cincinnati: William Moore.

Gorman, M. E. (1992) *Simulating Science: Heuristics, Mental Models, and Techno-Scientific Thinking.* Bloomington: Indiana University Press.

Greising, D., and L. Morse. (1991) *Brokers, Bagmen, and Moles: Fraud and Corruption in the Chicago Futures Markets.* New York: Wiley.

Griffin, K. (1998) "Friction in Economics." In *The Necessity of Friction,* ed. N. Åkerman, pp. 119–131. Boulder: Westview Press.

Grimmett, G. (1998) *Percolation.* Berlin: Springer.

Haag, G. (1994) "The Rank-Size Distribution of Settlements as a Dynamic Multifractal Phenomena." *Chaos, Solitons, and Fractals,* vol. 4, pp. 519–534.

Haag, G., and H. Max. (1993) "Rank-Size Distribution of Settlement Systems: A Stable Attractor in Urban Growth." *Papers in Regional Science,* vol. 74, pp. 243–258.

Haken, H. (1977) *Synergetics: An Introduction.* Berlin: Springer-Verlag.

_____. (1998) "Decision Making and Optimization in Regional Planning." In *Knowledge and Networks in a Dynamic Economy*, ed. M. J. Beckmann, B. Johansson, F. Snickars, and R. Thord, pp. 25–40. Berlin: Springer-Verlag.

Hardin, R. (1982) *Collective Action*. Baltimore: Resources for the Future.

_____. (1995) *One for All: The Logic of Group Conflict*. Princeton: Princeton University Press.

Harker, P. (1988) "Multiple Equilibrium Behaviours on Networks." *Transportation Science*, vol. 22, pp. 39–46.

Hegselmann, R. (1996) "Understanding Social Dynamics: The Cellular Automata Approach." In *Social Science Microsimulation*, ed. K. G. Troitzsch, U. Mueller, G. N. Gilbert, and J. E. Doran, pp. 282–306. Berlin: Springer.

Hinton, G. E., and S. J. Nowlan. (1987) "How Learning Can Guide Evolution." *Complex Systems*, vol. 1, pp. 495–502.

Holland, J. H. (1988) "The Global Economy as an Adaptive Process." In *The Economy as an Evolving Complex System*, ed. P. W. Anderson, K. J. Arrow, and D. Pines, pp. 117–124. Reading, MA: Addison-Wesley.

_____. (1998) *Emergence: From Order to Chaos*. Reading, MA: Addison-Wesley.

Holland, J. H., K. J. Holyoak, R. E. Nisbett, and P. R. Thagard. (1986) *Induction: Processes of Inference, Learning, and Discovery*. Cambridge: MIT Press.

Horowitz, I. A. (1964) *Chess Openings: Theory and Practice*. London: Faber and Faber.

Hume, D. (1957) *An Inquiry Concerning Human Understanding*. New York: Library of Liberal Arts.

Jacobs, J. (1969) *The Economy of Cities*. New York: Random House.

Johansson, B., and L.-G. Mattsson. (1995) "Principles of Road Pricing." In *Road Pricing: Theory, Empirical Assessment, and Policy*, ed. B. Johansson and L.-G. Mattsson. Boston: Kluwer.

Johnson, J. (1995) "The Multidimensional Networks of Complex Systems." In *Networks in Action*, ed. D. F. Batten, J. L. Casti, and R. Thord, pp. 49–79. Berlin: Springer Verlag.

Johnson-Laird, P. N., and R. M. J. Byrne. (1991) *Deduction*. Hove: Lawrence Erlbaum Associates.

Katz, J. S. (1993) "Geographical Proximity and Scientific Collaboration." *Scientometrics*, vol. 31 (1): pp. 31–43.

Kauffman, S. (1993) *The Origins of Order: Self-Organization and Selection in Evolution*. New York: Oxford University Press.

_____. (1995) *At Home in the Universe: The Search for Laws of Complexity*. London: Penguin.

Kobayashi, K. (1993) "Incomplete Information and Logistical Network Equilibria." In *The Cosmo-Creative Society*, ed. Å. E. Andersson, D. F. Batten, K. Kobayashi, and K. Yoshikawa, pp. 95–119. Berlin: Springer.

Kobayashi, K., S. Kunihisa, and K. Fukuyama. (2000) "The Knowledge Intensive Nature of Japan's Urban Development." In *Learning, Innovation, and Urban Evolution*, ed. D. F. Batten, C. S. Bertuglia, D. Martellato, and S. Occelli. Boston: Kluwer.

Krugman, P. (1993) "On the Number and Location of Cities." *European Economic Review*, vol. 37, pp. 293–298.

_____. (1994a) "Complex Landscapes in Economic Geography." *American Economic Association, Papers and Proceedings*, vol. 84, pp. 412–416.

_____. (1994b) *The Age of Diminished Expectations*. Cambridge: MIT Press.

_____. (1994c) *Peddling Prosperity: Economic Sense and Nonsense in the Age of Diminished Expectations*. New York: W. W. Norton.

_____. (1996) *The Self-Organizing Economy*. New York: Blackwell.

Kuhn, T. (1962) *The Structure of Scientific Revolutions*. Chicago: University of Chicago Press.

Kulkarni, R., R. R. Stough, and K. E. Haynes. (1996) "Spin Glass and the Interactions of Congestion and Emissions: An Exploratory Step." *Transportation Research C*, vol. 4 (6), pp. 407–424.

Lane, D. (1993) "Artificial Worlds and Economics, Part I." *Journal of Evolutionary Economics*, vol. 3, pp. 89–107.

_____. (1997) "Is What Is Good for Each Best for All? Learning from Others in the Information Contagion Model." In *The Economy as an Evolving Complex System II*, ed. W. B. Arthur, S. N. Durlauf, and D. A. Lane, pp. 105–127. Reading, MA: Addison-Wesley.

Langton, C. G. (1996) "Artificial Life." In *The Philosophy of Artificial Life*, ed. M. A. Boden, pp. 39–94. Oxford: Oxford University Press.

Le Roy, S. F., and R. D. Porter. (1981) "Stock Price Volatility: Tests Based on Implied Variance Bounds." *Econometrica*, vol. 49, pp. 97–113.

Lindgren, K. (1992) "Evolutionary Phenomena in Simple Dynamics." In *Artificial Life II*, ed. C. G. Langton, J. D. Farmer, S. Rasmussen, and C. Taylor, pp. 295–312. Redwood City, CA: Addison-Wesley.

Lindsay, C. L. (1991) *Trident: A Trading Strategy*. Brightwaters, NY: Windsor Books.

Lösch, A. (1944) *The Economics of Location*. Translated from the 2nd revised edition by William H. Woglom. New Haven: Yale University Press, 1954.

Machlup, F. (1962) *The Production and Distribution of Knowledge in the United States*. Princeton: Princeton University Press.

Mandelbrot, B. (1963) "The Variation of Certain Speculative Prices." *Journal of Business*, vol. 36, pp. 394–419.

_____. (1997) *Fractals and Scaling in Finance*. New York: Springer-Verlag.

_____. (1999) "A Multifractal Walk Down Wall Street." *Scientific American*, February, pp. 50–53.

Marshall, A. (1920) *Principles of Economics*. London: Macmillan.

Maruyama, M. (1963) "The Second Cybernetics: Deviation-Amplifying Mutual Causal Processes." *American Scientist*, vol. 51, pp. 164–179.

Marx, K. (1973) *Grundrisse: Foundations of the Critique of Political Economy*. Translated by Martin Nicolaus. Harmondsworth, UK: Penguin.

de la Maza, M., and D. Yuret. (1995) "A Futures Market Simulation with Non-Rational Participants." In *Artificial Life IV: Proceedings of the Fourth International Workshop on the Synthesis and Simulation of Living Systems*, ed. R. A. Brooks and P. Maes, pp. 325–330. Cambridge: MIT Press.

Mees, A. (1975) "The Revival of Cities in Medieval Europe." *Regional Science and Urban Economics*, vol. 5, pp. 403–425.

Monod, J. (1971) *Chance and Necessity*. London: Penguin.

Nagel, K., and S. Rasmussen. (1995) "Traffic at the Edge of Chaos." In *Artificial Life IV: Proceedings of the Fourth International Workshop on the Synthesis and Simulation of Living Systems,* ed. R. A. Brooks and P. Maes, pp. 222–235. Cambridge: MIT Press.

Nagel, K., and M. Schreckenberg. (1992) "A Cellular Automaton Model for Freeway Traffic." *Journal de Physique I,* vol. 2, p. 2221.

Nelson, R. R., and S. G. Winter. (1982) *An Evolutionary Theory of Economic Change.* Cambridge: Harvard University Press.

Neumann, J. von. (1966) *Theory of Self-Reproducing Automata.* Edited and completed by Arthur Burks. Urbana: University of Illinois Press.

Nicolis, G., and I. Prigogine. (1977) *Self-Organization in Nonequilibrium Systems.* New York: Wiley.

_____. (1989) *Exploring Complexity: An Introduction.* New York: W. H. Freeman.

North, D. C., and R. P. Thomas. (1973) *The Rise of the Western World: A New Economic History.* Cambridge: Cambridge University Press.

Nowak, M., and K. Sigmund. (1993) "A Strategy of Win-Shift, Lose-Stay That Outperforms Tit-for-Tat in the Prisoner's Dilemma Game." *Nature,* vol. 364, pp. 56–58.

Ohmae, K. (1991) *The Borderless World: Power and Strategy in the Interlinked Economy.* New York: HarperPerennial.

Olson, M. (1965) *The Logic of Collective Action.* Cambridge: Harvard University Press.

Pareto, V. (1896) *Oeuvres Completes.* Geneva: Droz.

Pigou, A. C. (1927) *Industrial Fluctuations.* London: Macmillan.

Pirenne, H. ([1925] 1952) *Medieval Cities: Their Origins and the Revival of Trade.* Translation by F. D. Halsey. Princeton: Princeton University Press.

_____. ([1936] 1965) *Economic and Social History of Medieval Europe.* Translation by I. E. Clegg. London: Routledge & Kegan Paul.

Portugali, J., I. Benenson, and I. Omer. (1994) "Sociospatial Residential Dynamics: Stability and Instability Within a Self-Organizing City." *Geographical Analysis,* vol. 26, pp. 321–340.

_____. (1997) "Spatial Cognitive Dissonance and Sociospatial Emergence in a Self-Organizing City." *Environment and Planning B,* vol. 24, pp. 263–285.

Pred, A. (1966) *The Spatial Dynamics of U.S. Urban-Industrial Growth, 1800–1914.* Cambridge: Harvard University Press.

Prigogine, I., and R. Herman. (1971) *Kinetic Theory of Vehicular Traffic.* New York: Elsevier.

Puu, T. (1997) *Mathematical Location and Land Use Theory.* Berlin: Springer.

Rapoport, A., and A. M. Chammah. (1965) *Prisoner's Dilemma: A Study in Conflict and Cooperation.* Ann Arbor: University of Michigan Press.

Rasmussen, S., and C. L. Barrett. (1995) "Elements of a Theory of Simulation." In *ECAL 95, Lecture Notes in Computer Science.* New York: Springer.

Ray, T. S. (1992) "An Approach to the Synthesis of Life." In *Artificial Life II,* ed. C. Langton, C. Taylor, J. D. Farmer, and S. Rasmussen, pp. 371–408. Redwood City, CA: Addison-Wesley.

Rhea, R. (1932) *The Dow Theory.* New York: Barron's.

Rostow, W. W. (1960) *The Stages of Economic Growth*. New York: Cambridge University Press.

Rothstein, M. (1982) "Frank Norris and Popular Perceptions of the Market." *Agricultural History*, vol. 56, pp. 50–66.

Rouse, W. B., and N. M. Morris. (1986) "On Looking into the Black Box: Prospects and Limits in the Search for Mental Models." *Psychological Bulletin*, vol. 100, pp. 349–363.

Rubinstein, M. (1975) "Securities Market Efficiency in an Arrow-Debreu Economy." *American Economic Review*, vol. 65, pp. 812–814.

Ryle, G. (1949) *The Concept of Mind*. London: Hutchinson.

Saari, D. (1995) "Mathematical Complexity of Simple Economics." *Notices of the American Mathematical Society*, vol. 42, pp. 222–230.

Sakoda, J. M. (1971) "The Checkerboard Model of Social Interaction." *Journal of Mathematical Sociology*, vol. 1, pp. 119–132.

Samuelson, P. (1976) *Economics*. New York: McGraw-Hill.

Sanders, L., D. Pumain, H. Mathian, F. Guérin-Pace, and S. Bura. (1997) "SIMPOP: A Multiagent System for the Study of Urbanism." *Environment and Planning A*, vol. 24, pp. 287–305.

Sargent, T. J. (1993) *Bounded Rationality in Macroeconomics*. New York: Oxford University Press.

Scheinkman, J. A., and M. Woodford. (1994) "Self-Organized Criticality and Economic Fluctuations." *American Journal of Economics*, vol. 84, p. 417.

Schelling, T. S. (1969) "Models of Segregation." *American Economic Review, Papers and Proceedings*, vol. 59 (2), pp. 488–493.

_____. (1978) *Micromotives and Macrobehavior*. New York: W. W. Norton.

Schrödinger, E. (1956) *Mind and Matter*. Reprinted together with *What Is Life?* Cambridge: Cambridge University Press, 1992.

Schroeder, M. (1991) *Fractals, Chaos, Power Laws: Minutes from an Infinite Paradise*. New York, W. H. Freeman.

Schumpeter, J. (1934) *The Theory of Economic Development*. Cambridge: Harvard University Press.

_____. (1942) *Capitalism, Socialism, and Democracy*. New York: Harper and Row.

Scott, J. W. (1876) *A Presentation of Causes Tending to Fix the Position of the Future Great City of the World in the Central Plain of North America: Showing that the Centre of the World's Commerce, Now Represented by the City of London, Is Moving Westward to the City of New York, and Thence, within One Hundred Years, to the Best Position on the Great Lakes*. Toledo.

Sendut, H. (1966) "City-Size Distributions of South-East Asia." *Asian Studies*, vol. 4, pp. 165–172.

Sheffi, Y. (1985) *Urban Transportation Networks*. Englewood Cliffs, NJ: Prentice-Hall.

Shiller, R. J. (1981) "The Use of Volatility Measures in Assessing Market Efficiency." *Journal of Finance*, vol. 36, pp. 291–304.

_____. (1989) *Market Volatility*. Cambridge: MIT Press.

Simon, H. (1987) "Giving the Soft Sciences a Hard Sell." *Boston Globe*, 3 May.

Singer, H. W. (1936) "The 'Courbes des Populations': A Parallel to Pareto's Law," *Economic Journal*, vol. 46 (182), pp. 254–263.

Soros, G. (1994) *The Alchemy of Finance: Reading the Mind of the Market*. New York: Wiley.

Spence, A. M. (1981) "The Learning Curve and Competition." *Bell Journal of Economics*, vol. 12, pp. 49–70.

Stauffer, D. (1985) *Introduction to Percolation Theory*. London: Taylor and Francis.

Taylor, G. R. (1951) *The Transportation Revolution: 1815–1860*. New York: Rinehart.

Thünen, J. H. von. (1826) *Der Isolierte Staat in Beziehung auf Landtschaft und Nationalökonomie*. Hamburg. English translation by C. M. Wartenburg. *Von Thünen's Isolated State*. Oxford: Pergamon Press, 1966.

Turner, F. J. (1920) *The Frontier in American History*. New York: Holt, Rinehart and Winston.

Vickrey, W. S. (1969) "Congestion Theory and Transport Investment." *American Economic Review*, vol. 59, pp. 251–260.

Vries, J. de. (1984) *European Urbanization: 1500–1800*. London: Methuen.

Ward, M. (1999) *Virtual Organisms*. London: Macmillan.

Yang, H., and M. G. H. Bell. (1998) "A Capacity Paradox in Network Design and How to Avoid It." *Transportation Research*, vol. 32 (7), pp. 539–545.

Zhang, W.-B. (1993) *Synergetic Economics*. Berlin: Springer-Verlag.

Zipf, G. K. (1941) *National Unity and Disunity*. Bloomington, IN: Principia Press.

_____. (1949) *Human Behavior and the Principle of Least Effort*. New York: Hafner.

Index